Vegetable Cooking of All Nations

Vegetable Cooking

OF ALL NATIONS

Edited by Florence Schwartz

ILLUSTRATED BY MARY NORTON

Gramercy Publishing Company

NEW YORK

The international recipes in this book were selected from the following books of the International Cook Book Series:

The Balkan Cook Book
  by Inge Kramarz

The Chinese Cook Book
  by Wallace Yee Hong

The Czechoslovak Cook Book
  by Joza Brízová, et al.

The Escoffier Cook Book
  by A. Escoffier

The Finnish Cook Book
  by Beatrice A. Ojakangas

German Cookery
  by Elizabeth Schuler

The Great Scandinavian Cook Book
  by Karin Fredrikson

The Greek Cook Book
  by Sophia Skoura

The Israeli Cook Book
  by Molly Lyons Bar-David

Jewish Cookery
  by Leah W. Leonard

Polish Cookery
  by Marja Ochorowicz-Monatowa

The Talisman Italian Cook Book
  by Ada Boni

Viennese Cooking
  by O. and A. Hess

The Yogi Cook Book
  by Yogi Vithaldes

Copyright © MCMLXXIII by Crown Publishers, Inc.
All rights reserved.

This edition is published by Gramercy Publishing Company,
distributed by Crown Publishers, Inc.
h g f e d c b a
1981 EDITION

Manufactured in the United States of America

Designed by George Hornby

Library of Congress Cataloging in Publication Data
Main entry under title:

Vegetable cooking of all nations.

  Includes index.
  1. Cookery (Vegetables)   2. Cookery, International.
I. Schwartz, Florence.
TX801.V415   1981   641.6′5   81-6743
ISBN 0-517-35703-8   AACR2

Contents

Editor's Note

Despite the acknowledged merits of vegetables for the daily diet, a disproportionately large number of people still object to them—and justifiably so. Soggy carrots, watery potatoes, or sand-strewn spinach cause one to forget the great potential benefits of vegetables, and yet their preparation can make them the tastiest of foods.

In *Vegetable Cooking of All Nations* we have selected the most interesting recipes from the cuisines of the eastern and western hemispheres, showing how to dress up a menu with the palate-appeal of tempting vegetable dishes, and even how to combine them for an entire vegetable meal. No vegetable is neglected and the variety is immense.

Here are the recipes that will grace tables, fill stomachs, and add the essential nutrients for good health.

This book is dedicated to
Herbert Michelman
for his wisdom

A

Artichokes

Soak artichokes, stems up, in salted cold water at least 10 minutes. Drain and plunge into boiling salted water to cover. Cook covered 30 to 45 minutes, depending on size. They are done when a toothpick will easily pierce the stem end. Drain and serve hot with melted butter, mayonnaise or Hollandaise sauce, or serve plain. Allow one medium artichoke per serving, or cut large one into halves through stem. The leaves are dipped into the sauce and only the tender inside layer of pulp is eaten. The fuzzy part near the stem is called the "choke" and is discarded.

Artichokes

Artichokes should be freshly picked; leaves and stems should be green, not brown, and the leaves tight together. The secret of good artichoke cooking is to be sure they are very well done; unlike other vegetables, they should be almost mushy. Trim stems, cut top leaves off with a sharp knife (about 1 inch) since tops are not edible, and if possible scoop out chokes before cooking. This, however, is not essential. Cook in boiling water to cover. Add juice of half a lemon, a teaspoon of sugar, and salt to taste. Stand upside down to drain before serving. Artichokes are also excellent if, in addition to lemon and sugar, the following are added to cooking water: 1 tablespoon olive oil, 1 clove garlic, 1 teaspoon thyme, marjoram, or oregano. Cook 30 to 40 minutes. Serve artichokes hot with drawn butter, butter and lemon, Bread Crumb Sauce, mayonnaise, or Hollandaise. Serve artichokes cold with mayonnaise or french dressing.

Artichokes Au Gratin GREECE

1 lemon, juice only
  coarse salt
8 to 10 small globe artichokes
½ cup butter, melted
  salt and pepper to taste

1 recipe Thick Béchamel Sauce
2 cups grated kefalotiri cheese
3 to 4 tablespoons toasted
  bread crumbs

Add some coarse salt and the lemon juice to a large pot of water; bring to a boil. Meanwhile, clean the artichokes; put them into the boiling water. Cover the pot, and cook over high heat until they are tender (35 to 45 minutes); remove with a slotted spoon. Cut them into cubes, pour half the melted butter over them, and season. Prepare the béchamel sauce.

Butter a small pan and spread a thin layer of the sauce in it; sprinkle generously with the cheese. Spread the artichokes evenly on top and sprinkle additional cheese over them. Pour the remaining béchamel over the whole, then top with the rest of the cheese and the bread crumbs. Drizzle the remaining butter over the top. Bake in a preheated (350°) oven for about 20 minutes or until golden brown. Serves about 6.

Omelet with Artichoke Bottoms FRANCE

Finely mince two small artichoke bottoms (raw if possible), season them, and slightly brown them in butter. Add beaten and seasoned eggs, and make the omelet in the usual way.

Artichoke Bottoms Au Gratin
with Vegetable Filling

10 *canned artichoke bottoms*
  Filling
2 *tablespoons butter*
¼ *cup flour*
½ *cup milk*
2 *egg yolks*
  dash salt
½ *cup asparagus tips, cooked*
½ *cup green beans, frenched*
  and cooked

2 *mushrooms, diced*
1½ *tablespoons butter*
  white sauce
1½ *tablespoons butter*
2 *tablespoons flour*
½ *cup water or soup stock*
1 *egg yolk*
¼ *cup milk*
¼ *teaspoon salt*
1½ *tablespoons cheese, grated*

Cook artichoke bottoms in canned stock 5 minutes. Place in buttered ovenproof dish. Prepare filling.

Melt butter; blend in flour; add milk. Cool; add egg yolks and salt. Add cooled asparagus tips, beans, and mushrooms sautéed in butter.

Heap on top of artichoke bottoms. Prepare white sauce. Pour over filling. Sprinkle with cheese. Bake in 375° oven 10 minutes. Serves 5 to 7.

Artichoke Bottoms Sauté

Remove the leaves and the chokes from the artichokes, trim the bottoms, and slice them up raw. Season them with salt and pepper; toss them in butter; set them in a vegetable dish, and sprinkle them with herbs.

Fried Artichokes

2 artichokes
2 cups water
  juice of ½ lemon
1 cup flour

2 eggs, lightly beaten
1 teaspoon salt
½ teaspoon pepper
1½ cups olive oil

Cut off tips and stalks of artichokes, discard tough outer leaves, and cut in halves, removing chokes from centers. Cut into very thin slices. Dip into 2 cups of water to which lemon juice has been added, drain, dry and roll in flour. Add salt and pepper to beaten eggs. Dip floured artichoke slices into egg mixture and fry in hot olive oil until golden brown. Serve hot. Serves 4.

Artichoke Hearts Florentine

4 to 8 boiled, hot globe artichoke hearts
¾ to 1 pound fresh spinach or 1 packet deep-frozen, whole spinach
  (9 ounces)
2 tablespoonfuls butter or margarine
  salt
  full quantity of Hollandaise

Clean and wash the fresh spinach. Blanch it and let it drain. Thaw deep-frozen spinach. Fry the spinach in the fat and add salt.

Make the Hollandaise.

Arrange the hot artichoke hearts in a dish, cover with the spinach and pour the Hollandaise on top.

The dish may be garnished with slices of truffle. Serves 4.

Artichokes with Green Beans

4 artichokes
  salted water

1 pound green beans
4 tablespoons butter, melted

Wash artichokes; cut off stems and leaf ends, and boil in salted water to cover for about 40 minutes, or until tender. Drain. Remove artichokes, cube, and cook in ¼ cup water for 5 minutes. Wash beans and cook for 15 to 30 minutes in salted water to cover. Drain and place in a dish; pour melted butter over and place artichoke cubes around the edges. Serves 4 to 6.

Artichoke Hearts with Sauce   SCANDINAVIA

4 to 8 boiled, hot globe artichoke hearts
full quantity Hollandaise

Arrange the hearts in a dish and pour the selected sauce or creamed vegetable over them.

The dish may be garnished with asparagus tips or mushrooms fried in butter.

Serve as a vegetable entrée or as a supper or luncheon dish with boiled rice. Serves 4.

Jerusalem Artichokes   JEWISH

These vegetables are very unlike the other artichokes. They are edible roots that look like small clusters of new potatoes. Italians call it *girasole*, but it must have been some early American Puritan colonist who named it Jerusalem Artichoke. If you have to combat a starch allergy or plan a diabetic diet, this starch-free vegetable will be of great help.

Wash, scrape and boil, in very little salted water, till tender. Drain. Add butter or grated cheese. Or cream with a white sauce made of butter, flour and milk or vegetable liquid.

Jerusalem Artichokes Au Gratin   SCANDINAVIA

with cream-fil or sour cream
1½ to 2 pounds cooked Jerusalem artichokes
1½ to 2 gills cream-fil or sour cream (1 to 1¼
  cups)
3 to 4 tablespoonfuls grated cheese

Put the Jerusalem artichokes into a greased, fireproof dish. Pour the cream-fil on top and sprinkle with grated cheese.

Brown in oven (450°) for about 15 minutes.

Serve with boiled rice. Serves 4.

Fried Jerusalem Artichokes FRANCE

Peel and cut the Jerusalem artichokes into thick slices. Cook these in butter; dip them in batter, and fry them at the last moment.

Artichokes ISRAEL

12 small artichokes
2 cloves garlic, crushed (optional)
2 tablespoons chopped parsley

2 tablespoons chopped mint
1 cup olive oil
lemon wedges
salt

Trim the tops off the artichokes, working around and around so as to retain the shape. Soak in salt water for an hour, then drain dry. Meanwhile lightly fry the garlic and herbs (this is a *battuto*) in a tablespoon of the oil and tuck a little of this mixture into the center of each artichoke. Heat the remaining oil and place the artichokes in it, upside down, 2 or 3 at a time. Cook until crisp on the outside (about 10 minutes) and serve hot with lemon wedges and salt. The artichokes open up like a rose, are crunchy on the outside and tender within. Serves 6.

Purée of Jerusalem Artichokes FRANCE

Peel, slice, and cook the Jerusalem artichokes in butter. Rub them through a sieve, and work the *purée* over the fire, with two ounces of butter per pound. Add enough mashed potatoes to thicken the preparation, and complete with a few tablespoons of boiling milk.

Stachys or Japanese Artichokes FRANCE

Whatever be their mode of preparation, Japanese artichokes must be cleaned, parboiled, and kept firm, and cooked in butter without browning.

Sauté of Stachys or
Japanese Artichokes in Butter   F R A N C E

After having parboiled, drained, and dried the Japanese artichokes, put them in an omelet pan containing some very hot butter, and toss them over a hot fire, until they are well frizzled. Serve in a *timbale*, and sprinkle moderately with chopped parsley.

Stachys or Japanese Artichokes in Cream   F R A N C E

After having parboiled the Japanese artichokes and three-quarters cooked them in butter, moisten with boiling cream, and complete their cooking while reducing the cream. Add a little thin, fresh cream at the last moment, and serve in a *timbale*.

Purée of Stachys or Japanese Artichokes   F R A N C E

Cook the Japanese artichokes in salted water, keeping them somewhat firm, and add 4 ounces of quartered potatoes per pound of Japanese artichokes.

As soon as they are cooked, drain the Japanese artichokes and the potatoes; rub them through a sieve, and dry the *purée* over a very hot fire. Add the necessary quantity of milk to bring the *purée* to its proper consistency; heat; add butter away from the fire, and serve in a *timbale*.

Artichokes with Mint   I T A L Y

4 *artichokes*	1 *teaspoon chopped mint*
3 *tablespoons olive oil*	*leaves*
½ *teaspoon salt*	3 *tablespoons water*
½ *teaspoon pepper*	

Cut off stems and tips of artichokes and remove outer leaves. Cut each into about 10 slices, removing center chokes. Place in skillet with oil, salt, pepper, and mint and cook slowly 30 minutes, or until artichokes are tender. Add a little water during cooking, if necessary. Serves 4.

Croquettes of Stachys or Japanese Artichokes

Having cooked the Japanese artichokes in salted water, and kept them somewhat firm, thoroughly drain them and mix them with a very reduced Allemande sauce in the proportion of one-fifth pint per pound of Japanese artichokes. Spread this preparation on a buttered dish, and cool. Now cut this preparation into portions weighing about 2 ounces; shape these portions like balls, pears, cakes, or otherwise, dip them in beaten eggs, and roll them in very fine bread crumbs.

Plunge these *croquettes* into very hot fat five or six minutes before serving; drain them on a piece of linen; salt moderately, and set them on a napkin with very green, fried parsley.

Artichokes Sicilian Style

4 artichokes
½ small onion, chopped
1 clove garlic, chopped
1 tablespoon chopped parsley
2 tablespoons grated Roman cheese

1 cup bread crumbs
½ teaspoon salt
½ teaspoon pepper
¼ cup olive oil
2 tablespoons water
2 tablespoons olive oil

Cut off stalks and tips of artichokes and remove some of the tough outer leaves. Spread remaining leaves open. Mix onion, garlic, parsley, cheese, bread crumbs, salt and pepper, moisten with ¼ cup olive oil and 2 tablespoons water and fill each leaf with a tiny bit of this mixture. Fill the center of each artichoke with this mixture also.

Place artichokes in baking dish, sprinkle with olive oil and pour a little water in bottom of the dish. Bake in slow oven (325°) 45 minutes, or until the bottoms of the artichokes are soft to the fork. Serves 4.

Artichokes with Tartare Sauce   ISRAEL

The Artichokes
8 artichokes
4 quarts water
2 tablespoons salt
2 tablespoons vinegar
The Tartare Sauce
½ teaspoon chopped tarragon

1 cup mayonnaise
4 tablespoons sour cream (optional)
1 tablespoon chopped pickles or capers
1 tablespoon chopped chives
1 tablespoon chopped parsley

Trim the spikes (if there are any) off the top of the artichokes. Bring the water to a boil and add the salt and vinegar. Cook the artichokes for 40 to 50 minutes (leaves should pull out easily). Drain, cool, and serve cold.

Mix the ingredients for the tartare sauce. Serves 8.

Note: Artichokes can also be served hot, with butter or Hollandaise sauce.

Turkish Artichokes   ISRAEL

10 artichoke hearts
    juice of 1 lemon
1 teaspoon salt
½ cup water

¼ cup olive oil
1 small clove garlic
2 teaspoons sugar
1 tablespoon cornstarch

Soak the artichoke hearts in the lemon juice, salt, and water for an hour. Put them, and the liquid in which they were steeped, into a little pot with the oil, garlic, and sugar. Simmer gently until tender (about 30 minutes). Remove the artichokes to a serving dish. Thicken the sauce with cornstarch and pour over the hearts. Cool. Serve cold. Serves 4.

Artichokes Tuscan Style ITALY

4 small tender artichokes
  juice of 1 lemon
2 tablespoons flour
1 cup olive oil

4 eggs
½ teaspoon salt
½ teaspoon pepper
2 tablespoons milk

Cut off tips and stems of artichokes and remove tough outer leaves. Cut into thin slices, removing chokes from centers. Place artichoke slices in water and lemon juice and let stand 5 minutes. Drain, dry well, and roll in flour. Fry in olive oil until nicely browned.

Place fried slices in buttered shallow baking dish. Mix eggs, salt, pepper, and milk and beat lightly with fork. Pour egg mixture over artichoke slices and bake in moderate oven (375°) 15 minutes. Serve immediately. Serves 4.

Tuscan Style Omelet ITALY

2 artichokes
2 tablespoons flour
3 tablespoons olive oil

4 eggs, lightly beaten with fork
¼ teaspoon salt
⅛ teaspoon pepper

Cut outer leaves off the artichokes, cut in half, remove chokes, and slice lengthwise in very thin slices. Flour the artichoke slices and fry in olive oil until crisp. When crisp, add eggs which have been beaten lightly with salt and pepper. Continue frying 12 minutes on each side. Serves 4.

Artichokes in Wine POLAND

4 medium artichokes
2 tablespoons melted butter

1 cup dry white wine
salt and pepper to taste

Cook artichokes 20 minutes. Drain half-cooked artichokes, and when cool enough to handle, cut in quarters, scoop out hairy centers, and arrange tightly in casserole. Add butter and wine, season lightly, and simmer tightly covered another 20 minutes. Serve with olive oil and vinegar, or other sauce according to preference. Serves 4 to 8.

Asparagus POLAND

Asparagus should be very fresh—never wrinkled or with dry or soft tops. Wash thoroughly, and scrape lower part of stems. The best cooking method is to tie the spears into a bunch and stand them in the lower half of a double boiler in about 5 inches of water to which 1 teaspoon salt and 1 teaspoon sugar are added. Reverse upper part of double boiler and use as cover so that the more tender tips will steam while the tougher lower stems cook in water. Allow 20 to 30 minutes, depending on thickness of stems. Serve with Hollandaise sauce or with White Sauce or cold with mayonnaise or french dressing. Allow ½ pound per portion.

Asparagus FRANCE

The best-known varieties of asparagus in Europe are:

1. The Lauris asparagus, which is par excellence the early-season kind.

2. The green, Parisian asparagus, which is very small, and of which the most diminutive sticks serve for garnishes.

3. The Argenteuil asparagus—very much in demand while it is in season.

4. English asparagus, which is somewhat delicate in quality, but inclined to be small. During the season there are, besides, several other kinds of asparagus imported from Spain or France, which, though not equal to the four kinds above mentioned,

may nevertheless be used for soups or garnishes instead of asparagus tips.

(Asparagus is grown all over the United States but the best kind comes from California. There are two varieties grown, the green and the white. The taste of most Americans goes to the green asparagus which grows to be as thick as any of the white type, so much appreciated in Europe. The tips of both kinds are used for salads and garnishes. If the asparagus is not absolutely young it is best to peel the stalks thinly and remove the ends that are tough.)

Asparagus should be had as fresh as possible; it should be cleaned with care, quickly washed, tied into bunches, and cooked in plenty of salted water.

Asparagus is served on special silver drainers, or on napkins.

Asparagus   INDIA

2 pounds fresh asparagus
salted water
4 tablespoons ghee (or more)

Wash the asparagus. Cut off the lower stems, which may be quite tough. Do not skin them. Tie securely around their middles with any stout, clean string, and stand them on their bottoms.

Steam them in a pot filled about halfway up the stalks with boiling salted water, and cover. (If your pot is not tall enough, then invert another pot over the tops.) Covered, the steam will tenderize the tops, which cook faster than the bottoms, while the bottoms are boiling. Cook anywhere from 10 to 15 minutes (depending upon the thickness of the asparagus).

When done, remove from the water. Untie and place in a serving bowl. Spread the ghee over the asparagus. Serves 4.

Note: Other vegetables may be prepared just this simply, of course. Boil in salted water until tender, then spread with ghee.

When making vegetables this way, never substitute butter for the ghee, for it wrecks their finer natural flavors.

Asparagus au Gratin   FRANCE

Lay the asparagus in rows, and coat the heads of each row with a little Mornay sauce. When all are placed, two-thirds cover the bunch with a band of buttered parchment paper, and coat the uncovered portion with the Mornay sauce. Sprinkle with grated Parmesan cheese; *glaze* quickly at the *salamander*, remove the paper, and serve at once.

Baked Asparagus   CZECHOSLOVAKIA

3 tablespoons flour   dash of nutmeg
¼ cup butter   1 pound asparagus, boiled
1 cup milk or water   ½ cup grated cheese
  salt to taste

Brown flour in half the butter. Add milk, salt, and nutmeg. Simmer sauce for 5 minutes. Arrange asparagus in a greased casserole in layers with sauce, and sprinkle with cheese. Dot with the remaining butter and bake in 350° oven for 30 minutes. Serves 2.

Asparagus   GERMANY

  2 pounds asparagus
    salt
  2 tablespoons bread crumbs in 4 tablespoons butter or Hollan-
    daise sauce or sauce vinaigrette

Clean fresh asparagus and remove hard end of stems. Bundle together and cut to assure even length. Set in lightly salted boiling water and cook until done, about 20 to 25 minutes. Asparagus is done if it bends when lifted out of water. Drain well (saving liquid) and serve on a hot platter. Cover with bread crumbs browned in butter or with Hollandaise sauce or sauce vinaigrette. The cooking water may be used as a soup base or, cool, as a wholesome vegetable juice drink. In the latter case, do not salt too heavily. Serves 2 to 4.

Boiled Asparagus

10 ounces asparagus for each portion water
2 teaspoonfuls salt to 1 quart (5 cups) water

Cooking Time: freshly picked asparagus: about 20 minutes, other asparagus, 40 to 50 minutes.

Scrape (or peel) the asparagus from the top downwards.

Cut off the lowest part if it is woody. Rinse the asparagus.

Use an asparagus boiler: this is a tall, cylindrical pan with an inner, perforated cylinder fitted with hooks or handles for lifting it in and out. The pan is fitted with a lid.

Trim the stalks to a suitable length so that the asparagus stands upright in the inner cylinder of the boiler. Place the cylinder inside the pan and half fill the boiler with boiling water. Add salt. Cover and cook until tender. In this way the tips are cooked in steam and not in the sulphurous water below.

If an asparagus boiler is not available, the following method may be used.

Put the asparagus on to a rack or a piece of foil with the tips pointing in the same direction.

Lower them into the boiling salted water and cook until tender. Lift out the asparagus and let it drain.

Serve as a separate course with (creamed) butter, to which lemon juice may be added, or with Hollandaise, mousseline, or Maltese sauce. Asparagus can also be served hot on a vegetable platter or cold with mayonnaise or vinaigrette dressing.

Note: Green asparagus is prepared in the same way but it is not peeled. It requires slightly less cooking time.

Argenteuil Poached Eggs

Garnish the bottom of some *tartlet-crusts* with asparagus cut into pieces and cooked, and six green asparagus tips, about one and one-half inches in length, arranged like a star. Place an egg, coated with cream sauce mixed with half its volume of asparagus *purée*, upon each *tartlet*.

Asparagus Tips with Butter   F R A N C E

Green asparagus is chiefly used for garnishing or as a garnishing ingredient, but it may also be served as a vegetable with perfect propriety. Cut the asparagus into two-inch lengths, and tie them together in bundles.

Cut what remains of them into bits the size of peas. After having washed the latter, plunge them into boiling salted water, and cook them quickly, that they may keep green.

This done, thoroughly drain them; let their moisture evaporate by tossing them over the fire; mix them with butter, away from the fire, and serve them in a *timbale* with the asparagus bunches on top.

They are usually served in small patty crusts, or in small *tartlet crusts*, with a few tips on each small patty or *tartlet*.

Asparagus with Hollandaise   I S R A E L

2 bunches asparagus,	3 egg yolks
trimmed	1 tablespoon lemon juice
water as required	¼ teaspoon salt
1 teaspoon salt	½ cup hot asparagus liquid
Sauce:	cayenne pepper, if desired
½ cup butter	

Cook the trimmed asparagus, standing up, in quickly boiling water with the salt. The tips should not be in the water, but should be steamed for about 15 minutes by putting a smaller pot over the top of the one with the water. Drain well, reserving the liquid.

For the sauce, work the butter until creamy, adding the egg yolks one at a time, then the lemon juice and salt. Just before serving, add the asparagus liquid and stir quickly. Cook in top of a double boiler until thick, stirring constantly. Add a dash of cayenne pepper if you wish. Serve over the drained asparagus. Serves 6 to 8.

Creamed Asparagus

1 pound asparagus, cut
   into 2-inch pieces
1⅓ cups water
   salt to taste
2 tablespoons flour

2 tablespoons butter
½ cup cream
1 egg yolk
1 tablespoon minced parsley or
   chives

Simmer asparagus in salted water until tender (10 to 20 minutes). Drain, reserving the liquid. Brown flour in butter, add drained liquid to it, and simmer for 5 minutes. Blend in cream mixed with egg yolk, and add asparagus. Heat almost to boiling, but do not boil. Before serving, add parsley or chives. Serves 2 to 4.

Creamed Asparagus on Toast

Steam tips of asparagus as in basic recipe. Make a cream sauce, using the vegetable liquid and milk, add grated cheese and asparagus tips just before serving on toast points. Dust with paprika or minced parsley.

Variation: Place 3 or 4 steamed asparagus tips on toast and cover with sliced hard-cooked eggs. Top with cream sauce and a dash of paprika.

Asparagus with Eggs Milanese

1 small bunch asparagus
4 poached eggs
½ cup butter, melted

4 tablespoons grated Parmesan cheese
1 teaspoon salt
½ teaspoon pepper

Clean asparagus and cut off tough part of stalk. Boil briskly about 15 minutes, or until tender. Exact time for boiling depends on thickness and tenderness of the asparagus. Drain very well. Place poached eggs in center of baking dish, arrange asparagus around eggs, sprinkle with melted butter, Parmesan, salt and pepper and bake in very hot oven (450°) 3 or 4 minutes. Serves 4.

Flamande Asparagus FRANCE

According to Flemish custom, asparagus is served with one hot, hard-boiled egg, cut in half, and one ounce of melted butter per person. The egg yolk is crushed, seasoned, and finished with the butter by the diners themselves. This accompaniment may also be prepared beforehand and served in a sauceboat.

Deep-Fried Asparagus GERMANY

2 pounds asparagus	*1 to 2 cups flour*
salt	*fat*
2 eggs, beaten	

Cook asparagus in slightly salted water until half done. Chop off top half of stalks and tie together in bundles of 5 or 6. Dip in beaten egg and then roll in flour. Fry in deep fat. The stubs and cooking water can be used for soup. Serves 4.

Asparagus, Hungarian Style HUNGARY

2 pounds asparagus	*3 tablespoons butter*
salted water	*1 pint sour cream*
1 teaspoon sugar	*½ cup bread crumbs*

Peel asparagus and boil until soft in salted water to which a little sugar has been added. Drain. Butter an ovenproof dish. Place in it half of sour cream and bread crumbs, then asparagus, then cream and bread crumbs again.

Bake in 325° oven for about 30 minutes. Serves 4 to 6.

Asparagus, Polish Style

2 pounds asparagus
⅓ cup bread crumbs
⅓ cup butter

Prepare asparagus. Cook gently in salted water 20 minutes. Drain. Fry bread crumbs in butter. Pour on top. Serves 4.

Note: If asparagus is not cooked at once, wrap in wet towel and place in refrigerator.

Long white radishes, string beans, wax beans, cabbage, cauliflower, and Brussels sprouts may be prepared the same way.

Asparagus with Various Sauces

Butter sauce, Hollandaise, *Mousseline*, and Maltese sauces are the most usual accompaniments to asparagus. Béarnaise sauce without herbs is also served occasionally, likewise melted butter.

When eaten cold, it may be served with oil and vinegar or a mayonnaise—more particularly a Chantilly mayonnaise, one to which whipped cream has been added.

Asparagus in White Sauce

3 pounds asparagus *1 cup asparagus stock*
2 tablespoons butter *dash salt*
2 tablespoons flour

Peel asparagus; cut off tough ends. Place in cold water; drain. Cut into small pieces; cook in salted water 10 minutes (or until tender). Drain. Melt butter; blend in flour; add stock. Cook gently 3 minutes, stirring constantly. Add asparagus (except tips) and cook until tender (about 10 minutes). Add tips last to prevent overcooking. Serves 6.

Note: Cauliflower may be prepared the same way.

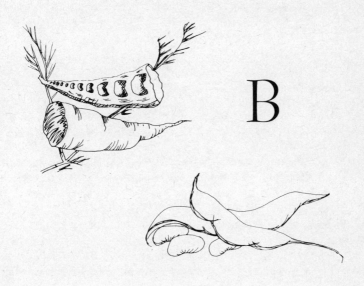

B

Sauté 3 Kinds of Bamboo Shoots with Chinese Red Cheese

CHINA

1 tablespoon peanut oil
1 clove garlic, crushed
1 cup bamboo shoots, cut into wedges
1 cup dried bamboo shoots, soaked in cold water overnight;
* cut off hard ends, chop into sections*
1 cup dried golden shoots, soaked in cold water overnight; cut
* off hard ends, chop into sections*
1 cake red cheese, mashed

Put peanut oil and a few drops of sesame seed oil in hot skillet; add garlic. Add bamboo shoots, dried bamboo shoots and dried golden shoots. Stir-fry 2 minutes.

Add red cheese. Stir 1 minute. Add 2 cups of water. Bring to a boil, reduce heat very low and let simmer 1 hour. Add more water if necessary. Serves 2.

Stuffed Bananas

1 cup chick pea flour
2 teaspoons salt
2 teaspoons turmeric
¾ teaspoon cayenne
1 tablespoon sugar
3 teaspoons peanut oil

3 to 4 firm bananas (the skins
   should be clear yellow and
   without brown freckles)
4 tablespoons peanut oil
½ teaspoon cumin seed
½ teaspoon mustard seed

In a small bowl, mix together the chick-pea flour, 1 teaspoon each of the salt and turmeric, ½ teaspoon of the cayenne, and the sugar. Add the 3 teaspoons oil. Blend well with the fingers until crumbly. Set aside.

Slice the stem ends from the bananas. Do not peel. Cut them into thirds, crosswise. Take each banana chunk and make a slit about halfway down (not across) the middle. Place in this pocket as much of the chick-pea mixture as will comfortably fit. Some will hang onto the end of the banana chunk, but this is okay. After all the banana pieces are stuffed, heat the 4 table-spoons oil, and to it add the cumin and mustard seed, and the rest of the salt, turmeric, and cayenne. When the mustard pops, add the banana chunks, one at a time, placing them on their sides, until the bottom of the pot is tightly packed. *Do not stack* them. Turn the heat quite low; cover. Shake the pot once or twice, to spread the oil over all. After 6 minutes, turn the bananas gently, using a fork (it is easier than a spoon), taking care not to puncture the skins. Cook another 6 minutes. Then eat, skin and all. Serves 4.

Banana and Eggplant Casserole

3 bananas
1 eggplant

Prepare the bananas exactly as in Stuffed Bananas. Use 3 bananas, and prepare twice as much stuffing.

Prepare an eggplant for stuffing—you should have as many eggplant chunks as banana chunks. Do not peel the eggplant, but simply cut it into chunks about the same dimensions as the banana and proceed to stuff it the same way.

Fry the stuffed eggplant first, since it takes longer to cook. Allow about 20 minutes—10 minutes on each side. Set the cooked eggplant aside and keep warm, then cook the bananas.

Arrange the stuffed eggplant and stuffed bananas in a casserole. Here you can have more than one layer. Pour juices from the pot over all. Place in the oven (350°) long enough to heat through. Serves 4.

Beans from Damascus   ISRAEL

2 cups small brown beans	1 cup prepared tahina
6 cups water	(sesame seed paste)
6 eggs	juice of ½ lemon
salt and pepper to taste	dash of cayenne
3 tablespoons olive oil	parsley
3 cloves garlic	dash of turmeric

Put the beans, water, unshelled raw eggs, salt, and pepper in a heavy pot and bring to the boil. Add the oil and the garlic. Simmer, covered, overnight on very low heat. Serve the beans with the whole eggs, shelled, and next to it the tahina sprinkled with lemon juice and garnished to taste, with parsley and a sprinkling of cayenne. Sprinkle turmeric on the egg. Serves 4 to 6.

Bean—or Lentil or Dried Pea—Patties   POLAND

2 cups beans, lentils, or dried peas	salt and pepper
2 whole eggs, lightly beaten	bread crumbs for rolling
3 tablespoons bread crumbs	butter for frying

Cook beans and purée. The purée for patties should be rather dry, which is the reason for omitting bouillon. When the purée has cooled, add beaten eggs, bread crumbs, and seasoning. Make patties. Roll in crumbs and fry in butter. Serves 5 to 6.

Baked Beans with Apples ISRAEL

1 cup white navy beans
3 large apples, peeled and quartered
1 cup sugar
½ pound fat

1 teaspoon salt
  dash of cinnamon
½ cup red wine
2 tablespoons wine vinegar

Soak the beans overnight, change the water, and cook until tender (2 to 3 hours). Drain, add the remaining ingredients, and stew gently over low heat for 1 hour. Serves 4 to 6.

Baked Beans JEWISH

2 cups navy beans
½ teaspoon salt
1 onion

4 tablespoons shortening
¼ tablespoon molasses
½ cup tomato sauce

Beans should be soaked in cold water for several hours or overnight. Drain, cover with fresh cold water, add salt and onion and cook over moderate heat until the skins of beans fill out and beans begin to soften enough to crush between thumb and forefinger. Add molasses and tomato sauce. Turn into a casserole, cover, and bake 1 to 1½ hours at 325°. Uncover and bake 10 to 25 minutes longer till reddish brown on top.

Serves 4 to 6.

Variation: Use tenderized navy beans (marked on package). These do not require soaking. Cook as above.

Variation 2: Black-eyed round beans or red kidney beans may be substituted.

Beans in Tomato Sauce ISRAEL

3 cups white navy beans
3 large onions
3 cloves garlic
3 carrots
6 large tomatoes

4 tablespoons olive oil
  water
½ cup chopped parsley
  dash of paprika or cayenne
  salt and pepper to taste

Soak the beans overnight. Boil 2 to 3 hours, or until tender. Drain. Cut up the vegetables fine and fry in oil until golden. Add a very little water and cook to a pulp (about 10 minutes). Add the seasonings. Put the sauce into the beans and simmer together for about 15 minutes more. Serves 8 to 10.

Bean Curd with Soy Sauce CHINA

6 cakes bean curd
3 tablespoons best light soy sauce
1 teaspoon seasoning powder and pinch of pepper
4 tablespoons peanut oil, heated until smoking
2 fresh scallions (white part only), cut into 1½ inch sections, then split
½ cup parsley

Cut bean curd into 4 slices each and place in deep dish, or divide into 2 portions and place on individual plates.

Mix light soy sauce with seasoning powder and pinch of pepper. Pour over bean curd.

Pour heated peanut oil over bean curd. Garnish with scallions and parsley. Serve hot or cold. Serves 2.

Boiled Beans or Peas SCANDINAVIA

6 to 8 ounces beans or peas for each portion
water
2 teaspoonfuls salt to each quart (5 cups) of water

Cooking Time: Young tender beans or peas: 8 to 12 minutes. Coarser beans or peas: 15 to 20 minutes. Deep-frozen beans or peas: 5 to 7 minutes.

Top and tail the beans or peas (such as French beans, wax beans, runner beans, sugar peas) and remove the stringy threads along the sides. Wash them thoroughly. Slice runner beans into pieces. Put the vegetables into boiling salted water. Deep-frozen beans or peas are put into the water unthawed. Boil them until they are tender.

Strain the vegetables.

Fried Bean Curd with Mushrooms CHINA

6 cakes bean curd
1½ cups black or white mushrooms,
  shredded (soak black mushrooms
  in warm water 15 minutes)
1 teaspoon light soy sauce
1 teaspoon sugar
1 teaspoon seasoning powder

1 teaspoon rice wine or 2 tablespoons
  sherry wine
1 teaspoon salt
  pinch of pepper
½ cup water
1 tablespoon cornstarch
½ teaspoon heavy soy sauce

Cut cakes of bean curd into 4 pieces each. Fry in deep fat until light brown. Put into deep dish. Mix light soy sauce, salt, pepper, sugar, seasoning powder, rice wine or sherry wine together; add ½ cup water. Stir well before using. Mix water, cornstarch, and heavy soy sauce together. Stir well before using.

Mushroom Sauce: Soak shredded mushrooms in light soy sauce preparation (if black mushrooms are used soak in warm water for 15 minutes before adding to preparation); cook in frying pan for 5 minutes.

Add cornstarch preparation slowly and cook until mixture becomes translucent. Pour sauce over bean curd.

Garnish with chopped parsley. Serves 2.

Beans, Tuscan Style ITALY

¾ pound white beans
2 tablespoons olive oil
½ teaspoon sage
2 cloves garlic, sliced
4 cups water

1 large fresh tomato, peeled
  and cut into pieces
1 teaspoon salt
½ teaspoon pepper
2 tablespoons olive oil

Place well-washed beans in large saucepan with oil, sage, garlic, water, and tomato. Cover pan, and cook over low flame 3 hours, or until tender. Add salt, pepper and olive oil before serving. Serves 4.

Broad Beans or Pole Beans FRANCE

Broad beans should be shelled just before being cooked, and it is quite the rule to peel them. Boil them in salted water containing a bunch of savory, the size of which should be in proportion to the quantity of broad beans. When they are cooked and drained, add the leaves of savory (chopped) to them.

Broad Beans in Butter   F R A N C E

Having well-drained and shelled the broad beans, toss them
over a hot fire to dry, and then finish them, away from the
fire, with three ounces of butter per pound of beans.

Creamed Broad Beans   F R A N C E

After having dried and shelled the broad beans, combine them
(per pound) with three tablespoons of thick, fresh cream.

Bean Sprouts—Plain   I N D I A

A little oil (1 tablespoon—no
    more)
1 teaspoon salt

¼ teaspoon mustard seed
¼ teaspoon cayenne
1 cup bean sprouts (not methi)

Heat the oil. Add the seasonings, stir, and when heated, add
the bean sprouts. Cook and stir rapidly for 3 to 5 minutes. Serves
4.

Brown Beans   S C A N D I N A V I A

¾ pint dried brown beans (1 pound or 2¼ cups)
1¾ to 2 pints water (4¼ to 5 cups)
1 to 1½ teaspoonfuls salt
2 to 4 tablespoonfuls syrup
2½ to 5 tablespoonfuls table vinegar (7½ teaspoons)
1 tablespoonful potato flour (optional)

Cooking Time: 1 to 1½ hours.
Clean and wash the beans. Soak in the salted water for about
12 hours.
Cook the beans in the same water until tender. Stir occasionally
and add more water if required.
Flavor the beans with the syrup and vinegar. If they are not
sufficiently thickened, they can be thickened after cooking.
Serves 4.

Fava Beans   ISRAEL

1 pound fava or butter beans (dried)
salt

Soak the beans overnight in cold water. Drain. Cook in fresh water over low heat for about 45 minutes. Drain and sprinkle with salt while still warm.

French Beans   POLAND

1 pound snap or wax beans
1 small onion, blanched and
* grated*
1 tablespoon butter
salt and pepper to taste

1 tablespoon chopped fresh dill
* and parsley*
dash of nutmeg
lemon juice to taste

Steam beans 10 minutes in a little salted water. Cook grated onion in butter until golden brown, add drained beans, seasoning, herbs, and lemon juice to taste. Simmer tightly covered 10 minutes longer. Serves 3 to 4.

Oven-Baked Giant Beans   GREECE

2 pounds dried giant white
* beans*
2 cups oil
1 head garlic, cleaned
3 medium onions, chopped
1 tablespoon chopped celery
½ cup minced parsley

salt and pepper to taste
1 cup hot water
1¾ pounds ripe tomatoes,
* peeled and strained, or 1 ta-*
* blespoon tomato paste*
* diluted with 1½ cups water*
water as needed

Wash the beans, place in water, and soak them overnight. Drain them, then place in a pot of fresh cold salted water; cook for 45 minutes; drain. Meanwhile, place the oil, garlic, and onions in a baking pan and bake in a preheated 350° oven until golden. Add the beans, celery, parsley, salt, pepper, and hot water. Bake 30 minutes longer. Remove from oven, stir the beans, pour in the tomatoes (or diluted tomato paste). Return to oven and bake until only the oil remains. Serves 6.

Potted Giant Beans

2 pounds dried giant white
    beans
2 cups oil
3 to 4 medium onions,
    chopped
½ cup chopped parsley

1¾ pounds ripe tomatoes,
    peeled and strained, or 1 ta-
    blespoon tomato paste
    diluted with 1½ cups water
salt and pepper to taste

Wash the beans and soak them overnight. Drain, then put into a pot and cover with fresh cold, salted water. Bring to a boil; pour off all the water. Add the oil, onions, parsley, salt, and pepper; stir over medium heat until the onions are golden. Add 2 cups hot water. Cover and simmer for 1 hour. Add the tomatoes (or diluted tomato paste); stir. Cook until the beans are tender and only the oil remains (about 30 minutes). Serves 6.

Green Beans

2 pounds green beans
2 tablespoons fat
2 onions, chopped
    salt to taste
1 tablespoon flour

paprika to taste
2 cloves garlic, mashed
½ cup hot meat bouillon or
    water
1 tablespoon dill, chopped fine

Wash beans; clean and cut lengthwise; simmer in 1 tablespoon of the fat with chopped onion for 10 to 15 minutes. Season with salt when they are almost done. Make a blond roux from remaining fat and flour; color with paprika; add garlic; pour in bouillon or water and add to beans. Sprinkle with dill. Serve with yogurt. Serves 4 to 6.

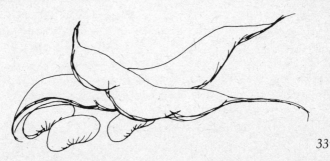

Green Beans, Bulgarian Style BULGARIA

2-3 onions
¼ cup oil
  paprika to taste
1 pound green beans, broken
  in pieces
2 carrots, peeled and sliced
  thin

4 tomatoes, peeled and quartered
2 green peppers, membrane
  removed, seeded and chopped
chopped herbs to taste

Cut onions into rings, and cut rings in half. Fry in hot oil until golden; sprinkle with paprika, then add beans and carrots. Simmer for about 45 minutes. Add tomatoes and peppers. Simmer for another 15 minutes. Sprinkle with herbs. Serves 4 to 6.

Green Beans in Oil GREECE

3 pounds green beans
1½ cups oil
2 medium onions, minced
1½ pounds ripe tomatoes,
  peeled and strained, or

1 tablespoon tomato paste
  diluted with 2 cups water
2 tablespoons minced parsley
salt and pepper to taste
water as needed

Wash the beans and break them in half or slice them lengthwise. Place in a large pot of cold water. Heat the oil in a large pot and sauté the onions in it until soft and limp; add the tomatoes (or diluted tomato paste), and bring to a boil. Drain the beans and add them to the pot. Add the parsley, salt, pepper, and enough water to barely cover the beans. Cook over medium heat until the liquid is absorbed but the oil remains (30 to 45 minutes). Serves 6.

Green Beans Paprika   CZECHOSLOVAKIA

1 medium onion, chopped   salt to taste
¼ cup butter   ½ cup water
¼ teaspoon paprika   2 tablespoons flour
1 pound green beans cut into   ½ cup sour cream
  1-inch pieces (3 cups)

Fry onion in butter, add paprika, beans, salt, and water. Simmer until tender (20 to 30 minutes). Mix flour with sour cream, stir into beans. Simmer for 5 minutes. Serve with hard-cooked eggs and potatoes. Serves 4.

Spiced Green Beans   JEWISH

1 pound green beans   1 clove garlic
2 tablespoons vinegar or   1 bay leaf
  lemon juice   Dash of allspice
  Brown sugar to taste

Cut beans diagonally or lengthwise. Cook in very little water 5 minutes, in a covered saucepan. Add the other ingredients, cook 3 minutes longer. Remove garlic and bay leaf. Serve hot or cold. Serves 6 to 8.

Fresh Lima Beans   JEWISH

2 cups fresh limas   1 teaspoon salt
  water to cover   2 tablespoons butter

Cook limas in salted water over moderate heat 45 minutes or till tender. Add butter just before serving. Serves 4 to 5.

Dried Lima Beans   JEWISH

1½ cups dried lima beans   1¼ teaspoon salt
  water to cover   1 onion

Soak dried beans overnight. Drain and cover with cold water. Boil slowly 2 to 2½ hours in a covered pot, adding onion and salt after one hour of cooking. Remove onion, drain, and serve with butter. Serves 4 to 5.

Steamed Green Beans

1 pound beans	¼ teaspoon salt
½ cup water	2 tablespoons butter

Wash. Cut beans slantwise or lengthwise. Cook in pressure cooker, or cook in top of double boiler without additional water until steamed through and tender. Or cook in a well-covered saucepan with a little water 5 to 8 minutes. Season with salt and butter before serving.

Serves 6.

Variation 1: Add Creole sauce after beans are tender. Simmer 3 minutes and serve hot.

Variation 2: Add thick white sauce and top with grated cheese and a dash of paprika.

Variation 3: Add canned tomato sauce or stewed tomatoes, season with lemon juice and brown sugar, simmer 5 minutes and serve hot or cold.

Variation 4: Combine with steamed brown rice, season with butter and grated American cheese.

Variation 5: Add browned sliced onions and green peppers.

Sweet-Sour Green Beans

1 pound green beans	1 tablespoon flour
water to cover	salt and pepper
1 teaspoon salt	2 tablespoons sugar
2 tablespoons fat	2 tablespoons lemon juice

Wash the beans and split them lengthwise through the pods. Cook until tender in just enough water to cover (15 to 20 minutes). Drain, reserving liquid, and add the salt. Melt the fat and add the flour, then 1 cup of the liquid in which the beans were cooked (add water if necessary to make 1 cup), then the remaining ingredients. Add to the beans and heat through. Serves 4.

Lima Beans with Honey   ISRAEL

2 cups dried lima or other
  beans
  water to cover
2 onions, cut up

4 tablespoons fat
½ cup honey
2 teaspoons salt

Soak the beans overnight, cover with water, and cook over a low heat until beans are soft (2 to 3 hours). Drain off the water. Fry the onions in the fat, then add the honey and salt and mix with the beans. Bake in a 350° oven for about an hour, or until beans are glazed. Serves 6 to 8.

Snap Beans or Wax Beans   POLAND

Snap beans can be cooked whole or sliced (frenched). Steam in a little salted water and drain. Then add a lump of butter and allow to stand covered a few minutes while butter melts.

Snap Beans with Sour Cream   POLAND

2 pounds snap beans
1 cup court bouillon
1 tablespoon butter
1 cup sour cream

1 teaspoon flour
lemon juice, salt, and pepper
  to taste

Blanch beans, season, then simmer in court bouillon until tender (about 10 minutes). Add other ingredients and simmer another 5 minutes. Serves 6.

String Beans   INDIA

2 pounds string beans
4 tablespoons ghee
1 tablespoon mustard seed
1½ teaspoons salt

1 tablespoon cumin seed
2 teaspoons turmeric
¼ teaspoon cayenne

Sliver the string beans Indian style, as in String Beans with Coconut.

In a saucepan, warm the ghee, and add the seasonings to it. Stir until the mustard pops, then add the string beans. Stir until they are well coated, then lower the heat, cover, and simmer very, very gently for 10 minutes. Shake the pan a time or two so the beans don't stick, or lift the cover and stir. Serves 4.

String Beans with Coconut INDIA

2 pounds fresh young string
  beans (not so old that the
  beans are fat enough to split
  their pods)
4 tablespoons ghee

1 teaspoon salt
1 teaspoon turmeric
¼ teaspoon cayenne
¼ cup fresh coconut, grated
1 teaspoon coriander

Wash the string beans well, snap off the ends, and slice into two lengthwise. For the true Indian touch, cut them into four lengthwise slivers. Set aside.

In a saucepan, heat the ghee, and add the salt, turmeric, and cayenne to it. Add the beans. Stir until they are well coated. Cook, covered, for about 5 minutes, giving the pot an occasional shake. Then add the coconut and coriander.

Cover again, and cook gently for another 5 minutes. You won't need to add water. If the ghee seems a bit too much, leave most of the ghee in the pot when you turn the vegetables into a dish for serving. Serves 4.

String Bean Pudding ITALY

1 pound string beans
2 tablespoons butter
¼ teaspoon salt
1 cup cream sauce
2 eggs, lightly beaten with 2

tablespoons grated Parme-
  san cheese
2 tablespoons fine bread
  crumbs
2 tablespoons butter

Wash string beans and cut into very small pieces. Boil in water 18 minutes and drain. Place beans in saucepan with butter and salt and cook gently 5 minutes. Remove from fire and add cream sauce, eggs and Parmesan.

Grease a 1-quart mold and sprinkle with bread crumbs. Pour in bean mixture, top with more bread crumbs and dot with butter. Bake in hot oven (400°) 45 minutes, or until mixture is firm. Remove from oven and let stand 4 minutes before unmolding. Serves 4.

Fried String Beans

1 pound tender string beans
1 cup flour

1 cup olive oil
salt

Parboil string beans 10 minutes and drain well. Roll in flour and fry in hot olive oil until crisp and golden brown. Sprinkle with salt and serve immediately. Serves 4.

String Bean Soufflé

1 pound string beans
2 quarts boiling water
½ teaspoon salt
1 cup thick cream sauce

2 tablespoons grated Parme-
    san cheese
4 egg whites

Wash beans and cook in boiling salted water 20 minutes, or until tender. Drain and pass beans through strainer. Mix with cream sauce and cheese. Beat egg whites until stiff and fold gently into bean mixture. Pour into greased casserole and bake in moderate oven (375°) 25 minutes. Serve immediately. Serves 4.

Buttered White Beans

Having well drained the dried white beans, season them with salt and pepper and add to them 2 ounces of butter per pound of cooking beans. Serve in a *timbale* and sprinkle with chopped parsley.

Beets JEWISH

Scrub beets well after removing tops 2 inches from root. Cook beets of uniform size in cold water to cover, adding ½ teaspoon salt to 1 quart of water. The smaller the beets the less time it takes for boiling till tender enough to pierce with a toothpick. Drain and use beet liquid for borsht. Slip skins from beets, cut away stems and slice or dice. Add butter and serve hot.

Variation 1: Add 1 tablespoon prepared horseradish. Omit butter.

Variation 2: Add 1 tablespoon lemon juice or vinegar for each cup sliced beets, 1 tablespoon sugar and 1 tablespoon flour or cornstarch. Cook 3 to 5 minutes without stirring but shaking the saucepan to prevent scorching. Add butter or other shortening and serve hot. Generally called Harvard beets.

Creamed Mashed Beets JEWISH

3 cups cooked, mashed beets
1 tablespoon lemon juice
½ teaspoon salt

½ cup heavy cream or sour cream
½ cup crumbs
1 tablespoon butter

Cooked or canned beets, drained, put through the ricer may be used. Add lemon juice and salt, fold in sour cream or stiffly beaten heavy cream. Top with crumbs and dot with butter. Slip under broiler flame to brown lightly and serve hot. Serves 4.

Ginger Beets

1 tablespoon flour
1 tablespoon shortening
½ cup beet liquid
2 cups cooked beets, cut in
   strips
1 tablespoon lemon juice or
   vinegar

2 tablespoons brown sugar
¼ teaspoon salt
1 teaspoon ground ginger
¼ teaspoon dry mustard (optional)

Blend flour and shortening and brown lightly. Add beet liquid and stir till smooth. Add the other ingredients. Cook 3 to 5 minutes. Serves 5 or 6.

Harvard Beets

8 medium beets
2 tablespoons margarine
1 tablespoon flour

½ cup sugar
⅓ cup lemon juice
salt and pepper to taste

Boil the beets in their skins until they can be pierced with a fork (30 to 60 minutes). Remove the skins and slice with a lattice or other fancy cutter. Melt the margarine and bring to bubbling. Add the flour. Add the sugar mixed with the lemon juice and cook until thick and transparent, stirring constantly. Add the beets, season to taste, and heat through. You can use a little water to dilute the lemon juice if you prefer it less piquant. Serves 6 to 8.

Beets in Orange Sauce

2 cups orange juice
1 tablespoon brown sugar
  dash salt
⅛ teaspoon pepper

2 teaspoons cornstarch
1 tablespoon butter
2 cups cooked and sliced beets

In a saucepan, combine all the ingredients except the beets. Bring to a boil, stirring constantly to keep the sauce smooth. Add the beets (these can be either freshly cooked or canned), and continue to cook over medium heat until they are heated through. Serves 4.

Red Beets in Butter

1¼ pounds beets, cooked
3 tablespoons butter
1 teaspoon parsley, chopped
1 teaspoon chives, chopped

½ section garlic
1 teaspoon flour
1 tablespoon vinegar
  salt and pepper

Peel and slice beets. Melt butter in stew pan and add parsley, chives and garlic. Sprinkle lightly with flour and let simmer. Add beets, vinegar, and seasoning and simmer for another 30 minutes. Serves 4.

Beet Tops

Wash leaves and stems thoroughly in cold water. Drain. Cut into inch pieces. Cook without additional water in a well-covered pot 5 minutes. Add ⅛ teaspoon salt to each cupful, 1 tablespoon butter, oil, 2 tablespoons dry bread or cracker crumbs. Toss lightly. Serve hot.

Variation: Add 1 tablespoon brown sugar and 2 tablespoons mild vinegar to above. Cook 2 minutes over moderate heat. Garnish with diced hard-cooked egg.

Beetroot Steaks

4 *large, cooked beetroots*	7 *tablespoonfuls browned bread crumbs*
salt	*butter, margarine, or oil*
white pepper	*lemon juice (optional)*
Coating	*chopped parsley*
1 *egg*	

Cut the beetroots into slices ¼ inch in thickness. Season. Dip the slices into beaten egg and toss them in raspings. Fry them on both sides for about 5 minutes.

Arrange the steaks on a serving dish. A little lemon juice may be sprinkled over them. Pour the fat from the frying pan over the steaks and sprinkle with parsley. Serve with fried onions and mashed potatoes or with mushroom sauce. Serves 4.

Broccoli

2 *pounds broccoli*
1 *teaspoon salt*
1 *small onion*

Remove fibrous section of stems. Wash and drain well. Cover with cold water and let stand 10 minutes before cooking. Pour off half the water, add salt and onion, boil 20 minutes in a well-covered pot. Drain when ready to serve.

Serves 6.

Variation 1: Add Hollandaise sauce and a dash of paprika.

Variation 2: Serve with cheese sauce and garnish with parsley.

Boiled Broccoli

8 ounces broccoli for each portion
water
2 to 3 teaspoonfuls salt to each quart (5 cups) of water

Rinse the fresh broccoli and remove the coarse stalks.

Put into boiling salted water. Frozen broccoli is put into the water while frozen. Cook the broccoli until it is just tender, 15 to 20 minutes for fresh broccoli, 10 to 15 minutes for frozen. Drain.

Serve with (creamed) butter or with Hollandaise or mushroom sauce.

Broccoli Flowerets

1 onion
1 clove garlic
2 tablespoons oil or vegetable shortening
3 pounds broccoli
1 teaspoon salt
2 tablespoons lemon juice
1 cup water

Use tender parts of stems with the flower or head. Cut stems into ¼-inch rounds, and separate the heads into flowerets. Brown diced onion and garlic in shortening. Remove the garlic. Add broccoli, salt and lemon juice and water. Cover and simmer 15 to 20 minutes. Garnish with boiled or roasted chestnuts. Serves 6 to 8.

Broccoli Roman Style

1 small bunch broccoli
3 tablespoons olive oil
2 cloves garlic, sliced
½ teaspoon salt
½ teaspoon pepper
1½ cups dry red wine

Trim broccoli of tough leaves and stems, cut into small flowerets, wash well and drain. Place olive oil and garlic in large skillet and brown garlic. Add broccoli, salt and pepper and cook 5 minutes. Add wine, cover skillet and cook over very low flame 20 minutes, or until broccoli is tender, stirring gently so as not to break flowerets. Serves 4.

Broccoli Sour   ITALY

1 bunch broccoli   ½ teaspoon pepper
¼ cup olive oil   juice 1 lemon
½ teaspoon salt

Wash and clean broccoli thoroughly. Cook in 2 quarts boiling water 15 minutes, taking care not to overcook, and drain. Place broccoli on serving dish, sprinkle with oil, salt, pepper, and lemon juice, and serve. Serves 4.

Brussels Sprouts   JEWISH

1 pint sprouts   water to cover
½ teaspoon salt   2 tablespoons butter or oil

Pick off wilted outer leaves and soak sprouts in cold water 10 to 15 minutes before cooking. Drain well. Cover with cold water, add salt, bring to a boil and cook 10 minutes or until sprouts can be pierced with a toothpick. Add shortening and serve. Serves 2 to 3.

Variation 1: Drain and serve with white sauce.

Variation 2: Combine with ½ cup boiled chestnuts, adding butter to taste before serving.

Variation 3: Serve Brussels sprouts with well-seasoned tomato sauce.

Brussels Sprouts   GERMANY

1 pound Brussels sprouts   ½ cup cooking water
  salt   3 tablespoons cream or milk
  baking soda   salt and pepper
1 tablespoon butter   nutmeg
1 tablespoon flour

Cook sprouts in slightly salted water with a pinch of baking soda for 10 to 20 minutes. Prepare a sauce with butter, flour, cooking water, cream or milk and seasoning. Add sprouts and bring to a boil again. Serves 4.

Brussels Sprouts

2 pounds Brussels sprouts
2½ tablespoons butter
2 tablespoons flour
1 teaspoon parsley, chopped

1 teaspoon onion, chopped
½ cup water or vegetable stock
  salt to taste

Clean Brussels sprouts; wash and cook in salted water about 20 minutes. (Do not overcook.) Drain. Melt butter; blend in flour; add parsley and onion. Add ½ cup water or vegetable stock (stock preferred) and cook 2 to 3 minutes. Pour over Brussels sprouts. Serves 6.

Note: If desired, add pepper and ¼ teaspoon lemon juice.

Brussels Sprouts

6 cups trimmed Brussels
  sprouts
2 teaspoons salt
3 quarts boiling water

6 tablespoons butter or 1½
  cups white sauce (see below)
  or 1 cup Hollandaise
  sauce

Soak the Brussels sprouts in water to cover, with the salt, for about 15 minutes. Discard the water. Cook in the boiling water until just tender (10 to 15 minutes). Do not overcook—the sprouts must not be mushy. Drain and serve hot with butter, or Hollandaise sauce, or the following white sauce. Serves 6 to 8.

White Sauce
2 tablespoons margarine
2 tablespoons flour

1 cup hot milk
  salt and white pepper to taste
  dash of nutmeg (optional)

Melt the margarine and add the flour. When the mixture begins to bubble, stir in the hot milk and cook, stirring constantly, until thick and creamy. Add the seasoning.

Boiled Brussels Sprouts   SCANDINAVIA

8 ounces Brussels sprouts for each portion
water
2 to 3 teaspoonfuls salt water to each quart (5 cups) of water
butter or margarine (optional)

Trim and wash the fresh Brussels sprouts.

Put them into boiling salted water. Deep-frozen Brussels sprouts are put into the water while still frozen. Cook the sprouts until tender, 10 to 15 minutes for fresh Brussels sprouts, 10 minutes for frozen. Drain the sprouts which may then be tossed in hot fat.

Creamed Brussels Sprouts   CZECHOSLOVAKIA

1½ pounds Brussels sprouts   salt to taste
  boiling water to cover   pepper to taste
¼ cup butter   dash of mace
1½ tablespoons flour   dash of nutmeg
1⅔ cups cream

Soak cleaned Brussels sprouts in cold water for 15 minutes. Drain, then place in boiling water for 5 minutes. Drain again. Melt butter, blend in flour; add cream, and stir until smooth. Add Brussels sprouts, salt, and pepper. Simmer for 10 minutes or until tender. Add mace and nutmeg to taste. Serves 6 to 8.

Purée of Brussels Sprouts   FRANCE

Three-quarters cook the sprouts; drain them well without cooling them, and complete their cooking by stewing them in butter. Rub them through a fine sieve, and add to the resulting *purée* one-third of its bulk of mashed potatoes.

Heat, add butter away from the fire, and dish in a *timbale*.

C

Cabbage

1 head cabbage, cored
3 tablespoons peanut oil
1 teaspoon turmeric

1 teaspoon black mustard seed
½ teaspoon salt

Chop the cabbage fine. (If this is done in advance, the cabbage should be stored in a plastic bag until ready for use.) Then heat the peanut oil, and add the turmeric, mustard seed, and salt to it. Simmer until the mustard seed sputters, and add 4 cups of the chopped cabbage. Stir briskly over high heat for 5 minutes. The cabbage will be hot through, but still crunchy. If it is kept at room temperature, it will still be delicious. If it must be refrigerated before serving, reheat very quickly.

Bavarian Cabbage

GERMANY

2 pounds cabbage
1 apple
2 tablespoons butter
1 bay leaf
  salt and pepper

juniper berries
1 tablespoon flour
½ cup white wine
  sugar
  vinegar

Wash and shred cabbage. Slice apple. Melt butter in pan and add cabbage and apple. Mix thoroughly. Season well with bay leaf, salt, pepper, and a few juniper berries. Cook in one cup of water, more if needed, over low heat until done, about 10 minutes. When liquid has evaporated, sprinkle with flour, add wine and sugar and vinegar to taste. Serve immediately. Serves 4.

Boiled Cabbage SCANDINAVIA

> 8 to 10 ounces cabbage for each portion
>   water
> 2 to 3 teaspoonfuls salt to each quart of water (5 cups)

Trim and wash the cabbage. White cabbage, savoy cabbage, or spring cabbage may be used. Cut it into sections and remove the core and tougher ribs.

Heads of spring cabbage may be cooked whole, if they are small. Put the cabbage into boiling, salted water and boil until tender, 15 to 20 minutes for summer cabbage, 35 to 40 minutes for winter cabbage. Drain the cabbage thoroughly.

Serve on a vegetable platter.

Boiled Celery Cabbage SCANDINAVIA

> 8 to 10 ounces celery cabbage for each portion

Cut the cabbage into pieces 2 inches in length.

Continue preparation as for boiled cabbage. Cooking Time: 4 to 5 minutes.

Caraway Cabbage

¼ cup butter
1 small head cabbage,
   shredded
1 small onion, sliced
½ cup water

3 fresh tomatoes, chopped
1 teaspoon salt
1½ tablespoons caraway seed
2 tablespoons sugar
   finely chopped parsley

Melt the butter in a large pan and add the cabbage and onion. Cook, turning with a fork, until the vegetables are limp but not browned. Add the water, tomatoes, salt, caraway seed, and sugar. Cover and simmer for 30 minutes. Serve hot, garnished with the parsley. Serves about 6.

Cabbage Dumplings

1 medium cabbage
2 tablespoons oil
4 hot rolls
½ cup milk
¾ pound (3 sticks) butter

2 egg yolks
2 eggs, beaten
¼ cup flour
2 quarts salted water
   grated cheese (optional)

Remove core and hard ribs from cabbage and chop leaves very fine. Fry in oil for 10 minutes. Cube 2 rolls and fry in 4 tablespoons butter until golden. Soak the other 2 rolls in milk and put through strainer. Beat 14 tablespoons butter with egg yolks until soft. Slowly add whole eggs, flour, and cabbage. Season and add fried roll cubes and strained roll mixture. Knead well. Shape small dumplings; cook in boiling salted water until they rise to the surface (about 10 minutes). Cook 3 to 4 minutes more. Remove and drain. Pour remaining melted butter over, or sprinkle with grated cheese, or use both. Serves 4 to 6.

Cabbage and Noodles

1 large cabbage
⅓ cup oil or fat
   salt to taste

1 pound broad noodles
   pepper to taste

Remove outer leaves from cabbage. Wash and shred it. Heat oil or fat in saucepan. Add cabbage; salt and sauté until light brown. Cook noodles in salted water about 9 minutes. Drain; rinse with cold water; drain again. Put the noodles into the saucepan with the cabbage. Add pepper; mix well; serve at once. Serves 6 to 8.

Cabbage Pockets   AUSTRIA

1 teaspoon onion, chopped	6 pancakes
1 teaspoon parsley, chopped	1 egg white for brushing
2 tablespoons butter	2 eggs, beaten
1 head cabbage	⅔ cup bread crumbs
dash of salt and pepper	¾ cup fat
1 egg	

Fry onion and parsley in butter. Add blanched, chopped cabbage, salt, and pepper. Simmer 25 minutes. Add egg. Use mixture as filling for pancakes. Serves 6.

Curly Cabbage   GERMANY

2 pounds cabbage	2 tablespoons flour
salt	1 cup milk
baking soda	salt and pepper
1 small onion, chopped	nutmeg
1 teaspoon parsley, chopped	extra butter and cream, as
2 tablespoons butter	desired

Divide up cabbage and remove stalk and ribs. Soak in strongly salted water. Rinse. Cook in slightly salted water, with a pinch of baking soda, until nearly done, about 10 minutes. Drain thoroughly and put through grinder. Brown onion and parsley lightly in butter. Add flour, stir in milk and cook briefly. Add cabbage and seasoning and heat through. This can be further enriched by adding extra butter or a little cream. Serves 4.

Variation: Remove and wash outer leaves and cook briefly in salted water. Drain, top with bread crumbs browned in butter, and serve immediately. Brussels sprouts may also be prepared in this way.

Fried Cabbage

3 small heads cabbage
  pepper to taste
1 cup flour

2 eggs, beaten
1½ cups bread crumbs
2 cups fat

Halve cabbages. Cut out cores. Cook 20 minutes in salted water. Squeeze dry and flatten like cutlets. Season with pepper. Dip in flour, beaten egg, and bread crumbs. Fry in deep fat until golden brown. Serves 6.

Note: Celery or eggplant slices may be prepared the same way.

Savoy Cabbage

Prepare like ordinary cabbage, but allow only 20 minutes cooking time after parboiling. Excellent with dill, or parboiled and then cooked smothered with butter and seasoned lightly. Serve with a generous topping of White Sauce. A medium-sized head of savoy cabbage makes 4 servings.

Cabbage with Chestnuts   AUSTRIA

2 ½ pounds cabbage (blue variety preferred)
2 tablespoons butter
3 tablespoons flour
½ cup water

½ teaspoon onion, chopped
1 teaspoon parsley, chopped
  dash salt
½ pound chestnuts
½ cup sugar

Clean and wash cabbage. Separate leaves; remove middle rib. Cook in salted water until tender. Drain. Melt butter; blend in flour; add water or soup; stir. Add onion and parsley; bring to a boil. Chop cabbage; add; season with salt. Cook gently 10 minutes. Peel and cook chestnuts; rub 6 chestnuts through strainer; add to cabbage. Caramelize remaining chestnuts; use as decoration. (Stick chestnuts on toothpicks or wooden sticks for caramelizing and dry on buttered plate or wooden board.) Serves 6.

Deep-Fried Savoy Cabbage   YUGOSLAVIA

2 pounds savoy cabbage
2 tablespoons flour
2 eggs, beaten

¼ cup bread crumbs
salt and pepper to taste
oil for frying

Wash cabbage and cook whole, in salted water, for 30 minutes, or until done. Cool; dip in flour, egg, and bread crumbs mixed with salt and pepper and fry in deep fat until crisp (5 to 8 minutes). Serves 4 to 6.

Health Cabbage   JEWISH

Grate or shred cabbage, allowing 1 cupful per serving. Melt 1 tablespoon butter in a heavy frying pan for each cupful of cabbage. Add grated cabbage, season with salt and grated onion to taste. Stir 5 minutes till steamed through. Serve at once. This loses flavor if cooked too long or allowed to stand overlong before serving.

Meatless Stuffed Cabbage Birds POLAND

1 large or 2 small heads white
  cabbage
salted boiling water
2 cups cooked-dry rice or pearl
  barley
2 medium onions, chopped
  and browned lightly in
  butter
2 to 3 tablespoons cooked

dried mushrooms,
  chopped fine
salt and pepper to taste
2 cups fermented rye liquid
  or bouillon with the mushroom cooking water added
1 heaping tablespoon butter
2 teaspoons flour
sour cream (optional)

Parboil cabbage in salted boiling water for 10 minutes. Separate individual leaves as soon as cabbage is cool enough to handle. Make a stuffing of the rice or barley mixed with onions, mushrooms, and seasoning. Spread leaves with it and roll up, securing with cotton thread. Arrange birds tightly in heavy casserole, add liquid and butter, and simmer tightly covered until tender (about 1 hour). There should be little sauce left. Dust with flour and baste. Add sour cream to pan gravy if desired. Serves 6. Excellent reheated in butter.

Cabbage Birds may be made with sauerkraut if this has been prepared in whole leaves instead of shredded, as is customary. This is a traditional Russian recipe.

Red Cabbage with Apples ISRAEL

1½ pounds red cabbage
4 tablespoons cooking oil
3 sour apples, peeled and
  cubed

salt and pepper
3 tablespoons sugar
3 tablespoons wine vinegar

Shred the cabbage and soak in cold water 30 minutes. Drain. Fry lightly in the oil. Add the apples, salt, pepper, sugar, and vinegar. Cover the pot tightly. If necessary, add a little water to keep the cabbage from burning. Cook on very low heat for 15 to 20 minutes. Serves 4 to 6.

Red Cabbage

4 portions
2 pounds red cabbage
2 tablespoonfuls butter or margarine
2 apples, peeled and cut into sections
1 onion, chopped
2 teaspoonfuls caraway seeds
1 teaspoonful salt
1 to 2 tablespoonfuls syrup or sugar
*2½ to 5 tablespoonfuls beetroot juice or table vinegar (7½ tea-
    spoons)*
2½ to 5 tablespoonfuls water

Trim and wash the red cabbage. Cut the cabbage in two lengthwise and remove the stalk. Shred the cabbage finely. Fry the cabbage in the fat. Add the apples, onion, salt, caraway seeds, and syrup. Moisten with vinegar and water.

Cover the pan with a tightly fitting lid and boil the cabbage gently on top of the cooker or in the oven (390°) for 45 to 60 minutes. Stir occasionally and add more liquid if necessary. Remove the lid toward the end of cooking so that the surplus moisture is reduced by evaporation. Taste the cabbage for seasoning. Serves 4.

Cabbage in Sour Cream

1 medium head cabbage (3 to
    3½ pounds)
½ cup cold water
2 cups sour cream
2 tablespoons butter

½ cup flour
½ cup mild vinegar
½ cup sugar
    Salt to taste

Shred cabbage and add water. Cook in frying pan for 5 minutes. Drain off excess liquid. Add sour cream and butter. Blend flour, vinegar, and sugar and stir in. Cook 3 minutes longer. Add salt. Serves 6.

Stir-Fry Chinese Cabbage

BASIC RECIPE

> 1½ tablespoons peanut oil or butter
> 1 teaspoon salt
> 1 clove garlic, crushed
> 1 pound Chinese cabbage, washed and cleaned; cut leaves into
>   1-inch sections with the stem slanting about 45°; drain
> ½ cup water
> 1 teaspoon light soy sauce
> 1 teaspoon seasoning powder
> 1 teaspoon sugar
> ½ teaspoon crushed ginger
> 1 teaspoon rice wine or 2 tablespoons sherry wine
> 1 teaspoon cornstarch

Mix water, light soy sauce, seasoning powder, sugar, ginger, rice wine or sherry, and cornstarch. Stir well before using.

Put peanut oil or butter into very hot skillet; add salt and garlic.

Put white part and stem of Chinese cabbage in skillet. Stir-fry for 2 minutes. Add green leaves; stir another minute.

Add prepared mixture. Stir thoroughly 1 minute. Cover and cook for 2 minutes. Serves 2 or 3.

Note: Following this basic recipe, any number of dishes can be made with almost any kind of vegetable being used instead of Chinese cabbage: mustard greens, pea pods, green peas, celery, onions, green peppers, American cabbage, etc. If broccoli or asparagus is used, cook in boiling water 2 minutes and rinse in cold water before adding to skillet. Broccoli should be cooked 5 minutes (and 2 teaspoons sugar should be used instead of 1); asparagus should be cooked 6 minutes.

Stuffed Cabbage Leaves

To prepare 30 cabbage rolls you will need:

*30 cabbage leaves (at least 2
    heads cabbage, because only
    the largest leaves can be
    used)*
1 pint boiling, salted water
3 large eggplants
3 tablespoons salt
1 cup oil
10 green peppers
5 carrots
*1 celery root (or 2 cups celery
    cut into thin slices)*

*30 small red or green peppers,
    very hot*
1 head garlic
*1 cup parsley, coarsely
    chopped*
2 quarts water
1 quart vinegar
3 cups oil
3 tablespoons salt
6 bay leaves
1 tablespoon peppercorns
1 tablespoon allspice

Scald cabbage leaves with boiling salted water; let stand for 10 minutes, then remove leaves from brine, cut off thick veins. Cut eggplants lengthwise into slices. Salt them and let stand for about 1 hour, then pour off liquid that has formed. Fry slices in oil until golden brown (for about 5 minutes on each side). Cut peppers lengthwise into narrow strips, removing seeds. Clean and cut carrots and celery root into narrow strips. Cut off stems of hot peppers. Clean garlic and cut individual cloves into thin slices.

On each cabbage leaf spread:
1 slice fried eggplant
5 to 6 strips green pepper
5 to 6 strips carrot

2 to 3 strips celery
1 hot small pepper, whole
½ teaspoon chopped parsley

Make cabbage leaf into roll; secure with thread if desired. Cook water, vinegar, oil, and spices for 20 minutes. Let cool completely. Arrange rolls in deep glass or earthenware jars, pour liquid over them to cover. After 3 days drain liquid and let it come to a boil. Cool again and pour over rolls. Repeat this a third time. Store in a cool place.

Cabbage in Yogurt

6 cups cabbage
3 tablespoons ghee
2 teaspoons cumin seed
½ teaspoon cayenne

1 teaspoon salt
2 teaspoons turmeric
½ cup yogurt

Chop the cabbage quite fine. Set aside. Heat the ghee and seasonings, and add the chopped cabbage to it. Stir until all is well coated. Cook gently for about 5 minutes.

Add the yogurt. Stir well until the yogurt is warm with the cabbage, and all is dry. And add perhaps a touch more salt.

Boiled Cardoons

Also known as Spanish artichokes.

This vegetable is related to the globe artichoke. The cooked root may be served with vinaigrette dressing. The cooked stalks may be used like celery. The uncooked stalks resemble celery in appearance except for their leaves which are more feathery and the presence of spines on the ribs.

2 to 4 cardoons
For Blanching
   water
1 teaspoonful salt to 1 quart (5 cups) of water
For Boiling
   water
2 teaspoonfuls salt to 1 quart (5 cups) of water and lemon juice

Pull the cardoons apart and rinse the stalks. Cut them into pieces 2 to 2½ inches in length and pull off the tough strings along the ribs with a knife.

Put the pieces into boiling salted water and parboil them, about 10 minutes. Rinse them with cold water and rub them with a rough cloth or against each other so that all the strings are detached.

Put the cardoons into boiling salted water containing lemon juice and boil until tender, about 30 to 40 minutes.

Drain the cardoons.

Serve with (creamed) butter, lemon sauce, or Hollandaise sauce.

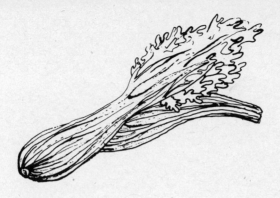

Cardoons with Parmesan FRANCE

After having drained the sections well, build them into a pyramid in successive layers. Sprinkle each row with a few drops of good half-*glaze* sauce and with grated Parmesan cheese. Cover the whole with the same sauce; sprinkle with grated Parmesan cheese, and set to *glaze* quickly.

Cardoons Mornay FRANCE

Proceed exactly as above, but replace half-*glaze* sauce by Mornay sauce. *Glaze* quickly, and serve immediately.

Carrots AUSTRIA

2 pounds carrots
3 tablespoons butter
1 to 2 tablespoons sugar

1 teaspoon parsley, chopped
water as needed

Scrape carrots; slice or cut in strips and cook in salted water until half done (about 10 minutes). Heat butter. Brown sugar slightly; add parsley and cook drained carrots in mixture until tender (10 to 15 minutes). Add 1 or 2 tablespoons water from time to time. Add more salt if needed. Serves 6.

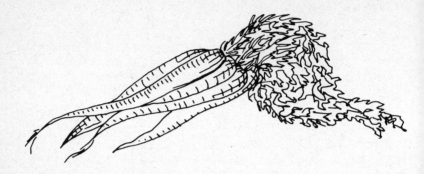

Boiled Carrots   SCANDINAVIA

> 8 ounces carrots for each portion
>   water
> 2 teaspoonfuls salt to each quart (5 cups) of water

Wash the carrots and peel or scrape them.

Put the carrots into boiling salted water and cook them until tender, about 8 to 15 minutes for young carrots, 20 to 30 minutes for winter carrots, and 10 to 15 minutes for carrots in pieces. Drain them.

Serve with (creamed) butter or on a vegetable platter.

Buttered Carrots   ITALY

4 large carrots	½ teaspoon sugar
¼ cup butter	1½ teaspoons flour
½ teaspoon salt	1 cup water

Scrape carrots and cut into ½-inch strips. Melt butter in skillet, add carrots and cook 5 minutes. Add salt and sugar and sprinkle with flour, mixing well. Add water, cover skillet, and cook gently 20 minutes. Serves 4.

Carrot Casserole   FINLAND

1 cup cooked rice	2 eggs
2 cups milk	3 tablespoons butter
5 medium carrots, shredded	⅓ cup fine bread or cracker
1 teaspoon salt	crumbs
1 tablespoon dark brown sugar	

Combine the rice, milk, carrots, salt, sugar, and eggs. Pour into a well-buttered 1½-quart casserole. Melt the butter in a separate pan and stir the crumbs into it. Sprinkle over the top of casserole. Bake in a moderately hot oven (375°) about 40 minutes or until the top is lightly browned. Serves 6.

Crusted Carrots   FINLAND

6 medium carrots, peeled	1 teaspoon sali
¼ cup milk	½ cup white flour
1 egg, beaten	1 tablespoon butter

Quarter the carrots lengthwise. Combine the milk and egg in a bowl. In another bowl combine the salt and flour. Dip the carrots first into the milk mixture, then into the flour-salt mixture. Arrange in a well-buttered baking dish in a single layer. Dot with the butter. Bake in a moderate oven (350°) until the carrots are tender (about 45 minutes). Serve hot. Serves 4 to 6.

Carrot Curry   INDIA

2 cups young carrots	1 teaspoon fenugreek
1 teaspoon salt added to	1 teaspoon mustard seed
4 cups water	3 to 4 whole cloves
3 tablespoons ghee	2 teaspoons cumin seed
2 cardamom pods (seeds only)	1 teaspoon (or more) cayenne
1 teaspoon turmeric	½ cup yogurt

Scrape and slice the carrots very thin. Boil them until tender in the salted water. Set aside. Do not drain.

In a saucepan, heat the ghee. Add the spices to it. Stir until very well blended. Then turn into the carrots. Add the yogurt. Let simmer, but do not boil, for 15 minutes. Serves 4.

Carrot and Turnip

6 young carrots (approxi-
   mately 1 pound), diced
6 young white turnips, diced
   water
½ teaspoon salt
¼ teaspoon sugar

2 tablespoons butter or other
   fat
dash of paprika
greens (tender tops of carrots and turnips) cut fine

Wash carrots and turnips after removing tops. Do not scrape
or pare them. Dice, then cover with cold water, add salt and
sugar and cook in a covered pot 6 to 8 minutes or till tender.
The liquid should be reduced by half. Turn into a large bowl
and mash with a fork. Add the melted shortening and serve
hot, heaped up in a vegetable dish or in individual portions,
garnished with greens and a sprinkling of paprika. Or form
into balls and garnish. Serves 4 to 6.

Carrot and Turnip Whip   JEWISH

1 cup cooked, mashed carrots	½ teaspoon sugar
1 cup cooked, mashed turnips	½ cup heavy cream
⅛ teaspoon salt	

Combine vegetables while hot, add salt and sugar, and beat with a rotary or electric beater 2 to 3 minutes or till fluffy. Fold in stiffly beaten cream and serve at once. Serves 3 to 4.

Carrots with Green Peas   AUSTRIA

2 pounds carrots	⅓ cup flour
4 tablespoons butter	¼ cup sugar
½ teaspoon parsley, chopped	½ teaspoon salt, or more
½ cup water	¼ cup water, or more
½ pound green peas	

Peel and wash carrots. Cut into thin strips. Cook with butter, parsley, and water until tender (about 20 minutes). Wash and cook peas in salted water 15 minutes; drain. Combine both vegetables; add flour, sugar, salt, and water. Bring to a boil. Serves 5-6.

Fried Carrots   POLAND

2 bunches carrots, blanched	¼ cup bouillon or water
1 to 2 tablespoons butter	sugar to taste (lemon juice
salt and pepper to taste	optional)

Very young carrots may be used whole, unpeeled; older ones should be scraped and cut in halves or quarters. Blanch, then simmer tightly covered with butter, seasoning, and bouillon. When steamed through, add sugar for a sweetish taste, lemon if desired, and cook uncovered, stirring constantly, until sauce thickens and carrots begin to brown. Serves 6.

Glazed Carrots

6 medium carrots
½ cup brown sugar

3 tablespoons butter

Scrape carrots. Cut into thin rounds or quarter lengthwise. Parboil in enough salted water to prevent sticking. Drain. Reserve liquid. Add butter and sugar, and bake 25 to 30 minutes (350°), basting with the liquid till glazed. Serves 4.

Marinated Carrots

1 bunch large carrots
2 cloves garlic, sliced
½ teaspoon salt
½ teaspoon pepper

¼ cup olive oil
2 tablespoons wine vinegar
1 teaspoon oregano

Scrape carrots and cut into thick slices. Boil in water 10 minutes, or until tender, taking care not to overcook. Drain well and place in bowl with garlic, salt, pepper, oil, vinegar, and oregano, stirring and mixing well. Let stand in marinade 12 hours before serving. Serves 8.

Carrots, Mazur Style

4 cups diced carrots
2 cups water
2 cups milk
1 tablespoon butter
  salt and pepper to taste

3 tablespoons sugar
1 heaping tablespoon butter
1 heaping tablespoon flour
1 cup heavy sweet cream
2 teaspoons chopped fresh dill

Simmer carrots in milk and water, adding butter, salt, and sugar. When tender, drain and reserve the liquid. Mix butter and flour and use to thicken the cream and 1 cup of the carrot cooking liquid. (Remainder may be used for a cream soup base.) Return carrots to sauce, add dill, and heat until sauce bubbles. Serves 8.

Carrots and Peas

INDIA

4 tablespoons ghee
½ teaspoon cumin seed
1 cup carrots, washed,
    scraped, and sliced
    into thin rounds

1 cup fresh green peas, hulled
1 teaspoon salt
½ teaspoon cayenne (optional)

Heat the ghee, and add the cumin seed to it. Fry for 1 minute. Add the carrots, peas, salt, and cayenne.

Mix well, cover, and cook over very low heat for 20 minutes or until tender. Cooked gently like this, no water is necessary. Shake the pot from time to time to prevent the vegetables from sticking and browning.

Carrots with Peas or Asparagus

POLAND

1 bunch carrots, scraped and
    diced
1 pound peas or 12 asparagus
    tips
    salt, pepper, and sugar to
    taste

1 tablespoon butter
2 teaspoons flour
1 tablespoon chopped fresh dill
    and parsley
2 egg yolks, slightly beaten
    (optional)

Cook each vegetable separately until done. Drain, reserving liquid for sauce. Combine vegetables and simmer another 10 minutes in white sauce made with the flour, butter, and ¾ cup vegetable water. Add herbs, season to taste, and bubble up once. When ready to serve, beat egg yolks into the sauce for added flavor. Serves 6.

Deep Carrot Pie FRANCE

This is served either as a vegetable or a sweet.

Line a spring-form mold with good, short paste, coat the inside of the ring with a round piece of paper, and fill it with rice or split peas. Bake it without letting it brown; remove the split peas or the rice (just to keep the form), as also the paper, and fill the crust with a slightly sugared *purée* of carrots. Cover this *purée* with half-slices of carrot cooked and kept unbroken. Coat with the cooking liquor of the carrots reduced to a syrup, and put the flan in the oven for 5 minutes.

Purée of Carrots FRANCE

Slice the carrots, and cook them in slightly salted water, with sugar and butter, as for *glazed* carrots, and a quarter of their weight of rice. Drain them as soon as they are cooked; rub them through a fine sieve; transfer the *purée* to a saucepan, and dry it over a hot fire, together with 3 ounces of butter per pound of *purée*.

Now add a sufficient quantity of either milk or consommé to give it the consistency of an ordinary *purée*. Serve in a *timbale* with triangular *croutons* of bread, fried in butter at the last moment.

Sautéed Carrots CZECHOSLOVAKIA

3 cups sliced carrots
1 cup water
½ cup butter
  salt to taste
½ teaspoon sugar

3 tablespoons flour
1 cup milk
  juice of ½ lemon
1 tablespoon minced parsley or
  chives

Cook carrots in water with butter, salt, and sugar until tender (15 to 25 minutes). Dust with flour, add milk, and simmer for 5 minutes. Before serving, add lemon juice and parsley or chives. Or cook carrots with green peas, kohlrabi, asparagus tips, or fresh mushrooms. Serves 4 to 6.

Smothered Carrots

2 bunches very young carrots,
   washed and blanched
2 tablespoons butter
salt and pepper to taste

dash of sugar
½ cup bouillon
flour for dusting

Very young carrots (3 inches long) need not be peeled or scraped. Wash carefully and cut off tops and tips. Blanch in salted water and simmer, tightly covered, with butter, bouillon, and seasoning until tender. When done, dust with flour and stir. Let cook a few minutes uncovered to reduce liquid. Older carrots should be scraped, sliced, and parboiled; then they may be prepared the same way. Allow ½ cup per portion.

Carrots Steamed in Butter

2 pounds carrots
3 tablespoons butter, melted
1 teaspoon sugar
½ teaspoon parsley, chopped

2 tablespoons flour
water as needed
salt to taste

Peel and wash carrots. Cut into cubes or strips. Boil in salted water 5 minutes; drain. Cook gently in butter, with sugar and parsley, 10 to 15 minutes. Add flour, water and salt. Bring to a boil. Serves 4 to 5.

Carrot Tzimmes (Glazed)   ISRAEL

8 large carrots
  salted water to cover
½ cup honey
4 tablespoons sugar

4 tablespoons cooking oil
lemon rind
dash of ginger (if desired)

Cut the carrots into slices and just cover with salted water. Boil 10 minutes. Add the honey, sugar, and oil. Cook gently until the liquid is absorbed and the carrots slightly glazed (about 30 minutes). Sprinkle with lemon rind and ginger, if desired. Serves 6 to 8.

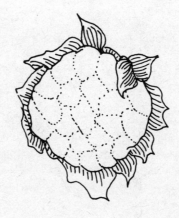

Cauliflower   INDIA

3 tablespoons peanut oil
1 teaspoon mustard seed
  (black or yellow)

3 cups cauliflower, cored and
  chopped very, very fine
1 teaspoon salt

Heat the peanut oil, and add the mustard seed to it. Stir for 1 minute, then add the cauliflower and salt.

Stir constantly over high heat for about 3 minutes. Cauliflower prepared like this may be served either hot or cold. You may want to add a pinch or two more salt before serving.

Cauliflower, Athenian Style   G R E E C E

2 pounds cauliflower	heaping ¾ cup flour
1 quart salted water	2 egg whites, beaten stiff
½ cup white wine	oil for frying

Clean cauliflower and divide into flowerets. Cook in boiling salted water for 10 to 15 minutes. Drain. Work wine, flour, and egg whites to a smooth batter. Dip flowerets in this batter. Fry in hot oil until golden. Serves 4.

Cauliflower Au Gratin   I T A L Y

1 small cauliflower	1½ cups thin cream sauce
1½ tablespoons bread crumbs	1½ tablespoons grated Parme-
¼ cup butter	san cheese

Break off flowerets and cook in 2 quarts boiling salted water 10 minutes. Drain well and place in buttered baking dish. Cover with cream sauce, sprinkle with cheese and bread crumbs and dot with butter. Bake in hot oven (400°) 20 minutes. Serves 4.

Baked Cauliflower   G E R M A N Y

1 medium head cauliflower	1 tablespoon cheese,
1 teaspoon salt in water to	grated
cover	3 tablespoons butter (to
Butter Sauce	grease dish and dot)
1 tablespoon bread crumbs	

Wash cauliflower and drop into boiling salted water. Cook until nearly done, about 20 minutes. Put it through a sieve and into a buttered baking dish. Cover with sauce, bread crumbs, and cheese. Dot with butter. Bake in moderate oven (350°) until nicely browned. Serves 4.

Boiled Cauliflower

*8 to 10 ounces cauliflower for each portion
    water
2 to 3 teaspoonfuls salt to each quart (5 cups) of water*

Trim and wash the cauliflower, leave it whole or divide it into flowerets. Put the cauliflower into acidulated water (1 tablespoonful vinegar to each quart (5 cups) of water for about 5 minutes. Rinse once again.

Put the cauliflower into boiling salted water and cook until it is just tender, about 10-15 minutes for the whole cauliflower and 8 to 10 minutes for flowerets. Drain the cauliflower.

Cauliflower in Cream

Separate the cauliflowers into flowerets; remove the small leaves which are attached, and cook the cauliflower in salted water.

Thoroughly drain; set the flowerets in a *timbale*, reconstructing the cauliflower in so doing, or on a dish covered with a folded napkin, and serve a cream sauce separately.

Cauliflower Creole

*1 medium head cauliflower
½ cup chopped onion
6 tablespoons butter or margarine
3 cups chopped tomatoes*

*3 tablespoons flour
1 or 2 green peppers, chopped fine
salt and pepper to taste
1 tablespoon chopped parsley*

Divide the cauliflower into flowerets and boil in plain water. Meanwhile brown the onion in some of the butter, add the tomatoes, and stew about ½ hour to make a smooth sauce. Mix the flour with the remaining margarine to thicken. Add to the sauce. Put in the green pepper and stew a few minutes. Season and add the cauliflower, to heat through for 5 minutes. Garnish with the chopped parsley. Serves 4 to 6.

Cauliflower Custard   FINLAND

1 medium cauliflower, separa-   1 tablespoon minced parsley
   ted into flowerets   2 cups milk
2 tablespoons butter   3 eggs
3 tablespoons flour   ¼ teaspoon white pepper
1 teaspoon salt

Cook the cauliflower until tender-crisp in salted water to cover. Drain. Arrange in a buttered 1½-quart casserole. Melt the butter in a pan, add the flour, ½ teaspoon of the salt, and the parsley, stirring until smooth. Slowly add 1 cup of the milk and cook until thickened, then pour over the cauliflower.

Beat the eggs in a bowl, add the remaining ½ teaspoon salt, the pepper, and the rest of the milk. Pour over the creamed cauliflower in the casserole and bake in a moderate oven (350°) for 30 to 35 minutes or until the custard is set. Serve hot. Serves 4 to 6.

Cauliflower with Eggs   CZECHOSLOVAKIA

1 medium onion, chopped   salt to taste
¼ cup butter   dash of powdered caraway
1½ cups chopped cooked   seeds
   cauliflower   1 tablespoon minced chives
4 eggs, lightly beaten

Fry onion in butter, add cauliflower, and heat thoroughly. Add eggs, salt, and caraway seeds, stirring until eggs are set. Sprinkle with chives before serving. Serves 2 to 3.

Fried Cauliflower   CZECHOSLOVAKIA

1 2-pound cauliflower   1 egg, lightly beaten
   salt to taste   ⅔ cup flour
½ cup milk   shortening for frying

Break cauliflower into flowerets and cook for 5 to 10 minutes in boiling salted water. Drain. Beat together milk, egg, and flour. Dip drained flowerets into mixture, and fry in deep fat to a golden brown. Serves 4 to 6.

Cauliflower with Mock Hollandaise ISRAEL

1 cauliflower
  pinch of sugar
  pinch of salt
8 cups boiling water
Sauce:
3 tablespoons butter

2 tablespoons flour
1 cup hot water
  salt
2 tablespoons lemon juice
2 egg yolks, well beaten

Boil the cauliflower, with sugar and salt, in an open pot in rapidly boiling water, until tender but not mushy (8 to 20 minutes). Drain.

To make the sauce, melt the butter, add the flour, and mix. Gradually add the hot water as you cook the sauce over very low heat or in a double boiler. Stir continuously until thick. Add salt and lemon juice. Pour the mixture over the egg yolks, stir very well, and pour over the cauliflower. Serve at once. Serves 4 to 6.

Cauliflower Kapamas, Calamata Style GREECE

6 pounds cauliflower
2 lemons, juice only
1¼ cups oil
1 medium onion, chopped

1 tablespoon tomato paste
  salt and pepper to taste
2 cups water

Wash the cauliflower well and break it into flowerets; drain. Place on a platter and pour lemon juice over all. Heat the oil in a frying pan and fry the pieces, one at a time, then carefully transfer these to a large pot. Fry the onions lightly in the same frying pan. Add the tomato paste and 1 cup water, stir, and bring to a boil. Cook for about 3 minutes, then pour the sauce into the pot with the cauliflower. Place over medium heat, bring to a boil. Add the second cup water. Continue to cook until all the liquid has been absorbed and only the oil remains (about 30 to 45 minutes). Serves 6 to 8.

Milanaise Cauliflower   FRANCE

Set the cauliflower on a buttered dish sprinkled with grated cheese. Also sprinkle the cauliflower with cheese; add a few pieces of butter, and set the *gratin* to form.

On taking the dish out of the oven, sprinkle the cauliflower with nut-brown butter and serve immediately.

Cauliflower and Peas   INDIA

2 cups cauliflower   ¼ teaspoon cayenne
3 tablespoons ghee   ½ teaspoon mustard seed
1 teaspoon cumin   1 cup fresh green peas, hulled
1 teaspoon salt

Wash and chop the cauliflower coarsely. Heat the ghee, and add the seasonings to it. Stir well, then add the cauliflower and peas.

Stir together thoroughly, then lower the heat, and continue to cook very slowly, covered, for 15 minutes, or until the peas are tender.

Cauliflower, Polish Style   GERMANY

1 head cauliflower   3 tablespoons butter
   salt, in water to cover   1 tablespoon bread crumbs
2 egg yolks

Divide cauliflower into several medium-sized sections and soak in cold salted water for 15 minutes. Bring water to a boil and cook cauliflower in it until tender, about 10 minutes. Drain and remove carefully so vegetable will not break up. Put on a hot platter. Beat egg yolks and pour over cauliflower. Melt butter and brown bread crumbs lightly in it. Top cauliflower with this and serve. Serves 4.

Cauliflower Pudding

3 tablespoons butter
3 egg yolks
¼ teaspoon salt
 dash pepper
6 mushrooms, chopped
1 tablespoon butter
½ teaspoon onion, chopped
 coarse

1 teaspoon parsley, chopped
1½ rolls
3 egg whites, stiffly beaten
1 head cauliflower
1 tablespoon flour

Cream butter; add egg yolks, salt, pepper. Sauté mushrooms in butter with onion and parsley; add. Soak rolls in water; squeeze dry; add and beat until blended. Fold in egg whites. Cook cauliflower; separate flowerets. Butter a pudding mold; sprinkle with flour. Place flowerets around bottom and sides of mold. Cover with layer of mushroom mixture. Repeat procedure until ingredients are used up. Cook in hot-water bath 45 minutes to 1 hour. Serves 4 to 5. *Side Dish:* white sauce or mushroom sauce.

Purée of Cauliflower, called Du Barry

Cook the cauliflower in salted water; drain it well; rub it through a fine sieve, and combine the resulting *purée* with one quarter of its bulk of somewhat firm, mashed potatoes with cream. Heat; add butter away from the fire, and serve in a *timbale.*

Cauliflower-Rice Casserole

1 small head cauliflower
½ cup cooked rice
3 eggs, beaten
1 cup milk

½ teaspoon salt
 dash allspice
 fresh chopped parsley

Cook the cauliflower in salted water to cover until tender-crisp (25 to 30 minutes). Separate the flowerets and arrange in a greased casserole. Combine the rice with the eggs, milk, salt, and allspice, and pour over the cauliflower. Bake in a moderate oven (350°) for 30 to 35 minutes or until the custard has set. Garnish with the parsley. Serve hot. Serves about 6.

Cauliflower Stifado

6 pounds cauliflower
6 small white onions
1¼ cups oil
3 to 4 cloves garlic, split
   lengthwise
1 tablespoon tomato paste
   diluted with 2 cups water

½ cup vinegar
½ tablespoon rosemary
1 bay leaf
6 peppercorns

Wash the cauliflower and break into flowerets. Skin and wash the onions; drain. Heat the oil in a pot and lightly brown the whole onions. Add the garlic and cook until golden. Add the diluted tomato paste, vinegar, rosemary, and bay leaf, and cook for 30 minutes. Bring a large pot of salted water to a boil; add the cauliflower. Cook for 5 minutes, then drain and add the cauliflower to the sauce. (Add a little water if necessary.) Add the peppercorns. Cover the pot. Simmer until all the liquid has been absorbed and only the oil remains (about 30 to 45 minutes). Serves 6 to 8.

Cauliflower in Yogurt

1 nice fresh young cauli-
   flower
1 cup yogurt
1 teaspoon sugar
1 clove garlic, minced very
   fine

1 tablespoon fresh ginger
   root, grated fine
2 tablespoons peanut oil or
   ghee
1 teaspoon Garam Masala
   (See Index)

Wash the cauliflower well. Remove the core and separate it into tiny flowerets. Place the yogurt, sugar, garlic, and ginger root in a deep bowl. Mix all together. Add the cauliflower. Let it stand for 2 or 3 hours.

Then heat the peanut oil or ghee and Garam Masala in a large frying pan or deep saucepan.

Throw in the cauliflower mix. Simmer slowly. If the vegetable glazes and becomes too dry before it is tender, add water, a small amount at a time. Serve from the pot, tender and elegant.

Boiled Celery

> 1 to 2 heads of celery
>   water
> 2 teaspoonfuls salt to each quart (5 cups) of water

Pull the celery apart. Cut off the green leaves. Scrape and wash the stalks. Cut them into pieces 4 to 5 inches long. Put the celery into boiling salted water and cook until tender, about 20 minutes. Drain the celery. Serve with (creamed) butter or sauce. Serves. 4.

Creamed Celery

2 cups diced celery
¼ cup water
  salt and white pepper to taste
1 tablespoon flour

2 tablespoons butter
½ cup milk or ¼ cup
  evaporated milk

Remove strings from celery stalks before cutting. Wash and drain. Add water; salt, and pepper to taste. Cook 3 minutes in a covered saucepan. Blend flour in hot melted butter. Add milk slowly, stirring till smooth. Add celery and cook 3 minutes. Serve hot. Garnish with sliced hard cooked eggs or parsley or both. Serves 2.

Leaf Celery

2 bunches white or Pascal celery
  salt and pepper

water or light bouillon
  for cooking

Cut off leaves, clean celery stalks, and cut into serving pieces. Simmer in salted water or bouillon until transparent, about 12 to 15 minutes. Serve like asparagus—with White Sauce, Hollandaise, or Dill Sauce. Serves 6 to 8.

Stewed Celery Y U G O S L A V I A

4 celery roots
1 tablespoon butter

1 tablespoon confectioners'
sugar
bouillon

Peel celery roots; soak for 30 minutes in water; then drain. Butter an ovenproof dish; sprinkle with confectioners' sugar. Place celery roots in it; pour in bouillon to almost cover them. Cover with aluminum foil and bake in (350°) oven for about 40 minutes. Serves 4 to 6.

Celery Root with Rice B U L G A R I A

1 celery root
5 to 6 tablespoons fat
¼ to ⅓ cup rice
1 tablespoon tomato paste

salt and pepper to taste
1 tablespoon chopped parsley
1¾ cups hot water
grated cheese

Peel and cube celery root. Simmer in fat until almost soft. Add rice, simmer 5 minutes. Add tomato paste, seasoning, parsley, and hot water. Boil for about 20 minutes or until rice is done. Serve sprinkled with grated cheese. Serves 4 to 6.

Creamed Celeriac (Celery Root) J E W I S H

Pare celeriac and dice or cut into strips or thin slices. Cover with cold water, add a little lemon juice and let stand 10 minutes before cooking 8 to 10 minutes. Drain. Add cream sauce. Season with salt and pepper, add minced parsley and serve hot. One medium-sized celery root will yield 1 cup, diced or sliced, and serve 2. Garnish with sliced hard-cooked eggs or grated cheese.

Boiled Celeriac or Root Celery SCANDINAVIA

Bulbous celery bases, known as celery root in USA.

> 4 to 6 ounces celeriac for each portion
> water
> 2 teaspoonfuls salt to each quart (5 cups) of water

Peel and rinse the celeriac. Cut it into slices about ½ inch in thickness.

Put the sliced celeriac into boiling salted water and boil until just tender, about 10 to 20 minutes. Drain the slices.

Serve with creamed mushrooms, Madeira sauce, or tomato sauce.

Fried Celery Root CZECHOSLOVAKIA

2 large celery roots (2
  pounds)
  salt to taste
  water
¼ cup vinegar

⅔ cup flour
1 to 2 eggs, lightly beaten
1 cup bread crumbs
1 cup shortening for frying

Clean and peel celery root; slice into pieces about ¾ inch thick. Simmer in salted water with vinegar 2 to 5 minutes.

Purée of Knob Celery (Celeriac) FRANCE

Peel the celeriac (knob celery); cut it into sections, and cook it in salted water.

Drain and rub it through a fine sieve, adding boiled, quartered potatoes the while in the proportion of one-third of the weight of the *purée* of celeriac.

Smothered Celery Roots POLAND

3 to 4 celery roots, cleaned and
  parboiled in salted water
1 cup bouillon
  lemon juice to taste

salt and pepper
1 tablespoon butter
2 teaspoons flour

Slice parboiled celery roots thin. Cover with bouillon, add a little lemon juice, season, and simmer tightly covered until tender. Combine butter and flour, dilute with the bouillon, and when smooth add to the celery roots. Let bubble up and then serve with croutons. Serves 4.

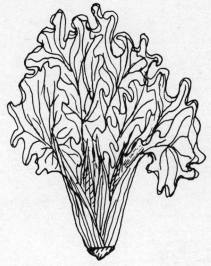

Chard   POLAND

Discard tops and leave only the stems or ribs. Cut into pieces 2 to 3 inches long. Boil in salted water with 1 tablespoon vinegar or juice of half a lemon until fibers may be removed. Drain, rinse in cold water, and remove fibers. Simmer until tender in 1 cup bouillon with a few drops of lemon juice added.

Swiss Chard   JEWISH

Wash carefully in several waters to remove dust, dirt, insects. Or cut into 2-inch lengths, using stems and leaves, and soak 10 minutes in cold water to which a little salt has been added. Drain well. Cook 5 minutes in very little water, adding lemon juice and salt to taste. Cook like spinach, and serve it in the same way. Allow 1 pound for 2 to 3 servings.

Swiss Chard, Genoa Style ITALY

1 large bunch Swiss chard
¼ teaspoon salt
¾ cup olive oil
2 medium onions, sliced
1 tablespoon chopped parsley
2 cloves garlic
¼ pound mushrooms, sliced

2 eggs, lightly beaten
½ teaspoon pepper
2 tablespoons grated Parmesan
  cheese
½ teaspoon salt
½ cup fine bread crumbs

Remove stalks from chard, wash and shred. Place in saucepan with ¼ teaspoon salt and no water, cover pan and cook over moderate flame 10 minutes, stirring often. Remove from fire and squeeze dry. Place onions and oil in saucepan and brown onions slightly. Add parsley, garlic, mushrooms, and chard, cook 5 minutes, remove from fire and cool. Add eggs, pepper, Parmesan, and salt. Grease casserole and sprinkle with some bread crumbs. Pour chard mixture into casserole and top with remaining bread crumbs. Bake in moderate oven (375°) 20 minutes. Serve either hot or cold. Serves 4.

Chayote FRANCE

This excellent vegetable, which has only become known quite recently, is beginning to be appreciated by connoisseurs. It is in season from the end of October to the end of March—, at a time when cucumbers and squash are over. It greatly resembles these last-named vegetables, and is prepared like them, while the recipes given for cardoons may also be applied to it.

Chestnuts

POLAND

Make incisions in shells and parboil for 10 to 15 minutes so that the nuts will peel easily. Peel off the shells and the dark-brown skin inside. Continue cooking until tender in milk to cover. Use for stuffings, purée, or pastry.

Chestnuts as a Side Dish

BULGARIA

1 pound chestnuts	*salt and pepper to taste*
½ cup water	*2 egg yolks*
2 ounces butter	

Cut crosses in chestnut shells and cook for 20 minutes in 400° oven. Remove outer shells and pour hot water over nut meats to make it easier to remove inner skin. Boil water with butter. Add chestnuts and cook until soft (about 20 minutes). Season and beat in egg yolks. Serves 4 to 6.

Chestnuts Fried in Sugar   POLAND

½ pound chestnuts   *½ pound sugar*

Prepare chestnuts but do not mash. Make a thick syrup of sugar and very little water. When syrup begins to bubble and brown, stick toothpicks in the chestnuts and dip each so that it becomes well glazed. Allow to cool on well-buttered dish. Then use as garnish for spinach, green peas, carrots, etc.

Glazed Chestnuts   SCANDINAVIA

1 pound chestnuts
For Parboiling
  water
2 teaspoonfuls salt to each quart (5 cups) of water
For Glazing
1 to 2 tablespoonfuls butter or margarine
½ to 1 teaspoonful sugar
  about ½ pint stock (about 1¼ cups)

Rinse the chestnuts and score them at the pointed end.

Put the chestnuts into boiling salted water and let them boil until the skins become light and loose, about 10 minutes. Peel them and also pull off the inner, dark membrane.

Melt the fat and add the chestnuts.

Sprinkle with sugar and pour on the stock. Cover with a lid and simmer the chestnuts gently, about 15 minutes. Remove the lid toward the end of cooking so that the stock is reduced and the chestnuts become shiny. Serves 4.

Chestnut Purée   SCANDINAVIA

> 1 pound chestnuts
> For Parboiling
>   water
> 2 teaspoonfuls salt to each quart (5 cups) of water
> Boiling Liquid
> 1 piece celeriac (celery root)
> 2 to 3 gills stock (1¼ to 2 cups)
> 1½ tablespoonfuls butter or margarine (4½ teaspoons)
>   about 1 gill cream (about ½ cup + 2 tablespoons)
>   salt
>   white pepper

Wash the chestnuts and score them at the pointed end.

Put the chestnuts into boiling, salted water and let them cook until the skins become light and loose, about 10 minutes. Peel them and also remove the inner, dark membrane.

Boil the skinned chestnuts and celeriac in the stock until they are tender, about 20 minutes. Sieve. Heat the purée and add the butter and cream while beating vigorously. Season to taste. Serves 4.

Chestnut Purée   POLAND

1 pound chestnuts   sugar to taste
1 to 2 tablespoons butter   dash of salt

Cook chestnuts. Mash with butter and sugar, adding a very little salt. Reheat in top of double boiler. Serves 3 to 4. For creamier purée, add a few tablespoons of sweet cream.

Stewed Chestnuts   FRANCE

As soon as they are peeled, cook them in enough consommé to just cover them, and add half a stalk of celery per pound of chestnuts.

Roasted Chestnuts SCANDINAVIA

4 to 8 ounces chestnuts for each portion (coarse salt)

Dry the chestnuts and score them at the pointed end. Place the chestnuts (on a bed of coarse salt) in a roasting or baking tin.

Roast them in the oven at (480°) until they are tender, about 20 to 30 minutes.

Serve with (creamed) butter.

Chicory GERMANY

1 *head chicory*	*juice of 1 lemon*
salted water, to cover	*salt and pepper*
butter, for baking dish	*gravy or cream*

Remove any wilted leaves and the stalks. Cook 5 minutes in salted water. Rinse in cold water. Place in a greased baking dish, sprinkle with lemon juice, salt, and pepper and add gravy or cream to cover. Cover with waxed paper and bake in moderate (350°) oven until well done, about 25 minutes. Serves 4.

Braised Chicory   SCANDINAVIA

4 to 8 heads chicory (Belgian endive)   *white pepper*
1 to 2 tablespoonfuls butter or margarine   *lemon juice*
  salt   *water*

Trim and wash the heads. Halve them lengthwise, if they are thick.

Melt the fat in a pan or fireproof dish and put the chicory into it. Season and add a few drops of lemon juice. Cover with a lid or aluminum foil.

Let the chicory simmer in its own liquid over a gentle heat or in the oven (390°) for about 20 to 30 minutes. Add water, if necessary. Toward the end of cooking remove the lid so that the liquid is reduced.

The dish may be garnished with chopped, hard-boiled egg and sprinkled with a little grated nutmeg or served with grated cheese. Serves 4.

Chicory or Escarole in Cream   FRANCE

Parboil the chicory for 10 minutes in plenty of boiling water. Cook it; press the water out of it, and chop it up.

Combine it with 4½ ounces of pale *roux* per 2 pounds of chicory; moisten with one quart of consommé; season with salt and a pinch of powdered sugar, and *braise* in the oven, under cover, for one and one-half hours.

Upon taking it from the oven, transfer it to another saucepan; add 3/5 pint of cream and 2 ounces of butter, and serve in a *timbale*.

Purée of Chicory   FRANCE

Braise the chicory, and rub it through a sieve. Mix it with one-third of its bulk of smooth mashed potatoes with cream; heat; add butter away from the fire, and serve in a *timbale*.

Soufflé of Chicory or Escarole FRANCE

Braise about ½ pound of chicory or escarole, keeping it somewhat stiff, and rub it through a sieve. Add to it the yolks of 3 eggs, also 2 ounces of grated Parmesan cheese and the whites of 3 eggs, beaten to a stiff froth.

Serve in a buttered *timbale*; sprinkle with grated Parmesan cheese, and cook after the manner of an ordinary *soufflé*.

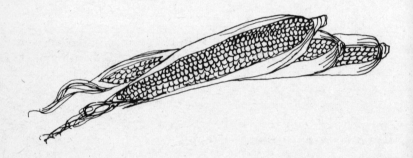

Boiled Corn-on-the-Cob SCANDINAVIA

1 to 2 cobs for each portion
  water

2 teaspoonfuls salt to each
  quart (5 cups) of water

Remove the husks and silky threads and rinse the cobs.

Put the cobs into boiling salted water and cook until the corn feels tender, about 10 to 20 minutes. Lift out the cobs and drain them.

Secure with special holders for corn-on-the-cob or with skewers or the prongs of forks, inserted at each end of the cobs.

Serve with creamed butter.

Corn Fritters

2 cups cooked corn kernels	½ cup flour
2 eggs	½ cup milk or water
½ teaspoon salt	shortening for frying

Beat eggs, add salt, flour and liquid to make a smooth batter. Add corn kernels and drop by the spoonful in deep hot melted shortening. Fry till nicely browned on both sides. Drain well. Serves 4.

Corn O'Brien

2 cups corn, cooked	1 tablespoon flour
1 onion	½ cup milk
1 large green pepper	¼ teaspoon salt
2 tablespoons butter	dash of white pepper

Cut corn from cob or use canned whole kernels. Dice onion and green pepper. Sauté in butter till lightly browned. Blend in flour, stirring lightly 1 to 2 minutes, add milk slowly to blend smooth. Add cooked corn and season to taste. Cook 3 minutes. If uncooked corn kernels are used, sauté with browned onion and pepper before adding milk in which flour has been blended smooth. Cook over low heat 5 to 10 minutes till corn is tender. Serves 4.

Corn Omelette

1 12-ounce can corn niblets	1 teaspoon salt
1½ tablespoons butter	pepper to taste
12 eggs	1 cup grated yellow cheese
1 cup milk	

Drain the corn, add the butter, and heat through in a large heavy skillet. Beat the eggs slightly, add the milk, salt, and pepper and pour over the corn. When the eggs begin to set, sprinkle on the cheese. Pull the egg from the edges with a spatula, so that the liquid will go down and cook. Remove from heat while the eggs are still moist but not raw. Serve with sliced tomatoes and buttered toast. Serves 6.

Soufflé of Creamed Corn FRANCE

Cook the cut corn in water or steam; rub it quickly through a sieve; put it into a saucepan with a small piece of butter, and quickly dry it.

This done, add sufficient fresh cream to this *purée* to make a somewhat soft paste. Thicken this paste with the yolks of 3 eggs, per pound of *purée*, and combine it with the whites of 4 eggs beaten to a stiff froth. Pour into a *soufflé form* and cook after the manner of an ordinary *soufflé*.

Soufflé of Corn with Paprika FRANCE

Before crushing the corn through a sieve, add to it 2 tablespoons of chopped onion fried in butter, and a large pinch of paprika per pound of corn.

Sautéed Sweet Corn and Sweet Pepper SCANDINAVIA

1 to 2 cans sweet corn (7 oz. can)   *salt*
1 green sweet pepper   *white pepper*
2 tablespoonfuls butter or margarine

Rinse the green pepper. Cut it in two, remove the seeds and cut it into dice.

Fry the diced sweet pepper in the fat for about 5 minutes. Stir in the sweet corn and heat it. Season to taste. Serves 4.

Cucumber Baskets GERMANY

3 large cucumbers   *salad dressing*
3 tomatoes   *lettuce leaves*

Without paring cucumbers, cut off each end squarely. Cut in half. Scoop out insides and dice. Chop up tomatoes. Add salad dressing to cucumber and tomato mixture and blend well. Fill each half. Set upright and serve on lettuce leaves. Serves 6.

Cucumbers in Cream

Peel and cut the cucumber into shapes resembling olives; parboil and drain these pieces. This done, three-quarters cook them in butter; moisten with boiling cream, and finish the cooking in reducing the cream. Serve in a *timbale*.

Stuffed Cucumber Au Gratin

1 green or white cucumber (1½ to 2 pounds)
  water
2 teaspoonfuls salt to each quart of water
Stuffing
1 medium-sized can of mushrooms, chopped (7½ oz.)
2 tablespoonfuls butter or margarine
  salt
  white pepper
Gratin Top
 1 tablespoonful butter or margarine
2 tablespoonfuls grated cheese

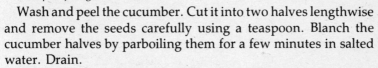

Wash and peel the cucumber. Cut it into two halves lengthwise and remove the seeds carefully using a teaspoon. Blanch the cucumber halves by parboiling them for a few minutes in salted water. Drain.

Fry the mushrooms in butter or margarine. Season to taste. Put the cucumber halves onto a greased, fireproof dish and fill them with mushrooms. Dot with pats of butter and sprinkle grated cheese on top.

Bake in oven (425°) until lightly browned, about 10 minutes. Serve with boiled rice or boiled potatoes. Serves 4.

Variation: The filling may be replaced by creamed mushrooms.

Cucumber Vegetable

2 medium cucumbers
4 tomatoes
  salt
  pepper

dill (chopped)
3 tablespoons butter
lemon juice or vinegar

Pare cucumbers, cutting toward stem end. Chop up cucumbers and tomatoes. Season well and sauté in butter. Before serving, add a dash of lemon juice or vinegar. Serves 4.

E

Eggplant

2 small eggplants
  salt
  flour
3 tablespoons butter
½ cup cheese, grated

1 cup tomato sauce
½ cup bread crumbs
  butter, to dot
  salt and pepper

Peel eggplants and cut into ¼-inch slices. Salt lightly, dip in flour, and fry lightly on both sides in butter. Grease a baking dish. Place slices in this and add part of the cheese, the tomato sauce, and seasoning. Sprinkle with bread crumbs, and again with cheese. Dot with butter. Bake in moderate (325°) oven for 20 minutes, or until nicely browned. Serves 2 to 4.

Variation: Peel eggplant and hollow out. Soak 10 minutes in a marinade of olive oil and lemon juice. Remove from marinade. Stuff with chopped leftover meat, sprinkle with grated cheese, dot with butter, and bake in 350° oven until done, about 30 minutes. Serve with tomato sauce. The hollowed-out insides can be fried lightly, combined with stewed tomatoes and baked for a subsequent meal. Serves 2 to 4.

Eggplant Plain

1 medium eggplant
4 tablespoons ghee or peanut
  oil
½ teaspoon cumin seed
1 clove garlic, chopped very
  fine

2 to 3 scallions, including
  green tops, chopped fine
½ teaspoon salt
⅓ teaspoon cayenne

Steam or boil the eggplant until just tender but not mushy. Set aside. In a saucepan, heat the ghee or peanut oil, and add the cumin seed, garlic, and scallions to it.

Stir and sauté for a few minutes, until the scallions are limp. Add the salt and cayenne.

Cut up the eggplant into bite-sized chunks. If the eggplant is young and tender, there is no need to peel it. If you are doubtful about this, slip off the skin before cutting the eggplant. Add the chunks to the pot, stir until well coated and thoroughly warm—about 5 minutes, no more. Serves 4.

Aubergine Au Gratin

1 to 2 aubergines (eggplants)
  salt
  white pepper
  butter, margarine or oil

Gratin Top
1½ gills cream-fil or 1 cup sour cream
3 tablespoonfuls grated cheese

Wash and dry the aubergines. Peel them and cut them into slices ¼ to ½ inch in thickness.

Fry the slices in butter, margarine, or oil and put them into a greased, fireproof dish. Pour the cream on top and sprinkle with cheese.

Brown in the oven (450°) for about 10 minutes. Serves 4.

Eggplant Baked in Cheese Sauce

2½ pounds eggplant
  oil for frying
1 tablespoon flour
1 egg

1 cup milk
½ cup grated yellow cheese
  salt and pepper to taste

Slice the eggplant thick (do not peel). Fry in very hot oil and remove before slices are soft. Put them into a casserole and dust each with flour. Mix the egg and milk, add the grated cheese and seasoning, and pour over the eggplant. Bake in a moderate oven until the eggplant is soft and the dish set in the sauce. Good hot or cold. Serves 6 to 8.

Broiled Eggplant

2 small eggplants, cut in
  halves
4 tablespoons olive oil

½ teaspoon salt
½ teaspoon pepper
1 clove garlic, sliced

Make little criss-cross cuts on inside part of eggplant halves. Brush well with oil, salt, pepper and garlic. Place eggplant, cut side up, in broiler and broil gently 30 minutes, brushing frequently with oil. Serves 4.

Eggplant Caviar   JEWISH

Wrap the eggplant in heavy waxed paper and brush the exterior with salad oil. Bake at 350° about 25 to 30 minutes, or till soft to the pressure of fingers or fork. Unwrap, remove the skin and chop fine in a wooden bowl. Add grated onion, garlic, and two or three skinned tomatoes while chopping to a fine pulp. Work in some salad or olive oil and season to taste with salt and pepper. Chill thoroughly and spread on rounds of hot toasted biscuits, crackers, or pumpernickel cut thin.

Cooked Eggplant   BULGARIA

10 pounds fleshy eggplant
1¼ cups salt
6 cups water
6 cups vinegar

3 cups oil
pepper (optional)
parsley, coarsely chopped
(optional)

Cut stalks from eggplants and slice about ½ inch thick without peeling. Sprinkle with salt; let stand 3 to 4 hours, then wash. Boil water and vinegar; place eggplant slices in a sieve and lower into boiling liquid. Boil for 8 to 10 minutes until soft. Remove and cool in a dish.

Meanwhile heat oil and allow to cool again. Dip eggplant slices in oil. Place in layers in a container, with pepper and coarsely chopped parsley in between, if desired. Pour remaining oil over slices and store in a cool place.

Eggplant with Cream

1½ pounds eggplant
  salt to taste
¼ cup butter
½ cup bouillon (optional)

lemon juice to taste
½ pint cream
scant pound each tomatoes
  and mushrooms (optional)

Peel eggplants and cut into slices ¼ inch thick. Sprinkle with salt and let stand for 1 hour. Squeeze out juice. Slowly simmer in hot butter until soft. If necessary, add a little bouillon. When soft, sprinkle with lemon juice and pour cream over. You may cook chopped tomatoes or mushrooms with them, or both. Serves 6.

Eggplant Croquettes

2 large eggplants
3 tablespoons grated
  Parmesan cheese
1 tablespoon chopped parsley
1 tablespoon chopped basil
¾ teaspoon salt
½ teaspoon pepper

dash nutmeg
2 slices bread, soaked in water
  and squeezed dry
2 eggs
½ cup flour
1 cup olive oil

Cut eggplants into 4 parts each and boil 20 minutes, or until tender. Drain well and chop fine. Mix together well with the Parmesan cheese, parsley, basil, salt, pepper, nutmeg, bread, and eggs and shape as croquettes. Flour and fry in olive oil until golden brown on all sides. Serve with tomato sauce or plain. Serves 4.

Eggplant Curry

3 tablespoons ghee or peanut
  oil
½ teaspoon cumin seed
1 teaspoon salt
1 teaspoon turmeric
1 teaspoon cayenne
1 eggplant, chopped, skin and
  all

1 onion, chopped
2 cups water
1 large ripe tomato, peeled
  and chopped (optional)
1 cup yogurt

Heat the ghee or peanut oil, and add the spices to it. When well heated, add the chopped eggplant and onion. Stir until well coated, then add the water and tomato. Cover and cook for 20 minutes, and add the yogurt.

Stir well, continue to cook until all is heated. Serves 4.

Eggplant with Eggs and Onions

1 large eggplant or 6 small
  ones
2 onions
2 tablespoons oil or other
  shortening
4 eggs

salt to taste
2 tablespoons grated Cheddar
  cheese
parsley or dill for garnish
  (optional)

Pare eggplant and cut into large cubes. Peel and dice onions and fry in oil to a golden brown. Add eggplant. Cover tightly. Let stew over a low flame until the eggplant is tender, about 10 minutes. Remove cover and shake frying pan. Beat eggs, season with salt, and pour over eggplant. Cook until the eggs are set. Turn onto a platter and sprinkle with grated cheese. Minced dill or parsley may be used to garnish this very nourishing dish. Serves 4 to 5.

Variation: Serve with sour cream, omitting eggs. Add more parsley or dill on top.

Patlijan Boereg
(An Egyptian Eggplant Specialty) JEWISH

1 large eggplant	3 eggs
salt to taste	½ pound dry pot cheese
¼ cup flour	1 teaspoon minced parsley
¾ cup oil	1 tablespoon lemon juice

Cut unpared eggplant into ¼-inch thick slices or rounds. Salt lightly and let stand approximately half an hour. Pat each slice dry, dust lightly with flour and fry in hot oil till nicely browned on both sides. Pour off surplus oil, leaving the fried eggplant slices in bottom of frying pan. Remove half the fried eggplant to a plate. Beat 2 eggs, add dry cheese and 1 teaspoon minced parsley and spread over the eggplant slices in the pan. Cover with remaining fried eggplant, and cook over low heat for 3 to 5 minutes. Beat remaining egg till light and frothy. Lift cover and pour beaten egg over top layer of eggplant. Let cook uncovered till set. Garnish with parsley or a sprinkling of lemon juice. Serve hot. Serves 4.

Fried Eggplant ITALY

1 medium eggplant, peeled	1 egg, lightly beaten
and cut into ½-inch	½ teaspoon salt
slices	½ teaspoon pepper
½ cup flour	½ cup olive oil

Flour eggplant slices and dip into egg to which salt and pepper have been added. Fry in olive oil 6 minutes on each side, or until slices are golden brown. Serves 4.

Fried Eggplant in Sauce GREECE

3 pounds (approx.) long eggplants	1½ pounds ripe tomatoes,
coarse salt	peeled and strained
oil for frying	

With a sharp knife, slash the eggplants lengthwise in 2 or 3 places; but do not cut off the stem. Fill a large pot with water, add a little coarse salt, and bring to a boil. Add the eggplants. Cook over high heat until tender but not soft. Remove and let drain.

Heat the oil in a frying pan. Lightly flour the eggplants, and fry them in the hot oil until golden brown. Remove to a platter. To the same oil, add the tomatoes; cook down to make a thick sauce. Add the eggplants to the sauce, reheat, and serve. Serves 6.

Eggplant, Gourmet Style   ITALY

1 medium eggplant, cut
   into 8 parts
1 cup olive oil
2 cups tomato sauce

2 tablespoons butter
3 tablespoons grated Parmesan cheese

Cut eggplant into 8 parts lengthwise and fry in olive oil until brown and tender. (Cooking time will be about 10 minutes for each part.) Place tomato sauce in casserole, add eggplant, sprinkle well with cheese. Dot with butter and bake in moderate oven (375°) 15 minutes. Serves 4.

Caviar of Eggplant and Cottage Cheese

BULGARIA

3 medium-sized eggplants
¼ cup white cheese (Sirene,
   Bulgarian white cheese, is
   firmer than cottage cheese)
4 to 5 tablespoons oil
4 to 5 cloves of garlic, grated

2 tablespoons vinegar
   salt to taste
   parsley, chopped
   tomato slices or sliced
   hard-cooked egg to garnish
   (optional)

Bake eggplant, then scrape out insides and mix with fork to a mush. Crush white cheese with fork and mix with eggplant. Stirring constantly, mix with oil, grated garlic, vinegar, and salt.

Heap mixture on a platter, sprinkle with parsley, and garnish, if desired, with slices of tomato or egg. Serves 4 to 6.

Eggplant Imam Baldi

3 pounds small oblong
  eggplants
  salt
2½ cups (approximately) oil
3 cups thinly sliced onions
5 to 6 cloves garlic, chopped
1½ pounds ripe tomatoes,
  peeled and strained

1 cup chopped parsley
  salt and pepper to taste
2 tablespoons Parmesan
  cheese
2 tablespoons toasted bread
  crumbs

With a sharp knife, slash each eggplant lengthwise, being careful not to cut all the way through and leaving at least a half inch on both ends uncut. (Do not cut away the stem.) Salt the cut and place the eggplants in a pot of salted water for 15 minutes. Drain, and rinse in clear water. Wipe dry. Fry the eggplants in ample oil and place them, split side up, side by side in a baking pan.

In the oil used for the frying, sauté the onions until golden. Add the garlic, tomatoes, parsley, salt, and pepper. Cook for 20 minutes, or until all the liquids are absorbed. Remove from the heat. Stuff this mixture into the cut in the eggplants; sprinkle with cheese and bread crumbs. Drizzle a little oil over them and bake for 30 minutes in a preheated 350° oven. Serves 6.

Note: This can also be made on top of the stove. After the eggplants are stuffed, place them side by side in a wide pot, add 2 to 3 tablespoons oil and 1 cup water, and cook over low heat for about 45 minutes.

Eggplant Marinara

1 large eggplant with skin
  on, cut into large cubes
½ cup wine vinegar
1 teaspoon salt
½ teaspoon pepper

2 cloves garlic, sliced
1 teaspoon chopped oregano
½ teaspoon chopped basil
1 cup olive oil

Boil large eggplant cubes in water 10 minutes and drain well. Place in large bowl with vinegar, salt, pepper, garlic, oregano, and basil. Mix well and let stand in this marinade at least 12 hours. Before serving add olive oil and mix well. This will keep for at least 1 week in refrigerator and is a good dish to have ready at all times. Serves 8.

Eggplant Mushrooms

1 large eggplant	*1 chopped onion or*
3 tablespoons butter	*2 tablespoons powdered mushroom soup*
1 cup sour cream	*dash of salt*

Peel the eggplant. Cut out balls with a melon cutter or cut into cubes. Melt the butter. Lightly fry the chopped onion and then add the eggplant. Stir often during frying. When the eggplant is slightly golden, put it into a baking dish, sprinkle with salt and sour cream. Heat in a 375° oven for 10 to 15 minutes. Serves 4 to 6.

Note: If you wish to use mushroom soup powder, omit the onions and add the soup powder to the sour cream before inserting into the oven.

Skewers Neapolitan Style

1 medium eggplant	*½ teaspoon salt*
8 small tomatoes	*¼ teaspoon pepper*
¾ pound mozzarella cheese, sliced	*½ cup milk*
	1 cup flour
16 slices French or Italian bread (long loaf)	*2 eggs, lightly beaten*
	2 cups olive oil

Peel eggplant and cut into ½-inch slices. Cut each slice in half. Peel tomatoes, cut off tops, drain off juice and cut in two. Cut mozzarella in slices about as large as eggplant slices. Have 8 skewers ready. Start skewer with slice of bread, then eggplant, mozzarella, half tomato, then eggplant, etc., until skewer is filled, ending with bread slice. Sprinkle with a little salt and pepper, dip skewers into milk, roll in flour and dip into egg. Fry in hot oil until golden brown on both sides. Serves 4.

Eggplants in Oil

10 pounds eggplants,
  peeled
3 cups oil
3 bunches parsley, chopped

2 large carrots, boiled
  until soft
5 cloves garlic, chopped
  fine

Cut eggplants lengthwise or crosswise into slices. Place in large dish. Pour salted water over them and let stand for 2 hours. Drain and squeeze out. Fry slices in oil on both sides to golden. Cool. Place in layers in preserving jars with parsley, pieces of carrot, and garlic in between.

Pour oil from frying over slices, adding more, if necessary, until they are completely covered. Seal with waxed paper and store in cool place.

Eggplant Pancakes

1 large eggplant
¼ teaspoon salt
2 eggs
  confectioners' sugar as
  required

shortening for deep frying
  (vegetable or salad oil)
½ cup fine cracker crumbs
  finely ground nuts (op-
  tional)

Pare eggplant and slice into ¼-inch thick rounds. Dust lightly with salt and let stand under a heavy plate while preparing the other ingredients. Beat eggs light and add a pinch of salt and a few grains of sugar. Heat enough shortening to be ½ inch deep when melted, in a heavy frying pan. Rinse eggplant slices in cold water and pat dry with a towel or paper towels. Dip each slice lightly in cracker crumbs then in beaten eggs, then dip into cracker crumbs on the under side.

Fry until well browned and crisp at the edges before turning to complete the process. Lift each pancake with a pancake turner and drain free of fat on paper towels. While the second panful is frying, dust each pancake with sugar and roll up. Fasten with a toothpick. Just before serving, dust generously with more sugar. Finely ground nuts may be added. Or, spread a little preserves of any kind lightly over the tops.

These pancakes may be served unrolled with the garnish in the centers, at least two per serving. Serves 4.

Eggplant Parmigiana ITALY

1 large eggplant, or
  2 small ones
1 cup olive oil
1¼ cups tomato sauce

3 tablespoons grated Parmesan cheese
½ pound mozzarella cheese, sliced thin

Peel eggplant and cut into thin slices. Fry in oil until brown and drain well on paper. Place 1 layer fried eggplant in casserole, cover with sauce, sprinkle with Parmesan, and cover with layer of mozzarella. Repeat procedure until all eggplant is used, ending with mozzarella. Bake in hot oven (400°) 15 minutes and serve hot. Serves 4.

Eggplant Potted with Butter GREECE

3 pounds eggplant
¾ cup butter
3 to 5 cloves garlic, chopped
3 tablespoons parsley, chopped

1½ pounds ripe tomatoes, peeled and strained, or 1 tablespoon tomato paste diluted with 1 cup water
salt and pepper to taste
1 cup water

Peel the eggplants, cut into 1½-inch cubes, and soak in lightly salted water for 15 minutes. Drain, and squeeze gently. Brown the butter in a large pot. Add the eggplant cubes and turn 2 to 3 times, to brown lightly on all sides. Add the garlic; cook until golden. Add the parsley, the tomatoes (or diluted tomato paste), salt, pepper, and 1 cup water. Cover. Simmer until all the liquid is absorbed and only the oil remains (30 to 45 minutes). Serves 6.

Eggplant à la Provençale

6 small eggplants
6 small shallots or 1 small
  onion, chopped fine
  olive oil
1 heaping tablespoon bread
  crumbs for stuffing
  bread crumbs for topping

1 heaping teaspoon each
  chopped dill and parsley
  salt and pepper to taste
2 egg yolks

Cut tops off eggplants and scoop out as much of the meat as possible without injuring skin. Parboil shells in salted water. Drain. Chop eggplant meat. Combine with shallots, bread crumbs, herbs, and olive oil, taking care not to make stuffing too greasy. Season and sauté until transparent and tender. Allow to cool, and then add egg yolks and mix thoroughly. Fill eggplants with stuffing, cover with their own tops, arrange tightly in a shallow baking dish, top with bread crumbs and olive oil, and bake in moderately hot oven for 30 minutes. Serves 6.

Eggplant Sandwiches

2 medium eggplants
½ cup flour
1½ cups olive oil
2 egg yolks
½ pound mozzarella cheese,
  diced fine

2 tablespoons grated Parmesan cheese
¼ teaspoon salt
1 egg, lightly beaten
½ cup bread crumbs

Peel eggplants and cut into ½-inch slices. Roll in flour and fry in olive oil. Drain well on paper. Save oil. Mix together well egg yolks, mozzarella, Parmesan cheese, and salt. Spread 1 tablespoon of this mixture on 1 side of each eggplant slice and cover with another slice. Dip sandwich into beaten egg, roll in crumbs and fry in oil until golden brown on both sides. Serves 4.

Whole Eggplant, Sicilian Style   ITALY

1 medium eggplant	¼ teaspoon salt
2 cups olive oil	¼ teaspoon pepper

Cut off stem and peel eggplant. Make vertical cuts in eggplant so as to make it resemble a tassel. Do not cut all the way to the top but leave top part whole. Heat oil and fry eggplant until dark brown. Sprinkle with salt and pepper and serve. Serves 4.

Eggplant and Squash   AUSTRIA

1 tablespoon onion, chopped	3 squash
⅓ cup oil	1 teaspoon salt
½ teaspoon garlic, crushed	dash pepper
1 tablespoon parsley, chopped	3 tomatoes, peeled and sliced
2 eggplants	

Fry onion in oil; add garlic and parsley. Peel and dice eggplants and squash. Season with salt and pepper. Simmer, covered, 10 minutes. Add tomatoes and cook gently 10 more minutes, or until soft. (Serve with grated cheese if desired.) Serves 6.

Note: If you serve the eggplant and squash as main dish, serve macaroni or potatoes on the side.

Eggplant Steak with Onions   JEWISH

1 eggplant	4 tablespoons oil or shortening
1 teaspoon salt	2 tablespoons grated cheese
2 eggs, beaten	1 tablespoon minced parsley
1 cup bread crumbs	1 large onion

Slice the eggplant in rounds ½-inch thick. Do not peel. Salt the slices lightly and allow to stand for 30 minutes. Drain or wipe each slice dry. Dip in beaten egg then in crumbs and fry till brown on both sides. Serve with grated cheese and minced parsley. Cut the onion into rounds and fry till light brown. Serve with the eggplant steaks. Serves 4 or 5 (depending on size of eggplant).

Stuffed Eggplant

4 small, long eggplants
1 pint salted water
½ pint oil
1 carrot, chopped
1 small celery stalk, grated
2 onions, chopped
1 tablespoon tomato paste

1 to 2 peppers, seeded and chopped
2 cloves garlic
5 tomatoes, peeled and
  chopped
  salt and pepper to taste
1 tablespoon minced parsley
1 tablespoon bread crumbs

Wash and dry eggplants, cut off stalk root. Peel off 4 alternate strips lengthwise, leaving 4 strips. Place in salted water for 30 minutes, then dry. Fry in oil for 10 minutes; remove and set aside.

In same oil fry carrot and celery for 10 minutes. Add onions, tomato paste, peppers, garlic, tomatoes, seasonings, and parsley. Simmer 15 minutes.

Cut eggplants open at peel strips and fill with stewed vegetables. Place in greased heat-resistant dish; add very little water; sprinkle with bread crumbs, and bake in 350° oven for 30 minutes. Serve cold. Serves 4 to 6.

Baked Stuffed Eggplant

6 to 7 eggplants
1 pound cream cheese
¼ cup sour cream

½ cup fat
salt to taste

Wash eggplants, remove stalks. Halve eggplants lengthwise, and boil until soft in salted water to cover. Drain, cool, and scrape out centers. Mix eggplant pulp with cheese, sour cream, fat, and salt. Fill hollowed-out halves with mixture. Pour hot fat into a casserole, place filled halves in it next to each other, and bake in (350°) oven until golden brown. Serves 6 to 8.

Serbian Vegetable Caviar

2 large eggplants
6 to 8 large green peppers
  salt and pepper to taste
1 clove garlic, crushed

juice of one lemon
vinegar to taste
¼ cup olive oil (about)
parsley to garnish

Bake eggplants and peppers in 375° oven for 20 to 25 minutes. Put them under a damp cloth and let stand for 10 minutes. Remove skins and seeds while still hot. Chop or mince fine; add salt, pepper, and garlic. Add lemon juice and vinegar, and pour on as much oil as the vegetables will absorb. Serve in a glass dish garnished with parsley. Serves 4 to 6.

Eggplant and Tomatoes

YUGOSLAVIA

3 7-inch-long eggplants
¼ cup butter
1 pound tomatoes, peeled
and sliced

1 onion, chopped
salt and pepper to taste

Peel and cube eggplants and fry in a flat pan (with lid) in butter. Add tomatoes and onion. Season. Simmer, covered, for 15 to 20 minutes. Serves 4.

Eggplant Yiaxni

GREECE

3 pounds long thin eggplants
1¼ cups oil
1 medium onion, chopped
4 to 5 cloves garlic, chopped
3 tablespoons parsley
1 cup water

1½ pounds ripe tomatoes,
peeled and strained, or 1
tablespoon tomato paste
diluted with 2 cups water
salt and pepper to taste

Peel the eggplants and cut each into 4 or 5 thick round slices. Put them into a pot of cold salted water and soak for 20 minutes. Heat the oil in a deep pot and sauté the onions and garlic until lightly golden. Add the tomatoes (or diluted tomato paste) and cook for 10 minutes. Drain the eggplants, squeeze them gently to remove the excess fluid, and add them to the pot. Add the salt, pepper, parsley, and water. Cover the pot. Simmer about 30 minutes to 1 hour until all the liquid has been absorbed and only the oil remains. Serves 6.

Note: Or you may fry the eggplant first, using half of the oil; use the rest to sauté the onions and garlic, then proceed as above.

Endive or Belgian Endive   FRANCE

Whatever the purpose for which they are intended, endives should always be cooked as follows:

After having washed and cleaned them, put them in a well-lined saucepan containing (per 3 pounds of endives) a liquor prepared from the juice of a lemon, a pinch of salt, 1 ounce of butter, and 1/5 pint of water. Cover the saucepan; boil quickly, and allow to cook at moderate heat for from 30 to 35 minutes.

Endives may be served plain, and constitute a favorite vegetable or garnish.

Endive or Chicory Salad with Oranges   GERMANY

2 large Belgian endives   *1 tablespoon mustard*
1 orange, seedless   *salt and pepper*
½ cup sweet cream

Remove outer leaves, using only those that are white. Cut leaves in half, along center. Place on platter. Peel oranges, removing inner white skin. Shred peels and cook for 5 minutes to eliminate any bitterness. Dry and cool. Mix cream with mustard, salt, and pepper and pour this marinade over endive. Sprinkle with shredded orange peels. Slice remainder of orange and garnish salad with orange slices. (Chicory may be substituted for the endive.) Serves 4.

F

Boiled Fennel

SCANDINAVIA

2 to 3 heads of fennel
water
2 teaspoonfuls salt to each
quart (5 cups) of water

Trim and wash the fennel. Cut it in two through the middle or into sections. Put into boiling salted water and cook until tender, about 30 to 40 minutes.

Drain the fennel.

Serve with (creamed) butter or cheese sauce or mushroom sauce.

Fennel in Skillet

ITALY

6 very small stalks fennel
1 clove garlic, sliced
2 tablespoons olive oil

½ teaspoon salt
½ teaspoon pepper
½ cup water

Cut off tough outer leaves and ends of fennels. Cut each into 4 parts and wash well. Drain, place in skillet with garlic, oil, salt, and pepper and cook 10 minutes, stirring frequently. Add water, cover skillet, and cook slowly 20 minutes, or until tender. Serves 4.

Sweet Fennel or Finocchio   FRANCE

This vegetable, commonly known as sweet fennel or finocchio, is not very well known. It is prepared like the cardoons and the squashes.

Fennel and Chard Au Gratin   ITALY

6 very small stalks fennel
1 bunch chard, cut into 2-inch pieces
2 cups cream sauce

4 tablespoons fine bread crumbs
3 tablespoons grated Parmesan cheese
2 tablespoons butter

Cut each fennel into 4 parts and boil with chard 10 minutes. Drain. Grease casserole and sprinkle some bread crumbs on bottom and sides. Place fennels and chard in casserole, pour cream sauce over them, sprinkle with bread crumbs and cheese, and dot with butter. Bake in moderate oven (375°) 20 minutes, or until cheese is melted and crumbs are light brown. Serves 4.

Stewed Garlic

BULGARIA

2 to 3 bunches young garlic
  (or onions or leeks)
½ pint lightly salted water

3 to 4 tablespoons oil
3 to 4 tablespoons vinegar
  dill to taste

Cut garlic, onion, or leeks into pieces about 1 inch long. Simmer for 5 minutes in lightly salted water, then arrange on plates. Mix oil with cooking liquid and vinegar, pour over garlic, and sprinkle with chopped dill. Serve warm or cold. Serves 4.

Stuffed Grape Leaves   JEWISH

8 grape leaves the size of a
  hand
  boiling water
4 large onions, diced or
  chopped
  vegetable shortening or oil

1 cup rice
⅓ cup or chopped seeded
  raisins
  salt to taste
  parsley

Wash grape leaves and cover with boiling water till the leaves are wilted. Drain well. Fry onions in shortening till light brown and transparent. Add washed rice and raisins and stir well over reduced heat for 2 minutes. Add salt to taste. Let cool before placing a spoonful of the mixture in the center of each leaf and rolling up, tucking in the ends or forming into a tightly wrapped ball. Arrange neatly in a heavy skillet, add water to cover and let simmer 30 minutes. Water may be added if necessary to prevent sticking. Slip under broiler flame to brown if desired. Serve with matzoun, yogurt, or sour cream topping, hot or cold and garnish with parsley. Serves 4.

Stuffed Grape Leaves

1 to 1½ pounds tender grape-
　vine leaves
1½ pounds onions
1 cup oil
1¼ cups raw rice
½ cup chopped parsley
2 tablespoons chopped dill
½ teaspoon chopped fresh
　mint leaves

salt and pepper to taste
1 lemon, juice only
water as needed
lemon wedges (optional)
pine nuts (optional)
raisins (optional)

If possible, buy the prepared grapevine leaves; wash them in clear cold water before using. If you are using fresh leaves, tenderize them first, as follows:

Cut the stems from the leaves with a sharp knife or scissors. Wash the leaves thoroughly, then throw them into a pot of rapidly boiling water. Boil for about 2 to 3 minutes, or until the leaves soften. Remove from the water and spread on a platter or tabletop.

To prepare the filling, peel and chop the onions. Put in a strainer and run cold water through them; drain. Sauté in the oil to a very light golden color. Add the rice; brown lightly. Add 1½ to 2 cups water, and the parsley, dill, mint leaves, salt, and pepper. Cook for 5 to 7 minutes, until the rice absorbs the liquid but is only half cooked (watch it carefully so it does not stick to the pot).

When filling the leaves, keep the shiny side of the leaf on the outside. Put 1 teaspoonful of filling in the center of the leaf and fold the sides up over it, covering it, then roll it up like a cigar. Lay the stuffed leaves in a pot (open side down so they do not swell open) in even, tight rows. When one layer is completed, make a second layer on top of the first, or a third layer, if necessary. Lay a plate directly on the top layer of dolmathes. Add enough water to the pot to half cover the stuffed leaves, and add the lemon juice. Cover the pot; cook until the liquid has been absorbed and only a slight amount of oil remains (this should take about 45 minutes). Serves 6 to 8.

Note: Although these are usually served cold with wedges of lemon, they can also be served hot. During the cooking, you may add pine nuts, and/or raisins.

Vine Leaves Stuffed with Mushrooms   BULGARIA

1 pound fresh mushrooms,
  preferably large ones
1½ cups lightly salted water
¾ cup rice

30 to 40 young vine leaves (about)
½ cup boiling water
6 to 8 tablespoons butter

Wash mushrooms and boil in lightly salted water for about 20 minutes. Drain, reserving stock. Chop remainder fine.

Boil rice until soft in mushroom stock, with a little water added if needed. Pour boiling water over young vine leaves so that they become soft. (If needed, this water can be added to rice.) Mix half of cooked rice with chopped mushrooms and place a spoonful of this mixture on each vine leaf. Make a small packet out of each individual leaf; place next to each other in a greased pan, and simmer in 3 to 4 tablespoons butter for 15 to 20 minutes. Brown remaining 3 to 4 tablespoons butter and pour over the dish. Place rolled leaves on remaining rice and serve hot. Serves 5 to 6.

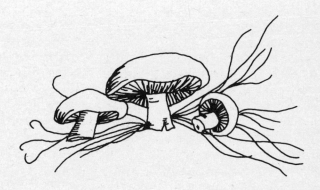

H

Hop Sprouts

The edible part is separated from the fibrous part by breaking off the ends of the sprouts, as in the case of asparagus. After having rinsed them in several waters, cook them in salted water containing, per every quart, the juice of one-half lemon.

Hop sprouts may be prepared with butter, cream, *velouté*, etc. When served as a vegetable, they are invariably accompanied by *poached* eggs, which are laid in a crown round them and alternated by comb-shaped *croutons* fried in butter.

Omelet with Young Shoots of Hops

Fill the omelet with two tablespoons of young shoots of hops, mixed with cream, and finish it in the usual way. Open it slightly along the top, and garnish with a few young shoots of hops put aside for the purpose.

The omelet may be surrounded with a ribbon of cream sauce, but this is optional.

K

Kale

These greens are at their best after frost. Wash and drain well any amount required. Cut or chop. Cook with very little water in a covered saucepan. Season with salt, pepper and plenty of fat. Serve like spinach. One pound serves 4.

Boiled Kale

1 1-pound head of kale
  water to cover
  salt to taste

½ cup bread crumbs
½ cup butter

Boil head of kale in salted water for 15 to 20 minutes, uncovered. Drain and quarter; sprinkle with bread crumbs browned in butter. Serves 4.

Creamed Curly Kale

2 stems curly kale (about 2¼
  pounds)

or 1 packet deep-frozen curly
  kale (about 15 ounces)

Prepare as creamed spinach. Cooking time for fresh curly kale is about 20 minutes.
Retain the vegetable water and use it in the sauce.
Serves 4.

Kale Patties

1 pound kale
2 rolls
1 medium onion, grated
  salt to taste
  pepper to taste

1 egg
2 tablespoons flour
1¼ cups (approximately)
  bread crumbs
⅔ cup shortening

Boil kale in salted water for 10 minutes. Drain. Soak rolls in water and squeeze dry. Chop kale and rolls together finely, or grind. Add onion, salt and pepper, egg, flour, and enough bread crumbs to make a soft dough. Form into patties, roll in the remaining bread crumbs, and brown in shortening. Serves 4.

Kale with Rice

2 cups chopped kale
1 cup cooked rice
1 grated onion

½ teaspoon salt
3 tablespoons butter

Combine all ingredients, turn into buttered baking dish and bake for 30 minutes (375°) or till nicely browned on top.

Scalloped Kale

1½ pounds kale
1 onion, diced
2 tablespoons butter
½ cup grated cheese
½ cup dry crumbs

1½ teaspoons salt
1 cup thin white sauce
2 hard-cooked eggs

Cut away fibrous stems and wilted tops from kale. Wash well. Drain. Chop or cut fine. Cook in a tightly covered pot over moderate heat 8 to 10 minutes. Sauté onion in butter till light brown. Combine cooked kale with onion and turn into a casserole or baking dish. Top with grated cheese mixed with crumbs. Bake 15 minutes at 375°. Pour on white sauce and garnish with sliced cooked eggs. Serves 4.

Scotch Kale, Spring Cabbage,
Broccoli Leaves, Turnip Tops   FRANCE

These various kinds of greens are boiled, or prepared with butter, like Brussels sprouts. These two methods of preparation are the only ones that suit them.

Sea Kale   FRANCE

This is one of the best and most delicate of vegetables.

It is trimmed with great care, washed, and then tied into bunches of from five to six plants, which are plainly cooked in salted water.

All cardoon recipes, and sauces given for asparagus, may be applied to sea kale.

Kohlrabi   AUSTRIA

8 medium-sized kohlrabi	½ teaspoon parsley, chopped
3 tablespoons butter	½ cup vegetable soup or stock
½ teaspoon sugar	or more
3 tablespoons flour	¼ teaspoon salt

Peel, halve, and slice kohlrabi. Cook in salted water until soft (about 10 to 15 minutes). Melt butter in pan; add sugar; brown slightly; blend in flour and parsley. Add stock or soup and salt; bring to a boil. Add kohlrabi. (Cooked green peas may be added, too.) Serves 6.

Note: If kohlrabi are young and tender, parts of the leaves may be cooked in salted water, chopped, and added to kohlrabi mixture.

Kohlrabi

This vegetable is sometimes called cabbage turnip. Buy small ones with fresh tops. Allow 2 to 3 per serving. Cut tops from stems and chop or mince. Dice or slice bulbs fine. Add cold water to barely cover. A few drops of lemon juice, minced parsley, or chives add a tangy flavor. Add salt to taste and cook in a covered saucepan 10 to 15 minutes or till tender. Add the chopped greens, cover, cook 5 minutes to tenderize. When ready to serve, add butter, grated cheese, cream or evaporated milk while hot.

Kohlrabi Kraut
CZECHOSLOVAKIA

1 medium onion, chopped
¼ cup butter
8 kohlrabi (2 pounds), peeled
and cut into thin strips
pinch of caraway seeds

salt to taste
1 tablespoon flour
½ cup water
vinegar to taste
sugar to taste

Fry onion in butter; add kohlrabi, caraway seeds, and salt. Sauté for 10 to 15 minutes. Dust with flour; add water, vinegar, and sugar; bring to a boil, and serve. Serves 6 to 8.

Sautéed Kohlrabi
CZECHOSLOVAKIA

8 kohlrabi (2 pounds), peeled
and sliced
⅓ cup butter
salt to taste

2 tablespoons flour
½ cup milk
1 tablespoon minced parsley
or dill

Sauté kohlrabi in butter, sprinkle with salt. When done, dust with flour and add milk. Bring to a boil. Before serving, add parsley or dill. Serves 6 to 8.

L

Leeks GERMANY

6 leeks
½ teaspoon salt in water to
  cover
2 tablespoons butter
2 tablespoons flour

½ cup milk
½ cup (or more) cooking water
  salt and pepper
  nutmeg
2 tablespoons cream

Remove green parts from stalks, cut the rest in finger-thick slices and grate. Cook 10 minutes in boiling salted water. Drain, reserving water. Prepare a light sauce from butter, flour, and milk, thin with vegetable water to desired consistency, and season. Add leeks to sauce and heat through. Add cream and serve hot. Serves 4.

Leek Au Gratin   BULGARIA

3 leeks
1 cup salted water
2 eggs, beaten

½ cup bread crumbs
  fat for frying

Cut leeks into pieces 2 to 3 inches long and cook in salted water for about 15 to 20 minutes or until tender. Take individual pieces, press flat with knife, place in beaten egg, then in bread crumbs, then in egg again. Fry in hot fat until golden brown. Serve with tomato sauce or salad of sour preserved vegetables. Serves 4 to 6.

Boiled Leeks

> 8 to 10 ounces leeks for each portion
> water
> 2 teaspoonfuls salt to each quart (5 cups) of water

Trim the leeks and wash them extremely well. Cut them into pieces. Put them into boiling salted water and cook until tender, about 10 to 20 minutes. Drain the leeks thoroughly.

Leek-Burgers

4 to 5 leeks
1 onion, chopped fine
3 tablespoons oil
½ cup bread crumbs or 4 slices
   white bread (about), cubed

¼ cup milk
1 to 2 tablespoons flour
   salt and pepper to taste
1 egg
   fat for frying

Clean leeks. Cook until soft in boiling, salted water and put through a sieve or grinder. Fry onion in oil. Mix leeks, onions, bread crumbs (or bread soaked in milk and squeezed out well), flour, seasonings, and egg. Shape balls. Press flat. Fry in hot fat until brown on both sides. Serve hot or cold. Serves 4.

Leeks in Lemon

1 pound leeks
   water to cover
1 teaspoon salt

1 tablespoon cornstarch
2 tablespoons olive oil
   juice of 1 large lemon

Clean the leeks well. Cover with water, add salt, and cook until tender (15 to 20 minutes). Drain off the liquid. To 2 cups of the hot liquid add the cornstarch, and cook, stirring constantly, until thick. Add the lemon juice and oil and pour over the leeks. Cool, then chill. Serve cold. Serves 3 to 4.

Leek with Olives

4 to 6 leeks
3 tablespoons oil
1 tablespoon meat bouillon
1 teaspoon flour

2 teaspoons vinegar
 salt to taste
20 to 25 olives

Cut leeks into pieces 1½ inches wide and soften for several minutes in boiling water. Drain well. Brown in hot oil. Make a smooth mixture out of bouillon and flour. Add vinegar and salt. In a baking dish mix with leeks and olives. Cook in 350° oven for about 20 minutes or until brown. Cool. Serve cold. Serves 4 to 6.

Leek with Rice

R U M A N I A , B U L G A R I A

5 leeks
1 onion, chopped
3 tablespoons oil

½ cup rice
¼ cup bouillon or tomato juice

Cut leeks into pieces. Fry first onion, then leeks in oil until golden. Add rice, fry 5 minutes, then pour in bouillon or tomato juice and cook for about 20 minutes. If necessary add a little more bouillon. Serves 4.

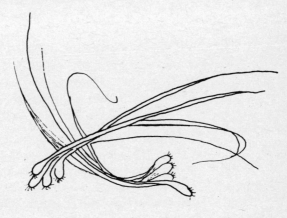

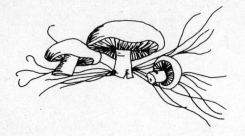

Mushrooms

2 pounds mushrooms
2 tablespoons olive oil
2 tablespoons butter

1 small onion, chopped
salt and pepper
parsley

Clean mushrooms carefully. Fry them lightly, 3 minutes, in olive oil. Add butter, onion, salt, and pepper. Cover and let simmer for 10 minutes. Garnish with parsley to serve.

Variation: Cook mushrooms until tender, sprinkle with flour and enrich the liquid with milk. Serves 4.

Mushrooms Au Gratin

1 pound mushrooms of even
 size
3 tablespoons butter
½ onion, minced
 salt and pepper

1 cup sour cream blended with
 1 teaspoon flour
 grated Parmesan
 bread crumbs for topping

Wash and clean mushrooms. Simmer with a little butter and the onion and seasoning, tightly covered, until transparent— about 10 minutes. Arrange in ovenproof *gratin* dish, cover with sour cream with the flour blended into it, sprinkle generously with grated Parmesan, then with bread crumbs, and top with remaining butter. Brown under broiler or in very hot oven for a few minutes. Serves 4.

Baked Mushrooms with Noodles   GERMANY

½ pound noodles
1 pound mushrooms
2 tablespoons butter
  salt and pepper

parsley, chopped
2 tablespoons bread crumbs
1 tablespoon butter

Cook and drain noodles. Slice mushrooms and sauté in butter 5 minutes. Season well. Add parsley. Arrange alternating layers of noodles and mushrooms in buttered baking dish, sprinkle with bread crumbs and dot with butter. Bake in 375° oven until golden brown, about 10 minutes. Serves 4.

Mushrooms in Batter   RUMANIA

3 to 4 large, firm mushrooms
½ cup milk
  heaping ¾ cup flour

1 egg
6 to 10 tablespoons fat
  salt to taste

Slice mushrooms very fine. Make a smooth batter out of milk, flour, and egg. Dip mushroom slices in it and fry in hot fat on both sides until light brown. Serves 4.

Breaded Mushrooms   POLAND

15 to 20 mushrooms of even
  size
½ minced onion
4 tablespoons butter

salt and pepper
1 egg, lightly beaten
  bread crumbs

Cook onion in a little butter until limp. Add mushrooms, season, and simmer tightly covered until transparent. Dip in egg, roll in bread crumbs, and fry evenly in hot butter. Serve with another vegetable. Serves 3 to 4.

Broiled Mushrooms JEWISH

Select large mushrooms, allowing 2 or 3 per serving. Wash, remove stems, and drain. Combine 1 cup dry bread or cracker crumbs with 2 tablespoons melted butter and 1 tablespoon grated cheese. Season with onion salt or salt and pepper. Stir in egg. Place a ball of this mixture in each mushroom cup. Broil 3 to 5 minutes or till lightly browned. Drizzle melted butter over each before serving.

Variation 1: Slice large or medium mushrooms and sauté in hot butter, or oil. Season with minced parsley, a dash of salt and pepper or paprika.

Variation 2: Sauté and serve with sour cream. Garnish with minced parsley or fresh dill.

Creamed Mushrooms FINLAND

4 tablespoons butter
4 cups sliced fresh mushrooms
1 medium onion, finely
  chopped

4 tablespoons flour
1½ cups cream
  salt to taste

Melt the butter in a frying pan, add the mushrooms and onion, and cook over medium heat, stirring constantly, until the mushrooms and onions are browned. Stir in the flour and the cream. Taste, and add salt. Simmer slowly for 30 minutes. Makes about 2½ cups.

Cultivated Mushrooms Smothered Whole POLAND

15 to 20 mushrooms of even
  size
  juice ½ lemon
  salt and pepper
½ medium onion, minced
1 tablespoon butter (approximately)

flour for dredging
3 to 4 tablespoons sweet or
  sour cream, according to
  preference
1 tablespoon chopped fresh
  parsley
2 egg yolks, lightly beaten

Wash and clean mushrooms and cut stems even with caps. (Reserve stems for other use. Sprinkle with a little lemon juice to avoid discoloration.) Season and smother with the onion in a little butter (cover tightly) until tender—about 10 minutes. Dust with flour, add cream and lemon juice to taste, add parsley, and let simmer another 5 minutes. When ready to serve, stir beaten egg yolks into sauce, taking care not to curdle egg. Serves 3 to 4.

Dried Mushrooms   POLAND

Imported dried mushrooms are tangier than domestic ones. Polish mushrooms, now readily available in the United States, are particularly recommended, since they are wild European mushrooms specially prepared. In Europe, where they are cheaper and more abundant, they are used as a vegetable. Here, however, this would be an impossible luxury, since good imported mushrooms cost about $12.00 a pound. But they are excellent in sauces and soups, for an ounce or even a half-ounce can "make" a dish. Dried mushrooms are best soaked overnight in milk or a little water, then simmered half an hour in the soaking liquid. If a recipe does not call for milk, be sure to soak in water. This water can then take the place of bouillon in sauce.

Mushroom Entrée   GERMANY

2 tablespoons butter
½ tablespoon lemon juice
    salt and pepper
¼ teaspoon finely chopped
    parsley

white bread
½ pound mushrooms
¼ cup cream
1 teaspoon sherry

Cream butter. Add lemon juice drop by drop, salt, pepper, and parsley. Cut two ½ inch thick rounds of bread and toast. Spread with butter mixture on both sides and put in individual buttered (greased) baking dishes. Clean and peel mushrooms. Heap on toasted sections and pour cream over. Bake, covered, in 350° oven for 25 minutes, adding additional cream if desired. Just before serving, add sherry. Serves 2.

Mushrooms with Egg AUSTRIA

¼ cup butter
½ teaspoon onion, chopped
½ teaspoon parsley, chopped

1 pound mushrooms
½ teaspoon salt
4 eggs, fried or poached

Melt butter. Fry onion and parsley. Add washed, sliced mushrooms; salt. Simmer 7 to 8 minutes. Arrange on serving dish. Decorate with eggs.
Serves 4.
Note: If desired, add 1 to 2 tablespoons sour cream and 1 teaspoon lemon juice.

Eggs with Creamed Mushrooms and Peas SCANDINAVIA

4 warm, boiled eggs
  (4 bread croûtons)

Sauce
1 small can mushrooms, sliced
  (7½ ounces)
1½ tablespoonfuls butter or
  margarine (4½ teaspoons)
2 tablespoonfuls plain flour

½ to ¾ pint cream, milk,
  mushroom or pea liquid
  (1¼ to 1¾ cups)
1 tablespoonful tomato purée
2 canned red sweet peppers
  (pimientos), sliced
1 medium-sized can of peas
  (15½ ounces)
  salt
  white pepper

Drain the mushrooms from their liquid. Fry the mushrooms in the fat, sprinkle with flour, add the liquid and boil the sauce for 3 to 5 minutes. Add the tomato purée, red peppers, and peas; season to taste.
Shell the eggs and cut into wedges. Arrange the wedges in four groups (on bread croutons, if liked) and pour the sauce over them. Serves 4.

Mushroom Omelet ISRAEL

2 tablespoons butter or margarine
2 cups sliced mushrooms
1 teaspoon fat

4 eggs
4 tablespoons milk
  salt and pepper to taste

Heat the butter, put in the sliced mushrooms, and fry until done (about 5 minutes). In another skillet, melt the fat. Beat the eggs lightly with the milk, season to taste, and pour into the pan. When the eggs begin to set, put on the mushrooms and fold the egg over. Serve at once. Serves 3 to 4.

Fried Mushrooms

ITALY

24 *small solid mushrooms*
½ *cup flour*
1 *egg, lightly beaten*

1 *tablespoon milk*
½ *teaspoon salt*
1 *cup olive oil*

Wash mushrooms well and dry. Roll in flour. Add milk and salt to egg and beat a little. Dip mushrooms into egg mixture and fry in medium hot olive oil until light brown in color. Drain on paper and serve hot. Serves 4.

Mushroom Fritters

SCANDINAVIA

10 *to* 12 *mushrooms, uniform*
  in size

Fritter Batter
2 *ounces plain flour (*½ *cup)*
½ *teaspoonful salt*

1 *egg*
7 *tablespoonfuls pilsner or*
  water
1 *tablespoonful melted butter*
  or margarine
  oil or coconut butter to fry

Clean the mushrooms.

Stir together the flour, salt, egg yolk, and liquid to make a smooth batter. Add the fat. Whisk the egg white to a stiff foam and carefully fold it into the batter.

Dip the mushrooms into the fritter batter and let them drain a little. Fry them in the hot fat (about 390°) a few at a time, until golden brown, about 1 minute. Lift them out using a fritter spoon and let them drain on absorbent kitchen paper. Serves 6.

Mushrooms, Genoa Style ITALY

¾ *pound mushrooms, sliced*
   thin
2 *tablespoons olive oil*
½ *teaspoon salt*

½ *teaspoon pepper*
1 *large clove garlic, chopped*
1 *teaspoon oregano*

Place mushrooms in frying pan with oil, salt, and pepper and cook until all water from mushrooms has evaporated. Add garlic and oregano, mix well, and cook 1 minute longer. Serves 4.

Glazed Mushrooms SCANDINAVIA

1 *pound mushrooms, uniform in size (8 cups)*
¾ *gill (7 tablespoonfuls) oil (scant ½ cup)*
   salt
   paprika
1 *clove garlic, crushed*
1 *small onion, chopped*
3 *tablespoonfuls chopped parsley*
1 *to 2 tablespoonfuls finely chopped dill (optional)*
2 *teaspoonfuls basil*

Clean the mushrooms. Cut large specimens in half.

Fry the mushrooms in the oil. Add the seasonings and herbs. Cover the pan and cook the mushrooms slowly, about 45 minutes. Moisten with more oil if necessary. Taste for seasoning. Serves 4.

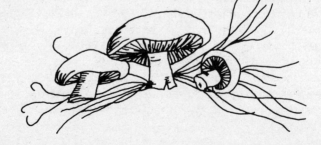

Marinated Mushrooms   POLAND

For marinating, choose only very young, small mushrooms with caps still tight around the stem. Wash thoroughly, then place in an earthenware casserole. If cooked in a metal pot they will discolor.

1 pound mushrooms	*wine vinegar to taste*
1 large onion, sliced	*10 peppercorns*
salt to taste	*10 whole allspice*
½ cup water	*2 bay leaves*

Combine mushrooms, onion, salt, and water. Simmer, tightly covered, until mushrooms are done—15 to 20 minutes. Add vinegar to taste (depending on how tart one likes the marinade), spices, and bay leaves. Allow to boil up a few times. When mushrooms have cooled enough to handle, transfer to glass jars and seal tightly. Refrigerate for use as required.

Mushroom-Macaroni Casserole   FINLAND

1 medium onion, finely chopped	*2 cups milk*
3 cups fresh mushrooms, chopped	*2 eggs, slightly beaten*
2 tablespoons butter	*1½ teaspoons salt*
2 cups cooked macaroni	*½ teaspoon pepper*
	⅓ cup fine dry bread crumbs

Brown the onion and mushrooms in butter in a frying pan over medium heat, stirring constantly. Butter a 2-quart casserole and place half the macaroni on the bottom. Spread the onions and mushrooms over it, and distribute the remaining macaroni evenly over all. Combine the milk, eggs, salt, and pepper and pour over the ingredients in the casserole. Top with the bread crumbs. Bake in a moderate oven (350°) for 30 minutes or until the casserole is set and the top slightly browned. Serve hot. Serves about 6.

Mushrooms Smothered in Butter POLAND

1 pound mushrooms	½ medium onion, minced
salt and pepper to taste	2 tablespoons flour

Wash mushrooms and slice thin both stems and caps, which do not need to be peeled. Season, add onion, and simmer, tightly covered, in their own juice for a few minutes, stirring to prevent burning. When mushrooms are limp, add butter, and continue cooking until thoroughly limp and dark. Although mushrooms may be served after 8 to 10 minutes, they will have more flavor if allowed to stew longer. Serves 4 to 6 as a side dish.

Mushroom Patties POLAND

1 pound mushrooms	2 whole eggs, lightly beaten
1 medium onion, grated	1 tablespoon chopped fresh
butter	parsley
salt and pepper to taste	bread crumbs for rolling
2 white rolls, moistened in	butter for frying
milk and mashed	

Wash, clean, and chop mushroom caps and stems. Cook grated onion in a little butter, and when onion begins to brown, add the mushrooms. Season and simmer, covered, for about 5 minutes. Mix thoroughly with the mashed rolls, eggs, and parsley, and shape into patties. Roll in bread crumbs and fry in hot butter to a golden brown. Serves 4. Serve with pan-fried potatoes.

Mushroom Pastries (Salty) YUGOSLAVIA

2½ cups flour	½ pound fresh mushrooms or
½ cup sour cream	2 ounces dried mushrooms,
½ cup butter	soaked, chopped fine
2 eggs	salt and pepper to taste
Filling	
1 small onion, chopped fine	
½ cup oil	

To make puff pastry mix flour, 6 tablespoons of the sour cream, butter, and 1 egg.

To prepare filling, sauté onion in oil until golden; add mushrooms, salt, and pepper and cook 5 minutes. Remove from heat; add remaining sour cream. Cool.

Roll out pastry ½ inch thick. Cut into 2-inch squares. Place a spoonful of the filling on each square. Brush the edges of the squares with second egg, slightly beaten. Fold four points toward the middle, one on top of the other. Brush the tops with egg. Arrange the pastries on a buttered baking sheet. Sprinkle with pepper. Bake in (475°) oven for about 15 minutes. The oven must not be opened for the first 7 minutes. Serves 8 to 10.

Mushroom Pudding   AUSTRIA

1 teaspoon onions, chopped
1 teaspoon parsley, chopped
2 tablespoons butter
½ pound mushrooms, cleaned
 and diced
3 tablespoons butter
5 egg yolks

½ cup sour cream
⅓ cup flour
1 teaspoon salt
5 egg whites, stiffly beaten
1 tablespoon bread crumbs
2 tablespoons butter
2 tablespoons bread crumbs

Fry onions and parsley slightly in butter. Add mushrooms and simmer 6 to 8 minutes. Beat butter until creamy. Add egg yolks, sour cream, flour, salt, and mushroom mixture. Fold in egg whites. Butter a pudding form; sprinkle with bread crumbs. Pour mixture in. Cook in hot-water bath 45 minutes. Turn out on serving dish. Sprinkle with bread crumbs fried in butter. Serves 5 to 6.

Mushroom Ramekins POLAND

12 to 15 medium mushrooms
  lemon juice
½ medium onion, minced
  butter
  salt and pepper to taste
1 heaping teaspoon flour

2 tablespoons grated Parmesan cheese
1 cup sweet cream
2 egg yolks, lightly beaten
  butter and bread crumbs for
  topping

Wash and clean mushrooms, slice thin, and sprinkle with lemon juice. Simmer, tightly covered, with the onion and a little butter until transparent. Season, dust with flour, add grated Parmesan, cream, and egg yolks. Mix thoroughly. Pour mixture into buttered ramekins, sprinkle with bread crumbs, and dot with butter. Bake in hot oven 5 minutes. Makes 3 to 4 servings.

Mushrooms with Rice YUGOSLAVIA

½ cup rice
¼ cup butter
1 cup water

½ pound fresh mushrooms, chopped
1 tablespoon chopped parsley
  salt and pepper to taste

In a skillet fry rice in half of butter until transparent. Pour in water and boil until water is completely absorbed. In another pan fry mushrooms in remaining butter for 10 minutes. Sprinkle with parsley. Mix with rice; season. Serves 4.

Mushrooms à la Russe JEWISH

4 cups sliced fresh mushrooms
1 heaping tablespoon flour
¼ teaspoon salt
1 cup sour cream

1 teaspoon onion juice or
2 tablespoons chopped chives
  or green onion tips
  generous dash of paprika

Do not peel fresh mushrooms but cut away the woody, fibrous stem section. Slice from the top down as thin as desired. Wash in slightly salted water and drain well. Enough water will cling to the slices to form sufficient steam. Place in saucepan or heated frying pan and cook over low heat 3 to 5 minutes. Rub the flour and salt with a little sour cream until smooth then stir into the remaining sour cream. Add to steamed mushrooms, stirring lightly to combine, then add the onion juice or chives. Cook 1 minute longer and serve hot on toast or Holland rusks. Garnish with a dash of paprika or a few bits of parsley. Serves 4.

Sautéed Mushrooms   FRANCE

After having washed the mushrooms, dried, and sliced them, and seasoned them with salt and pepper, toss them with butter in a frying pan over a hot fire. Sprinkle them with chopped parsley at the last moment, and serve them in a *timbale*.

Sautéed Mushrooms   CZECHOSLOVAKIA

1 medium onion, chopped	1 pound mushrooms, sliced
⅓ cup butter	½ teaspoon caraway seeds
	salt to taste

Fry onion in butter; add mushrooms, caraway seeds, and salt. Sauté for 10 to 15 minutes. Serves 4.

Sautéed Mushrooms in Sour Cream   ISRAEL

1 pound mushrooms	1 cup sour cream
2 tablespoons margarine or butter	salt and paprika to taste

Peel and slice the mushrooms and sauté in the margarine for 10 minutes, stirring often. Add the sour cream and cook 5 minutes more. Add the seasoning. These mushrooms are wonderful on toast. Serves 4.

Mushrooms with Spinach YUGOSLAVIA

2 pounds mushrooms, washed
  and chopped
1 teaspoon caraway seeds
1 tablespoon minced parsley
1 slice white bread, cubed

¾ pound spinach
1 onion, chopped
1 tablespoon oil
½ cup sour cream
  salt to taste

Simmer mushrooms in a little water with caraway seeds, parsley, and bread for 5 minutes. Chop spinach and add. Continue cooking until liquid evaporates almost completely. Fry onion in oil. Add mushroom-spinach mixture. Pour in sour cream. Season. Dish should be juicy but not soupy. Serves 4 to 5.

Stir-Fry Black Mushrooms CHINA

1½ tablespoons peanut oil; add a drop of sesame oil
1 teaspoon salt
1 clove garlic
2 ounces dried black mushrooms, soaked in warm water for 15
    minutes, sliced
½ cup water
1 tablespoon light soy sauce
1 teaspoon sugar
1 teaspoon seasoning powder
1 teaspoon rice wine or 2 tablespoons sherry wine
1 teaspoon cornstarch

Mix water, light soy sauce, sugar, seasoning powder, rice wine or sherry and cornstarch together. Stir well before using.

Put peanut oil into very hot skillet; add a drop of sesame oil. Add salt and garlic, then add black mushrooms. Stir-fry for 5 minutes. Add ¼ cup water. Cover and cook 5 minutes.

Add prepared mixture. Stir-fry thoroughly. When boiling, lower heat; let simmer until gravy becomes translucent. Serve hot with boiled rice or potatoes. Serves 2 or 3.

Mushroom and Sweet Corn Hash   SCANDINAVIA

1 medium-sized can mushrooms (7½ ounces)
1 large onion, chopped
2 tablespoonfuls butter or margarine
  salt
  white pepper or paprika
1 medium-sized can sweet corn (11 ounces)
  chopped parsley

Chop the mushrooms and fry them gently in the fat with the onion. Season. Strain off the liquid from the sweet corn.

Add the sweet corn to the mixture and reheat it thoroughly. Taste for seasoning.

Sprinkle with parsley and serve. Serves 4.

Turned or Grooved Mushrooms
for Garnishings   FRANCE

Take some very fresh mushrooms; wash and drain them quickly.

Cut their stalks flush with their heads; turn or groove the latter with the point of a small knife, and throw them, one by one, into a boiling liquor prepared as follows:

For 2 pounds of mushrooms, put 1/6 pint of water, ⅓ ounce of salt, 2 ounces of butter, and the juice of 1½ lemons, in a saucepan. Boil; add the mushrooms, and cook for 5 minutes. Transfer to a bowl immediately, and cover with a piece of buttered parchment paper.

Whole Fried Mushrooms   POLAND

1 pound small white mush-
rooms (or mushroom caps)
½ medium onion, minced

2 tablespoons butter
salt and pepper to taste

Wash and clean mushrooms, but do not peel. Lightly brown the onion in butter, add mushrooms, season, and cook about 10 minutes covered. When juice begins to form (mushrooms have a good deal of water in them), uncover and continue to fry until lightly brown. Serves 4.

Note: The same procedure may be used for broiling, in which case broil in a pan so that the juices will not drip away and leave mushrooms too dry. Dot with butter.

Mushrooms in Wine   BULGARIA

½ pound fresh mushrooms,
cleaned and chopped fine
1½ cups lightly salted boiling
water

½ cup white wine
pepper to taste
4 tablespoons flour
4 to 5 tablespoons fat

Simmer mushrooms for about 30 minutes in salted water with wine and seasoning to taste. Heat flour in hot fat until colored a little; pour in mushrooms and their liquid. Continue cooking for 8 to 10 minutes over low heat. If mixture becomes too thick, add a little hot water. Serves 3 to 4.

Morels   FRANCE

The spring mushroom or morel is the one most preferred by connoisseurs. There are two kinds of morels—the pale and the brown kind—both excellent, though some prefer the former to the latter, and vice versa.

In spite of what connoisseurs may say regarding the error of washing morels, I advocate the operation, and urge the reader to do it carefully, and without omitting to open out the underneath parts, so as to wash away any sand particles that may be lodged therein.

This type of mushroom does not generally grow in the United States.

Cooking Morels: If they be small, leave them whole; if large, halve or quarter them. After having properly drained them, put them in a saucepan with 2 ounces of butter, the juice of a lemon, and a pinch of salt and another of pepper per pound of morels. Boil, and then stew for 10 or 12 minutes. Never forget that the vegetable juices produced by the morels should be reduced and added to their accompanying sauce.

Creamed Morels   SCANDINAVIA

> scant ½ pound (1 ¾ pints) fresh morels, cleaned (4 cups)
> or 1 ¼ to 1 ½ ounces dried morels (about 1 cup)
>   water
> Sauce
> 1 ½ tablespoonfuls butter or margarine (4 ½ teaspoons)
>   salt
>   paprika
> 2 tablespoonfuls plain flour
> ½ to ¾ pint cream (1 ¼ to 1 ¾ cups)
> 1 to 2 tablespoonfuls Madeira or sherry (optional)

Rinse the morels thoroughly.

Put the fresh morels into a saucepan and just cover them with water. Bring the morels to the boil and boil for about 4 minutes. Discard the water. Rinse the morels carefully. Place the dried morels in water and let them soak for about 2 hours. Boil them in water until tender.

Chop the morels and fry them in the fat. Season. Sprinkle with the flour and add the cream. Cook the sauce for 3 to 5 minutes. (Add wine.) Taste for seasoning. Serves 4.

Sweet and Sour Mustard Greens — CHINA

½ cup water
2 tablespoons sugar
2 tablespoons vinegar
1 tablespoon cornstarch
1 pound sweet and sour mustard greens, cut into sections, squeezed dry
1½ tablespoons peanut oil

Mix water, sugar, and vinegar together. Mix cornstarch with ½ cup water. Stir well before using. Put mustard greens in hot skillet. Stir-fry 10 to 15 minutes, until very dry, then add the peanut oil. Stir thoroughly. Add the water, sugar, and vinegar mixture and stir 2 minutes. Add cornstarch preparation and stir-fry until gravy thickens and is smooth. Serves 2.

N

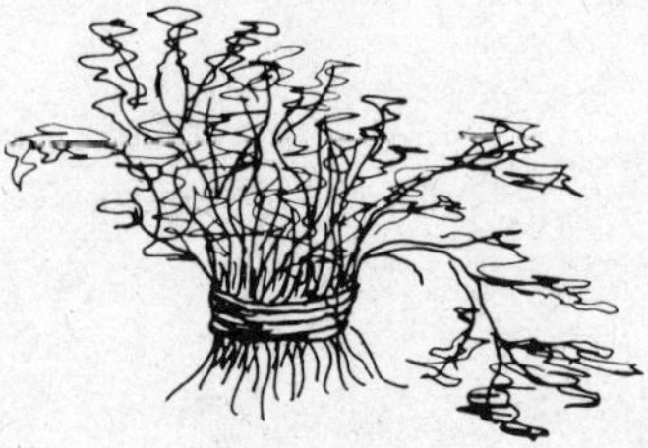

Young Nettles in Cream — RUMANIA

2 cups young nettles
salt to taste
1 tablespoon flour
1 tablespoon fat
1 cup bouillon
juice of ½ lemon
½ cup cream

Choose very young nettles; pour boiling water over. Drain. Cut or chop very fine and cook in salted water to cover for 10 minutes. Meanwhile heat flour in fat until golden; pour in bouillon and cook sauce for 20 minutes until thick. Add drained nettles, lemon juice, and cream. Serves 2.

Okra

1 pound okra
4 tablespoons peanut oil
2 teaspoons cumin seed
1 teaspoon salt

1 teaspoon turmeric
½ teaspoon cayenne
1 teaspoon ground coriander
(optional)

Wash and dry the okra. Cut it into thin slices, discarding the stem ends. Set aside. Heat the peanut oil, and add the cumin seed, salt, turmeric, and cayenne to it.

Throw in the okra and stir like mad until all is well coated with the oil. Cover, and cook over low heat for about 5 minutes. Do not add water. Lift the cover and stir again. In about 10 minutes, when it is done, add the coriander. Serve.

Creamed Gumbo or Okra

FRANCE

After having trimmed them, parboil them in salted water and drain them. Then cook them in butter, and, just before serving them, combine them with a cream sauce.

137

Okra with Mushrooms   BULGARIA

1 pound okra
½ cup chopped mushrooms
½ cup shallots
5 to 6 cloves garlic, chopped
    fine

¼ cup oil
¼ cup white wine
    salt and pepper to taste
1 tablespoon chopped parsley
3 to 4 tomatoes, sliced thin

In a pan place cleaned, washed okra, mushrooms, shallots, and garlic. Pour in oil and wine; add salt, pepper, and parsley; mix well. Place tomatoes on top. Simmer in (325°) oven about 20 to 30 minutes. Serve cold. Serves 4 to 6.

Okra Curry   INDIA

1 pound okra
3 tablespoons ghee
2 teaspoons cumin seed
1 teaspoon salt
1 teaspoon turmeric

1 teaspoon cayenne
1 teaspoon coriander
1 cup yogurt
4 cups water
2 tablespoons chick pea flour

Wash and dry the okra, cut it into thin slices. Set aside.

Heat the ghee, and add the spices to it. Heat and stir, and when warm, add the okra. Mix well. Lower the heat, and simmer slowly 10 minutes. Shake the pot from time to time to prevent sticking, but do not add water.

In a separate pot, mix the yogurt, water, and chick pea flour. Heat slowly until smooth and boiling. Add to the cooked okra and heat together for 10 minutes.

Okra in Oil   GREECE

3 pounds okra
    salt and pepper to taste
½ cup vinegar
1¼ cups oil or butter
4 to 5 cloves garlic
1 medium onion, chopped

1¼ pounds ripe tomatoes,
    peeled and strained, or 1
    tablespoon tomato paste
    diluted with 2 cups water
    water as needed

Wash the okra several times; clean carefully and remove the stems without cutting into the okra. Place them in a pan. Salt lightly, add the vinegar, and place in the sun for about 2 hours.

Heat the oil in a frying pan. Add the garlic and onion, and sauté until golden. Add the tomatoes (or tomato paste). Cook for 5 minutes. Rinse the okra well; discard the vinegar. Add okra, salt, pepper, and about 1 cup water to the tomatoes. Cover the pot. Simmer until the sauce is absorbed and the oil remains (45 minutes to 1 hour). Serves 6 to 8.

Note: After soaking the okra, you may rinse and fry it in half of the oil; use the rest of the oil as above. Then add the okra and 1 cup water to the sauce and cook for about 30 minutes.

Okra and Rice   JEWISH

2 cups cut okra
½ cup dry rice
1 cup cold water

½ teaspoon salt
2 tablespoons butter or oil
1 cup tomato sauce

Use only tender okra pods. Remove stem ends and tips. Cut into ½-inch slices. Add washed and drained rice, water, and salt. Cook in double boiler 30 to 45 minutes. Turn okra and rice into a greased baking dish and add tomato sauce. Bake 10 minutes (375°). Serves 4.

Stewed Okra and Tomatoes   JEWISH

1 pound okra
1 cup tomatoes, stewed
2 tablespoons butter, oil or
   chicken fat

1 tablespoon lemon juice
1 tablespoon brown sugar
½ teaspoon salt
   boiling water

Remove stems and tips from pods. Wash and drain. Slice pods if large. Add boiling water to barely cover and cook 15 minutes. Add the other ingredients and cook 5 minutes longer. Serves 4.

Baked Pearl Onions

1 pound pearl onions
¼ cup olive oil
½ teaspoon salt

½ teaspoon pepper
1 tablespoon wine vinegar
¼ clove garlic, chopped

Place onions on baking sheet with skins on and bake in moderate oven (375°) 15 minutes, or until tender. Remove from oven, peel and place in salad bowl with oil, salt, pepper, vinegar, and garlic. Mix well and serve either hot or cold. Serves 4.

Boiled Onions

4 large onions
1 teaspoon chopped parsley
½ teaspoon chopped oregano

½ teaspoon salt
½ teaspoon pepper
¼ cup olive oil

Peel onions, cut in halves crosswise and boil in water ½ hour. Drain well and place in serving dish. Sprinkle with parsley, oregano, salt, pepper, and olive oil. Serves 4.

Creamed Onions

8 medium-size white or yellow
  onions
  cold water to cover
¼ teaspoon salt
3 tablespoons butter

3 tablespoons flour
1½ cups milk
4 tablespoons grated cheese,
  sharp or mild Cheddar type
  dash of paprika (optional)

Peel onions and cut away root and stem ends. Cover with cold water, add salt and bring to a quick boil. Reduce heat and cook, uncovered, 20 to 25 minutes or until the onions are tender enough to pierce with a toothpick. Drain. Make a cream sauce by melting butter in a saucepan and rubbing in the flour till smooth. Stir in milk and cook over moderate heat 5 to 8 minutes, stirring constantly till thick. Add grated cheese and stir till smooth. Remove from heat. Add the cooked onions. Heat before serving. Add a dash of paprika for color if desired. Serves 4.

Variation: White pickling onions 1 inch in diameter may be used, allowing 4 to 6 per serving. Proceed as in basic recipe.

Fried Onions   SCANDINAVIA

> 3 to 4 onions
> 2 tablespoonfuls butter or margarine
>   salt

Peel the onions and cut them into thin slices.

Melt the fat, add the onions and fry them gently until they are tender, about 15 minutes. Turn them occasionally but do not let them brown until cooking is almost completed. Season with salt. Serves 4.

Fried Whole Onions   SCANDINAVIA

1 pound small onions or shallots or freshly pickled onions
2 tablespoonfuls butter or margarine

1 to 2 teaspoonfuls sugar or syrup
salt
7 tablespoonfuls water or stock

Peel the onions. Small onions are easier to peel if they are scalded in hot water first of all.

Heat the fat and add the onions. Brown them gently and add the sugar and salt. Add the liquid when the onions are golden brown, about 15 to 20 minutes for small onions, about 30 minutes for larger ones. Cover with a lid and let them simmer gently until tender on top of the cooker or in the oven (200°C, 390°F). Shake the pan now and again so that the entire surface of the onions becomes shiny.

Serve on a vegetable platter. Serves 4.

Note: The onions may be parboiled before frying. The frying time is then slightly reduced.

Grilled Onions ITALY

4 *large onions*   ½ *teaspoon salt*
1 ½ *teaspoons chopped parsley*   ½ *teaspoon pepper*
2 *tablespoons olive oil*

Peel onions and boil in water 10 minutes. Drain well and cut into halves crosswise. Place on grill and sprinkle with parsley, olive oil, salt, and pepper and cook under low flame 30 minutes, adding more oil before serving. Serves 4.

Onions and Potatoes ALBANIA

2 *pounds potatoes*   2 *tablespoons oil*
2 *onions, chopped*   *salt and pepper to taste*

Boil potatoes in salted water for 20 to 40 minutes, depending on size. Peel and put through a potato ricer. Fry onions in oil; mix with potatoes; season. Serves 4 to 6.

Onions and Prunes ISRAEL

1 ½ *pounds firm onions*   1 *pound prunes*
4 *tablespoons margarine*

Select onions about the size of prunes. Peel and sauté them gently in the margarine over low heat. Soak the prunes for half an hour and then add to the onions. Cook until tender (20 to 30 minutes). If necessary, a very little water may be added to keep the ingredients from frying quickly. Serves 6.

Onions in Tomato Sauce YUGOSLAVIA

1 ½ *pounds small onions*   *sugar to taste*
¼ *cup oil*   2 *tablespoons tomato paste*
2 *tablespoons butter*   2 *tablespoons water*
  salt and pepper to taste   ½ *cup bouillon, if needed*

Choose onions as small as possible; peel and place in cold water for 30 minutes. Quarter; fry in very hot oil with butter, salt, pepper, and sugar. Mix tomato paste with water; add to onions; simmer well covered until done. Pour in bouillon only if necessary. Sauce should remain thick. Serves 4.

Scrambled Eggs with Young Onions　　BULGARIA

5 to 6 onion stalks
¼ cup oil
2 teaspoons flour
½ cup milk

4 eggs
chopped parsley to taste
salt to taste

Cut onion stalks into small pieces and fry well in oil. Sprinkle with flour, cook until it changes color. Add milk and eggs, and mix everything well. Scramble and sprinkle with parsley and salt. Serves 2.

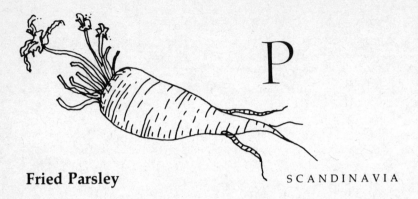

Fried Parsley SCANDINAVIA

parsley
oil or coconut butter to fry

Wash the parsley and dry it extremely well.

Lower the parsley into the hot fat and fry it quickly—just a few seconds. Lift it out with a frying spoon and drain it on absorbent paper.

Parsnips JEWISH

This root vegetable is very flavorful when young and tender. It should be scraped like carrots, cut lengthwise into quarters, and soaked in salted cold water 5 minutes before cooking. Allow 2 slender parsnips per serving, if fairly large. Cook parsnips 10 minutes in just enough water to prevent sticking. Add melted butter.

French Fried Parsnips JEWISH

Cut parsnips in strips or ¼-inch thick rounds. Soak in salted water. Drain and dust lightly with flour or fine crumbs seasoned with salt and pepper. Fry like french fried potatoes.

Sautéed Parsnips JEWISH

Parboil parsnips 5 minutes in slightly salted water. Drain well. Roll in flour or fine crumbs and fry in butter or oil till nicely browned on all sides.

Peas

2 tablespoons ghee
1 small white onion, very
    finely chopped
1 teaspoon turmeric
¼ teaspoon cayenne

2 cups fresh peas, hulled
1 teaspoon salt
¼ cup water
6 to 8 mint leaves,
    chopped fine

Heat the ghee, and add the onion, turmeric, cayenne, peas, and salt to it. Stir well, and add the water and mint leaves.

Bring all to a good boil, lower the heat, cover, and cook until the peas are tender. Since just enough water is called for to make steam and bring out the mint essence, take a quick look under the cover about 10 minutes after cooking. If too much water remains, remove the cover and continue to cook until the water evaporates. Serves 4.

Green Peas in Butter

As soon as the peas are cooked, drain them and toss them over a hot fire, to dry. Then season them with a pinch of powdered sugar, and mix them, away from the fire, with butter, in the proportion of 3 ounces per pint of peas.

Peas and Artichokes Latheros

3 pounds peas
6 medium artichokes
1 lemon
1¼ cups oil or 1 cup butter
5 scallions, chopped
1½ pounds ripe tomatoes,

peeled and strained, or 1
    tablespoon tomato paste
    diluted with 2 cups water
2 tablespoons chopped dill
salt and pepper to taste
water as needed

Shell and wash peas. Drain. Clean the artichokes, rub each one with lemon, and place in a pot of salted water. Squeeze half the lemon into this and let stand. Pour the oil into a pot, add the scallions; cook until soft but not browned. Add the tomatoes or the diluted tomato paste and bring to a boil. Add the peas. Rinse the artichokes and place them upside down (stem side up) on the peas. Add the dill and 1 cup hot water. Cover the pot. Cook over medium heat (about 30 to 40 minutes) until all the liquids are absorbed and only the oil remains as a sauce. Serves 6.

Note: You may omit the tomatoes, if you wish. In that case, substitute 2 cups water and the juice of another lemon.

Creamed Green Peas CZECHOSLOVAKIA

1 pound (2 cups shelled)
  fresh green peas
½ cup salted boiling water
¼ cup butter
½ teaspoon sugar
  salt to taste

pepper to taste
dash of nutmeg
1 cup cream
2 tablespoons flour
1 tablespoon minced
  parsley

Simmer peas in water for 5 minutes. Drain. Sauté with butter and sugar until tender (5 to 15 minutes). Stir in seasonings and cream mixed with flour; simmer for 3 minutes. Before serving, add parsley. Serves 4.

Omelet Clamart FRANCE

Fill the omelet with two tablespoons of fresh peas, bound by means of butter and combined with a portion of the lettuce used in cooking them, finely shredded. Roll the omelet, make an opening lengthwise in the center, and fill the space with a tablespoon of fresh peas.

Chick Peas in Tomato Sauce ISRAEL

2 cups chick peas
  water to cover
3 tablespoons olive oil
1 onion, chopped

1 clove garlic, crushed
1 cup tomato sauce
  salt and pepper to taste

Soak the peas overnight. Cover with fresh water and bring to a boil. Simmer slowly with the olive oil, onion, and garlic. When the peas begin to get tender, add the tomato sauce and finish cooking. Season to taste. Serves 6 to 8.

Note: The chick peas should be just covered with water during cooking.

Clamart Poached Eggs

Garnish some *tartlet-crusts* with small, green peas, cooked à la française, and mixed with finely shredded lettuce with the peas. Place an egg, coated with cream sauce which has been finished with fresh-pea butter, upon each.

Green Peas

> ¾ *pint dried green peas (1 pound) (2⅓ cups)*
> *1¼ to 1¾ pints water (3 to 4¼ cups)*
> *1 to 1½ teaspoonfuls salt*
> *1 tablespoonful butter or margarine*

Clean and wash the peas. Soak in the salted water for about 12 hours. Cook the peas in the same water until they are tender and the liquid well thickened, about 1½ to 2 hours. Stir occasionally and add water if necessary. Add the fat and taste for seasoning. Serves 4.

Peas Latheros

4½ to 5 pounds peas
1½ pounds ripe tomatoes,
  peeled and strained, or 1
  tablespoon tomato paste di-
  luted with 2 cups water

4 scallions
1¼ cups oil or 1 cup butter
3 tablespoons chopped dill
  salt and pepper to taste
  water as needed

Shell, wash, and drain the peas. Chop the white part of the scallions into small pieces and the green part into large pieces. Heat the oil in a large pot. Add the scallions and cook until soft but not browned. Add the peas and brown very lightly. Add the tomatoes (or the diluted tomato paste), dill, salt, and pepper. Add enough water to half cover the peas. Cover the pot. Cook over medium heat until only the oil remains and the liquid has been absorbed (about 45 minutes). Serves 6 to 9.

Note: You can make this without the tomatoes, if you wish. In that case, add just enough water to half cover the peas.

Chick Peas with Honey   ISRAEL

2 cups chick peas	2 teaspoons salt
2 tablespoons fat	½ cup honey
1 teaspoon cinnamon	water to cover

Soak the chick peas overnight and then cover with fresh water and simmer 2 to 3 hours, or until tender. Drain off the water. Mix with the remaining ingredients and bake in a 350° oven about 1 hour, or until peas are glazed. Serves 6 to 8.

Flamande Green Peas   FRANCE

Prepare ½ pound of new carrots as though they were to be *glazed*.

When half-cooked, add ⅔ pint of freshly shelled peas to them. Complete the cooking of the two vegetables together, and, at the last moment, add butter away from the fire.

Green Peas Française   FRANCE

Take a saucepan, of a size a little larger than would be necessary to just hold the following products, and put into it one quart of freshly shelled peas; a herb-bunch containing a heart of lettuce, two sprigs of parsley, and two of chervil; twelve small onions, 4 ounces of butter, ⅓ ounce of salt, and ⅔ ounce of sugar. Mix the whole together until it forms a compact mass, and place in the cool until ready for cooking. Add three tablespoons of water, when about to cook the peas, and cook gently with lid on.

When about to serve, take the herb-bunch; shred the lettuce; add it to the peas, and combine the whole with butter, away from the fire.

Note: Raw, shredded lettuce may be added to the peas; but, as various tastes must be allowed for, it is better to insert the lettuce whole, and to mix it with the peas afterwards, if it be so desired. The lettuce may also be quartered and laid on the peas without being mixed with them.

Minted Green Peas   JEWISH

2 cups shelled fresh peas or	½ cup cold water
1 tall can	2 tablespoons chopped fresh
¼ teaspoon salt	mint leaves
few grains of sugar	1 tablespoon butter

If canned peas are used, heat with liquid from can. If quick frozen peas are used, follow directions on the package. For fresh peas, add cold water, salt and sugar and cook in tightly covered saucepan 5 to 7 minutes over moderate heat. Or 2 minutes in pressure cooker. Just before serving add butter and chopped mint; shake the pan to distribute evenly. Remember when marketing that it takes about 3 pounds unshelled peas to serve 4.

Purée of Fresh Green Peas   AUSTRIA

1 pound green peas (fresh)	¼ teaspoon pepper
1 tablespoon parsley, chopped	1 egg yolk
3 tablespoons butter	½ cup light cream
½ teaspoon salt	

Cook peas in salted water. Drain; rub through strainer. Fry parsley in butter; combine with puréed peas. Add salt and pepper; bring to a boil. Blend in egg yolk and cream before serving. Serves 4 to 5.

Snow Peas   INDIA

½ pound fresh snow peas	1 teaspoon salt
4 tablespoons butter or ghee	½ cup water

Wash the snow peas. Remove the strings from the snow peas as you would from string beans. In a saucepan, heat the butter or ghee. Add the salt and the snow peas until well mixed. Then add the water.

Cook briskly, uncovered, for about 12 minutes, until all the water has evaporated. Serves 4.

Sautéed Green Peas

1 pound (2 cups shelled) fresh
  peas
½ cup salted boiling water
¼ cup butter

1 tablespoon flour
½ cup milk
1 tablespoon minced
  parsley

Simmer peas in water for 5 minutes. Drain. Sauté in butter until tender (5 to 15 minutes). Dust with flour, stir in milk. Bring to a boil, add parsley.

Peas may also be sautéed with other vegetables: carrots, kohlrabi, cauliflower, lettuce hearts, etc. Serves 2 to 3.

Split Pea Fritters

2 cups green or yellow
  split peas
1 onion, minced
1 tablespoon butter
4 tablespoons bread crumbs
1 heaping tablespoon chopped
  fresh dill and parsley

salt and pepper
1 whole egg, lightly
  beaten
bread crumbs for rolling
butter or fat for frying

Prepare peas. Simmer in water until tender, about 1½ hours. Purée them without diluting with liquid. Brown onion in butter and add to purée, together with bread crumbs, seasoning, herbs, and half the beaten egg. (The proportions should be—accurately—1 egg and 4 tbs. bread crumbs to 2 cups of purée.) Shape into patties or fritters, dip in remaining egg, roll in bread crumbs, and fry to a golden brown on all sides. Serve with a sharp sauce and in combination with other vegetables, such as stewed kohlrabi, spinach, carrots, etc. Serves 6.

Fried Peppers   ITALY

3 *large peppers*   ½ *cup flour*
2 *tablespoons oil*   1 *egg, lightly beaten*
½ *teaspoon salt*   1 *cup olive oil*
½ *teaspoon pepper*

Roast peppers in very hot oven (450°) 10 minutes, or until peppers peel easily. Peel, remove seeds, and cut into thin slices. Place in dish, add oil, salt, and pepper and let stand for ½ hour.

Drain off oil, roll in flour, dip into egg, and fry in very hot olive oil until golden brown. Serves 4.

Peppers with Cheese   YUGOSLAVIA

6 *large green peppers*   ¼ *cup kaimak (cottage cheese*
1 ¼ *pounds sheep's cheese*   *and sour cream)*
2 *eggs*   *salt to taste*
  vegetable oil

Remove stems, membrane, and seeds from peppers. Crumble cheese with fork, add eggs, and mix well. Stuff the peppers with this mixture. Oil a baking dish, put peppers upright in it, and top each pepper with some kaimak. Bake in 475° oven for about 15 minutes. Serve hot. Serves 3 to 4.

Sautéed Green Peppers   CZECHOSLOVAKIA

8 *green peppers, cut*   *salt to taste*
  into strips   *dash of ground caraway*
¼ *cup shortening*   *seed*

Add peppers to shortening with salt and caraway seed. Cook, covered, about 7 minutes. Serve with rolls, bread, or fried potatoes. Serves 4 to 6.

Grilled Marinated Peppers   ISRAEL

green peppers
sweet red peppers
salt and pepper

citrus or wine vinegar
olive oil
sugar to taste

Hold each pepper on a fork over an open flame, and when it is charred, turn to scorch the other side. This charred touch adds a delightful flavor to the dish. Rinse the peppers under cold water to blanch them. Put them into a bowl, sprinkle with salt and pepper and pour a little oil over each pepper. Prepare a marinade of citrus or wine vinegar and sugar to taste, and pour this over the peppers. After a few hours in the refrigerator the peppers will be ready. They keep very well for days. Some people add a hint of garlic to the marinade.

Stewed Peppers in Sour Milk   BULGARIA

12 to 15 long green peppers,
whole, seeded if desired
⅓ cup oil
salt to taste
2 tablespoons flour

¾ cup sour milk or yogurt,
slightly salted
chopped parsley for sprink-
ling
pepper to taste

Roast peppers in 375° oven 10 minutes, or pour boiling water over, and skin. Season and simmer in oil until tender, stirring. Sprinkle in flour. Stir in sour milk or yogurt. Simmer for 5 to 6 minutes. If desired, sprinkle with pepper or chopped parsley or both. Serves 4 to 6.

Note: If you seed the peppers, the dish will be less hot.

Stuffed Peppers   BULGARIA

8 peppers
2 carrots, peeled
½ celery root
1 potato, peeled
½ cup oil
2 to 3 tomatoes, peeled and
   chopped
2 to 3 cloves garlic, mashed
   salt and pepper to taste
1 onion, chopped
2 tablespoons chopped parsley
¼ pound sheep's cheese (white
   cheese)
½ cup water
Sauce
½ cup yogurt
3 eggs
2 tablespoons flour
   dash baking powder
   salt to taste

Cut a lid from stalk end of each pepper. Remove white membrane, seeds, and rinse out. Cube carrots, celery root, and potato; fry in oil for 10 minutes. Add tomatoes, garlic, salt, and pepper. Stew for 10 minutes. Add onion and parsley. Crumble cheese and add. Mix and stuff into peppers. Place next to each other in a baking tin; pour in water and cook in 350° oven for about 40 minutes.

Make a sauce out of yogurt, 3 eggs, flour, baking powder, and salt. Pour over peppers. Cook sauce until it is stiffened and lightly browned. Serves 4 to 6.

Fried Peppers   YUGOSLAVIA

Wash and dry small, round, sweet peppers. Fry in liberal amount of oil for 3 to 5 minutes. Drain and cool. Pack in a jar and cover with vinegar solution as in the recipe for peppers stuffed with cabbage.

Peppers Stuffed with Cabbage

2 pounds red cabbage	1⅓ cups vinegar
6 teaspoons salt	2⅔ cups water
8 teaspoons sugar	4 to 5 peppercorns
4 to 5 large green peppers	1 bay leaf

Shred the cabbage; sprinkle with 5 teaspoons salt and 7 teaspoons sugar and let stand for 2 hours. Wash the peppers and remove the stems, white membranes, and seeds. Fill them with the cabbage and pack into 2-quart glass jars. Boil the vinegar and water with 1 teaspoon salt, 1 teaspoon sugar, and the peppercorns. Cool and pour over the peppers.

This pickle is usually made in large quantities since it keeps fresh during the whole winter. Process in a pressure cooker made especially for preserving. If desired, process on two consecutive days, first for 30 minutes at a temperature of 225° and on the second for 15 minutes at a temperature of 180°.

Sweet Peppers for Garnishing

For this purpose, the large red, Spanish peppers are best. *Braise* them when they are peeled, and, when cooked, cut them up as the requirements may suggest.

Green Pepper Vegetable

4 sweet green peppers	2 teaspoons turmeric
3 tablespoons ghee	½ teaspoon cayenne
1 teaspoon salt	1 teaspoon ground coriander

Wash, core, and chop the pepper. In a saucepan, heat the ghee, salt, turmeric, and cayenne. Add the chopped peppers to it. Stir well, lower the heat, and cook gently for about 5 minutes. Test with a sharp knife for doneness. These are best slightly crisp. Add the coriander.

Mix all together well.

What is very pretty indeed is to use 2 sweet green peppers and 2 sweet red peppers. Serves 4.

Potatoes

Scrub potatoes and boil with jackets on, in enough water to prevent burning or sticking. Use a covered pot or saucepan and do not cook over a high flame. Boiling time depends on the size of potatoes. Add salt after boiling begins, ½ teaspoon to 1 pint water. Drain when tender. One pound serves 4.

Variation 1: Add butter, salad oil, or other shortening to peeled boiled potatoes and garnish with minced parsley or fresh dill.

Variation 2: Serve with thin or thick cream sauce to which grated cheese or minced parsley is added.

Variation 3: Roll peeled, boiled potatoes in flour seasoned with salt and white pepper. Brown in butter or other shortening.

Variation 4: Serve cooked whole small potatoes or diced large ones, hot or cold with sour cream and/or creamed cottage cheese, farmer cheese or pot cheese. Garnish with minced celery, chives, finely cut green onion or green pepper.

Variation 5: Fry thinly sliced cooked potatoes in hot melted shortening till lightly browned on both sides. Add 1 beaten egg for each cupful potatoes. Cover and cook over low heat 3 minutes. Turn out on heated platter underside up.

One cupful per serving.

Alsatian Fried Potatoes

4 large potatoes
fat to cover
salt to taste

Pare raw potatoes and cut lengthwise in strips ½ inch thick. Dry thoroughly in a towel. Fry small quantities at a time in hot deep fat, using a spatula to keep pieces from sticking together. When potatoes are golden brown, remove to strainer to drain, then sprinkle with salt.

Note: When preparing large quantities, the small initial lots may be fried lightly and stored in a strainer. Finish larger lots as above, in deep fat. It is practical to use a wire French fryer. Serves 4.

Anna Potatoes

Cut them to the shape of small cylinders; cut these into thin slices; wash them, and dry them in a piece of linen.

Set these slices in circles on the bottom of the mould proper to this potato preparation, or in a well-buttered thick-bottomed saucepan; let them overlap one another, and reverse each circle.

Season; spread a coat of butter upon the first layer, and proceed in the same way with a second layer.

Make five or six layers in this way, seasoning and spreading butter over each.

Cover the utensil; cook in a good oven for 30 minutes, turn the whole over, if necessary, to equalize the browning; turn out upon a saucepan lid, to drain off the butter, and then tilt onto a dish.

Potatoes Au Gratin

2 tablespoons butter
4 ½ cups diced cooked potatoes
4 tablespoons grated cheese
½ cup dry crumbs

1 egg
¼ teaspoon paprika
Salt and pepper to taste

Melt shortening in a shallow baking dish. Toss cheese, crumbs, egg and seasonings with potatoes. Bake 10 to 20 minutes at 400°. Serves 4.

Potatoes with Cheese Au Gratin

2 pounds potatoes
1 tablespoon butter
4 to 5 hard-cooked eggs, sliced

9 tablespoons grated
 cheese
½ cup sour cream

Cook unpeeled potatoes in boiling salted water for 20 to 40 minutes, depending on size; peel and slice. Butter a baking dish; place in it a layer of potato slices, then egg slices, then potatoes, sprinkling each layer with 3 tablespoons cheese. Pour in sour cream and bake in (350°) oven for about 45 minutes until brown on top. Serves 4 to 6.

Baked Potatoes

Idaho potatoes are best for baking. Scrub potatoes and wipe dry. Rub a little butter or oil into the skins. Bake at 350° for 1 hour or until soft enough to pierce with a toothpick. Slash lengthwise and across. Insert 1 teaspoon butter and a few grains salt.

Variation 1: Cut baked potatoes lengthwise. Scoop out. Mash thoroughly and season with butter or chicken fat, salt and pepper. Return to the half shells. Brush with melted butter or milk. Brown lightly under broiler flame.

Variation 2: Top filled half shells with grated cheese. Return to hot oven for 3 to 5 minutes before serving.

Note: Wrap baked potatoes in aluminum foil to keep hot if serving time is delayed.

Baked Potatoes

Wash the potatoes well, film lightly with ghee, and put into a slow oven (about 325°). Bake for about an hour—longer, if the potatoes are very large—until quite tender.

They may be baked wrapped in aluminum foil.

When ready to serve, simply pass the salt and pepper and a small saucer of warm ghee.

Or try:

Indian Topping
1 pint yogurt
6 sprigs fresh parsley leaves,
   finely chopped

2 scallions, including tender
   green tops, minced fine
1 teaspoon salt
¼ teaspoon cayenne

Beat all the ingredients together until smooth. This is best prepared ahead of time. Let it sit at room temperature while the potatoes bake, then place in a bowl and pass as a topping for the hot baked potatoes. Serves 4.

Baked Potatoes with Cheese CZECHOSLOVAKIA

8 medium baking potatoes
½ cup butter
2 egg yolks
½ cup grated cheese
   salt to taste
¼ teaspoon paprika

½ cup sour cream
2 tablespoons grated
   cheese
1 tablespoon minced
   parsley

Bake potatoes in a 450° oven until done (about 45 minutes). Cut a thin slice off, lengthwise; scoop out the inside and mash. Cream butter and egg yolks. Add the ½ cup cheese, mashed potato, salt, paprika, and sour cream. Mix well, and refill the potato shells. Sprinkle with cheese and parsley, and bake in a 350° oven for 30 minutes. Serves 4 to 8.

Baked Potato Custard   SCANDINAVIA

5 to 6 potatoes   Egg Custard
  salt   *2 eggs*
  white pepper   *about ½ pint milk (1¼ cups)*
  grated nutmeg
  (3 to 4 ounces grated cheese) (¾ to 1 cup)

Peel and wash the potatoes and slice thinly.

Put the slices into a buttered, fireproof dish. Sprinkle with seasonings and the grated cheese (optional).

Beat the eggs and milk together and pour over the potatoes. Bake at 390 to 435° until the potatoes are tender and the egg custard has set, about 35 to 40 minutes. Serves 4.

Potato Balls   AUSTRIA

2 pounds potatoes
½ cup fat
  salt to taste

Peel potatoes and cut into balls. Cook in salted water 5 minutes. Dry. Bake in hot fat in 400° oven until yellow all over (about 20 minutes). Remove; sprinkle with salt. Serves 5 to 6.

Potatoes and Barley   CZECHOSLOVAKIA

⅔ cup barley   *2 pounds potatoes, peeled*
1 cup water or milk   *1 medium onion, chopped*
2 tablespoons shortening   *¼ cup butter*
1 teaspoon salt

Cook barley in water or milk, shortening, and salt, until tender (45 minutes). Boil potatoes in water to cover; drain and mash. Mix barley and potatoes; brown onion in butter and pour it over mixture. Serves 4 to 6.

Potatoes in Brown Sauce AUSTRIA

2 pounds potatoes
3 tablespoons fat
4 tablespoons flour
½ teaspoon onion, chopped
¼ teaspoon parsley, chopped
1 cup water or more

1 to 2 tablespoons vinegar
½ bay leaf, chopped
dash thyme, chopped
salt to taste
3 tablespoons sour cream
4 to 6 pickles, sliced

Boil potatoes; peel and slice. Melt fat, add flour, and brown. Fry onion and parsley in same fat. Add water, vinegar, bay leaf, thyme, salt, and sour cream. Blend well. Bring to a boil. Add potatoes and pickles. Serves 5.

Buttered Potatoes GERMANY

4 large potatoes
4 tablespoons butter
salt

Select not too mealy potatoes. Peel and cut into wedges or thick slices. Melt butter, add potatoes, and cook over low heat. Turn over several times, adding more butter if needed. (Be careful that the potatoes do not fall to pieces in this process.) When nearly done, increase heat and add salt to taste. The finished potatoes should be golden brown on the outside, smooth and creamy on the inside. Serves 4.

Château Potatoes FRANCE

Cut them to the shape of large olives; season them; cook them gently in clarified butter that they may be golden and very soft; and, just before serving, sprinkle them moderately with chopped parsley.

Caraway Potatoes

8 medium potatoes
3 tablespoons butter
  salt and pepper
  dash of paprika

1 teaspoon caraway
½ cup sour cream
  (optional)

Boil the potatoes in their jackets, then peel and slice thickly. Heat the butter. Sprinkle the potatoes with salt, pepper, and, if you wish, a dash of paprika for color and extra flavor. Fry until golden. Sprinkle on the caraway seed, cook a minute more, and serve plain or with heated sour cream for a topping. Serves 8 to 10.

Potato Casserole

4 cups fluffy (not dry) mashed
  potatoes
¼ cup flour

4 tablespoons dark corn
  syrup (optional)

Beat the mashed potatoes with a rotary beater or a whip (if too stiff, add a little milk). Mix in the flour until well blended, then add the syrup (some Finns add the syrup, some do not). Turn the mixture into a heavy buttered casserole, cover tightly, and let cook in a warm oven (turn oven to the very lowest heat possible) for 5 hours. Check it occasionally to be sure that it does not get dry. Add milk if necessary. During this time the potatoes should become soft and sweet, and they will have a flavor similar to sweet potatoes. When they are yellowish in color, add a pinch of salt and stir to make smooth again. Leave uncovered, but dot the top with butter, and continue to bake in a moderate oven (350°) for 15 minutes or until browned on top. Serve hot. Serves 6 to 8.

Potato Chips   SCANDINAVIA

2 to 3 potatoes per portion
oil or coconut butter to fry

Potatoes fried in deep fat may be cut in several different ways and are named according to the shape. They are usually fried twice. The first frying at (345–360°) softens the potatoes but browns them very little. This process may be done in advance. The second frying at a higher temperature (390–400°) rapidly produces golden-brown crisp potatoes. They should be served at once.

Peel and wash the potatoes and cut in one of the ways listed below. Rinse and soak in cold water.

Dry the potatoes thoroughly and put a few at a time into a frying basket and fry in hot fat to soften. Drain.

Fry the potatoes once again in hotter fat, in 2 or 3 batches. Lift out the frying basket when the chips are golden in color, drain quickly and serve in a hot dish, sprinkled with salt.

Creamed Potatoes   ITALY

1½ pounds potatoes   *1 tablespoon butter*
½ teaspoon salt   *¼ cup milk*
¼ teaspoon pepper   *¾ cup heavy cream*
⅛ teaspoon nutmeg

Peel potatoes, quarter and cook in water 15 minutes, or until tender to fork. Drain, place back in pan over low flame and mash potatoes with masher. Add salt, pepper, nutmeg, butter, and milk and stir well 5 minutes.

Heat cream. Pour potatoes in covered vegetable dish, pour warm cream over potatoes, cover dish and let stand 3 or 4 minutes. Serves 4.

Creamed Potatoes and Celery Root   FINLAND

1 *large celery root*   1 *teaspoon salt*
5 *medium potatoes*   2 *teaspoons sugar*
2 *tablespoons butter*   ½ *teaspoon pepper*

Pare, cut up, and cook the celery root in enough salted water to cover. Peel, cut up, and cook the potatoes until tender. Force both vegetables through a potato ricer, or mash until smooth. Stir in the butter, and season with the salt, sugar, and pepper. Serve hot. Serves 6 to 8.

Potato Croquettes   AUSTRIA

2 *pounds potatoes*   ½ *teaspoon salt*
2 *tablespoons butter*   ¾ *cup flour*
2 *eggs*   1 *to 2 eggs, lightly beaten*
1 *teaspoon cheese, grated*   ⅓ *cup bread crumbs*
  dash nutmeg   1 *pound fat*

Boil and peel potatoes; rub through strainer. Cool. Work with butter, eggs, cheese, nutmeg, salt, and flour to a dough. With floured hands, form roll 1 inch wide. Cut into pieces 3 inches long. Dip in eggs and then in bread crumbs. Fry in deep fat until golden brown. Place on absorbent paper to drain. Serves 5 to 6.

Note: If desired, shape dough into small turnips instead of rolls.

Devonshire Fried Potatoes   GERMANY

4 *large potatoes*   2 *large onions*
  salt and pepper   4 *tablespoons butter*

Cook unpeeled potatoes until done; peel while still hot and mash. Add seasoning. Slice onions thinly and fry in butter until golden brown. Mix potatoes and onions together and add more seasoning. Spread 2 inches deep in a buttered baking dish, dot with more butter and bake 15 to 20 minutes in a moderate (350°) oven. Serves 4.

Potato Curry

6 medium potatoes
3 tablespoons peanut oil or
  ghee
1 teaspoon salt
1 teaspoon cumin seed
½ teaspoon mustard seed,
  black or yellow

1 teaspoon turmeric
2 cups water
1 teaspoon ground coriander
1 teaspoon cayenne
½ cup yogurt

Peel and chop the potatoes, and set aside. Heat the peanut oil or ghee. Heat the spices in warm oil, then add the potatoes. Stir well until the potatoes are coated all over, then add the water.

Simmer slowly for ½ hour, and add the coriander and yogurt.

Heat well and serve anytime. This keeps well. It is even better the next day, warmed over.

Napkin Roll of Potato Dough

1 pound potatoes
⅔ cup farina
3 white rolls, diced
1 egg

¼ teaspoon onion, chopped
¼ teaspoon parsley, chopped
½ teaspoon salt
1 teaspoon baking powder

Cook potatoes a day ahead. Grate potatoes; work all ingredients to a dough. Moisten hands and form a roll. Wrap in wet napkin. Cook in salted water 30 minutes. Use as a side dish for sauces or salads.

Serves 4 to 5.

Note: If desired, cut roll in pieces when cold and fry in fat.

Duchesse Potatoes

(Mashed potatoes with egg)
Used for gratin dishes and as the basis of potato croquettes

4 large potatoes
  water
  salt
1 to 2 tablespoonfuls butter or margarine

2 egg yolks or 1 egg
  salt
  white pepper

Boil the freshly peeled potatoes for about 20 to 30 minutes. Drain. Press the potatoes through a ricer or purée press. Beat thoroughly while adding the fat, egg yolks, or egg and seasoning. Bring to boil and continue to beat well. Taste.

When the potato purée is used for a gratin dish, brown it under a radiant grill. The mixture may be piped onto a fireproof dish containing the filling.

The time to brown will be about 10 to 15 minutes (430°).

Potato Dumplings   AUSTRIA

6 white rolls, diced
2 tablespoons butter
½ cup butter or fat
3 eggs

2 pounds potatoes,
  cooked and mashed
⅔ cup flour
  salt to taste

Fry rolls in butter. Cream butter or fat; add eggs and rolls, potatoes, flour, and salt. Mix well. Form dumplings; cook in salted water until they rise to the surface. Continue cooking 5 minutes longer. Serves 6 to 8.

Potatoes and Fenugreek   INDIA

1 pound potatoes
2 tablespoons ghee
½ teaspoon turmeric
1 cup fresh fenugreek, washed
  and chopped

1 teaspoon cayenne
1 teaspoon salt

Peel and chop the potatoes, and set aside. Heat the ghee in a pan, and add the potatoes and turmeric to it. Stir and fry for 3 minutes. Then add the fenugreek, cayenne, and salt.

Mix well, lower the heat, and cook for about 20 minutes covered, until the potatoes are tender. Serves 4.

Potato Fondant

3 ½ cups cooked potatoes, mashed
3 tablespoons butter
1 ½ teaspoons salt
  dash of pepper

¼ teaspoon parsley, chopped
⅔ cup milk, hot
½ cup sweet cream
¾ cup bread crumbs

Mix mashed potatoes, while still hot, with butter, salt, pepper, parsley and hot milk. Beat thoroughly for 3 minutes. Turn into a buttered baking dish. Pour cream over mixture and sprinkle with bread crumbs. Bake in hot (425°) oven until crumbs are well browned. Serves 6.

French Fried Potatoes

2 pounds potatoes
2 teaspoons salt
  water to cover

deep fat for frying
salt for sprinkling

Slice the potatoes very thin. Sprinkle with the salt and cover with water. After half an hour, drain and dry the potatoes thoroughly between towels. Have the deep fat very hot (400°) and fry a few potatoes at a time. Drain on paper and sprinkle with salt. Put the chips into the oven to crisp them for a few minutes. Serve hot or cold.

French fried potatoes are made in much the same way, except that the potatoes are cut into strips (about eight to a potato) and served right after frying in deep hot fat.

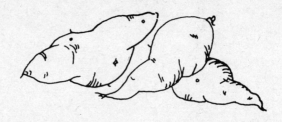

Fried Potatoes with Onion and Cheese
S C A N D I N A V I A

5 to 6 cold, boiled potatoes	salt
1 sliced onion	white pepper
5 to 6 ounces diced cheese (1 cup)	butter or margarine to fry

Cut the potatoes into uniform slices and fry with the onion until lightly browned. Season to taste.

Add the cheese and reheat the mixture. Serves 4.

Grated Potato Casserole
F I N L A N D

2 eggs	2 medium potatoes, grated
1 cup milk	2 tablespoons butter
2 tablespoons flour	parsley
1 teaspoon salt	

Beat the eggs and add the milk, flour, salt, and potatoes. Melt the butter in the bottom of a 1- to 1½-quart baking dish, and spread evenly over the bottom and sides. Pour in the egg-potato mixture and bake in a moderately hot oven (375°) for 45 to 50 minutes or until the potatoes are tender and the casserole is set. Serve hot, garnished with chopped parsley. Serves 4 to 6.

Potatoes in Their Jackets
G E R M A N Y

8 medium potatoes
1 teaspoon caraway seeds
1 teaspoon salt

Brush potatoes clean in cold water. Change water and cook together with caraway seeds and salt for 30 minutes. Test with fork to be sure they are done. Drain off water. Replace pot over low heat and systematically shake it so potatoes will dry. Serves 4.

Julienne Potatoes FRANCE

Cut the potatoes into a long, thin *julienne;* wash them and thoroughly dry them on a piece of linen.

Put them into hot fat; and, at the end of a few minutes, drain them in a frying basket. Just before serving them, plunge them again into smoking fat, that they may be very crisp; drain them on a piece of linen, and salt them moderately.

Potato Knishes JEWISH

1 cup mashed potato
1 egg
   Flour to make a stiff
   dough

salt to taste
1 tablespoon butter or
   vegetable shortening

Combine ingredients thoroughly. Form into 2 mounds. Brush with diluted egg yolk or evaporated milk and bake 20 minutes at 350° or till nicely browned.

Variation 1: Same proportions for larger quantities. Make a depression in center and fill with 1 tablespoon hard-cooked eggs. Or, pot cheese seasoned to taste with salt and white pepper and combined with 1 egg per cupful. Bake.

Variation 2: Add chopped nuts, raisins and sugar, a dash of cinnamon or nutmeg, or grated lemon rind to pot cheese to which egg has been added and combine well. Brush top of filled knish with melted butter, sprinkle with sugar and cinnamon or chopped nuts and bake.

Lyonnaise Potatoes FRANCE

Cut some peeled and boiled potatoes into slices, and toss these in butter in a frying pan. Likewise toss some sliced onions in butter, the quantity of the former measuring one-fourth of that of the potatoes. When the onions are a nice golden brown, add them to the *sautéed* potatoes; season with salt and pepper; *sauté* the two together for a few minutes, that they may mix thoroughly, and serve them in a *timbale* with chopped parsley.

Mashed Potatoes   POLAND

Mash potatoes that have been boiled. For each pound add 1 heaping tablespoon of butter and a few tablespoons of milk or cream. Continue mashing until fluffy. Season with salt, pepper, and a dash of nutmeg.

Variation 1: For a slightly varied taste, omit milk, increase the amount of butter, and brown the butter first with a little minced onion.

Variation 2: Prepare as above. Divide into three equal parts. Color one part with a little chopped spinach, one part with tomato juice, and leave one part white.

Mashed-Potato Casserole   FINLAND

6 medium potatoes, peeled	salt
	butter
2 eggs, beaten	6 tablespoons fine dry bread
1 cup cream or milk	crumbs

Cook, then mash, the potatoes. Whip in the eggs, cream or milk, salt to taste, and 4 tablespoons butter; beat until very fluffy. Turn into a buttered 1-quart casserole and sprinkle with the bread crumbs. Dot with more butter. Bake in a moderately hot oven (375°) for 20 to 25 minutes or until the top is nicely browned. Serve hot. Serves 6.

Potatoes and Squash Moussaka   GREECE

Prepare like Moussaka Potatoes (see page 170) but substitute squash for half the potatoes called for in the recipe. Serves 6 to 8.

Moussaka Potatoes   GREECE

3 *pounds potatoes*
1⅔ *cups oil*
  salt and pepper to taste
½ *cup chopped onion*
1½ *pounds tomatoes, peeled*
  and strained, or 1½ table-
  spoons tomato paste diluted
  with 1 cup water

½ *head garlic*
  (6 to 8 cloves)
½ *cup chopped parsley*
1 *cup grated cheese*
  bread crumbs

Clean and peel the potatoes; cut them into thin round slices. Fry in the oil, then season with salt and pepper. Sauté the onions to a light golden color in the pan in which you fried the potatoes, and add to them the tomatoes (or diluted tomato paste), garlic, parsley, and salt and pepper; cook for about 20 minutes, until you have a thick sauce. Remove from the heat. Add to the sauce ¾ cup of the cheese and 3 tablespoons bread crumbs.

Oil a medium-sized baking pan lightly. Spread a layer of the potatoes in it; cover them with part of the sauce. Top with another layer of potatoes and another layer of sauce. Continue this process until all the potatoes and sauce are used; sprinkle with the remaining cheese and additional bread crumbs; dribble a little oil over the top, and bake in a preheated oven at 375° for about 30 minutes. Serves 6 to 8.

Potato and Mushroom   CZECHOSLOVAKIA
Casserole

1 *medium onion, chopped*
½ *cup butter*
2 *pounds mushrooms,*
  sliced
  salt to taste
¼ *teaspoon caraway seeds*

2 *pounds cooked*
  potatoes, peeled and sliced
1 *cup milk*
2 *eggs, lightly beaten*

Sauté onion in butter, add mushrooms, salt, and caraway seeds. In a greased casserole arrange alternate layers of potatoes and mushrooms. Repeat layering, ending with potatoes. Mix together milk and eggs, and pour over casserole. Bake in a preheated (350°) oven for 20 to 30 minutes, or until eggs are set. Serves 4 to 6.

Potato Kugel   ISRAEL

10 medium potatoes	1 teaspoon salt
1 large onion, chopped	dash of pepper
4 tablespoons fat	5 eggs, separated

Boil and mash the potatoes. Lightly fry the onion in the fat and add to the potatoes with the salt and pepper. Beat the egg yolks well and whip into the potatoes. Beat the egg whites until stiff and fold into the potatoes. Bake in a greased baking dish in a 350° oven until the kugel is golden (about 30 minutes). Serves 6 to 8.

Crisp Fried Potato Noodles   INDIA

1 cup cooked mashed potatoes, unsalted	½ teaspoon turmeric
	½ teaspoon cayenne
¼ cup chick pea flour	Peanut oil or ghee
¾ teaspoon salt	

Place the mashed potatoes, chick pea flour, and seasonings in a mixing bowl. Mix together until thick and smooth. Place half the mixture in a potato ricer.

Heat the peanut oil or ghee in a deep fryer. The fat should not reach more than halfway up. When the fat is hot enough to brown a dribble of the potatoes in 2 minutes, all is ready.

Squeeze the potato mixture gently but firmly through the ricer into the deep fat. You will now see why a deep pot is necessary. The fat will boil up rapidly to surround the noodles—and may keep moving right on up and over and onto the stove before you can stop it. So easy does it. The fat settles quickly, however, and the skinny little noodles fry happily away and brown rapidly. Remove them with a slotted spoon as soon as they are brown, and drain on absorbent paper. They will be quite crisp. Fry the rest the same way.

These are just as good cold as hot. To serve with cocktails do not bother to warm them. Serves 4.

Maître d'Hôtel Potatoes FRANCE

Cook some medium-sized potatoes in salted water; peel them; cut them into round slices while they are still quite hot, and cover them with boiling milk.

Season them with salt and white pepper; completely reduce the milk, and serve them in a *timbale* with chopped parsley.

Potatoes Stuffed with Mushrooms POLISH

6 baked Idaho potatoes

Stuffing:
2 to 3 tablespoons cooked dried
   mushrooms, chopped fine
1 small or ½ medium onion,
   minced
1 tablespoon butter
2 whole eggs, lightly beaten
1 teaspoon each of chopped
   fresh dill and parsley

2 to 3 tablespoons of the
   mushroom cooking liquid

Sauce:
1 cup mushroom sauce or 1
   cup sour cream thickened
   with 1 teaspoon flour
grated Parmesan
bread crumbs and melted
   butter for topping

Bake potatoes until skins are crisp (45 to 60 minutes). Cut each lengthwise in half or cut off a thin top layer to use later as a cover. Scoop out centers and mash. Brown onion lightly in butter, combine with chopped mushrooms, mashed potato, eggs, herbs, mushroom liquid, and seasoning, and refill the shells. Cover with their own tops, arrange in shallow baking dish, and pour mushroom sauce or sour cream over them. Sprinkle with grated Parmesan and melted butter, and dot generously with bread crumbs. Bake in hot oven for 5 to 10 minutes. Serves 6.

Variation: May also be prepared with the addition of 2 tablespoons sour cream to the stuffing. Omit Parmesan and mushroom sauce. Top only with melted butter and bread crumbs. Bake 5 minutes.

O'Brien Potatoes

3 tablespoons margarine
  or butter
4 cups cubed, cooked potatoes
1 onion, chopped
1 large green pepper,
  finely cubed

2 sweet red peppers,
  finely cubed
salt and pepper to taste
2 teaspoons chopped
  parsley

Heat the fat and brown the potato cubes. Add the onion and peppers and fry together, being careful not to break the potatoes. (Or you can fry the peppers and onions separately from the potatoes, and then stir together for a heating through.) Serve hot, seasoned to taste, and sprinkled with parsley. Serves 6 to 8.

Cheese-Potato Omelet

1 pound potatoes
½ cup butter
5 eggs
3 tablespoons milk or water

dash of pepper
½ cup grated Parmesan cheese
1 tablespoon chopped parsley

Pare the potatoes and cut into thin, even slices; wash and drain. Melt half the butter in a large frying pan and spread the potato slices in an even layer in it. Fry gently but do not let brown. Add the remaining butter. Beat the eggs with the milk (or water), add the pepper and cheese; mix well. Pour over the potatoes. Lower the heat and cook slowly, stirring very little, until the eggs are set. Remove from the heat. Turn a platter upside down on the pan and turn the pan over quickly so the whole omelet drops onto the platter. Garnish with parsley. Serve immediately. Serves 2 to 3.

Parsley Potatoes

Boil the potatoes plainly; drain them well, and roll them in melted butter and chopped parsley.

Potato Pancakes (Raw Potatoes)

2½ pounds potatoes
  salt to taste
  milk as needed

1 to 2 eggs
1 cup flour
¾ cup shortening

Peel and grate potatoes, drain (measuring liquid drained off), and sprinkle with salt. Add milk (about the same amount as drained-off liquid) to potatoes, eggs, and flour; mix well. Drop pancake batter by spoonfuls into hot shortening and fry to a golden brown. Serves 4 to 6.

Grated Potato Pancakes

6 medium-sized
  potatoes
1 onion
2 eggs

½ cup flour
1 teaspoon salt
  vegetable shortening or
  oil for deep frying

Pare and grate potatoes into a mixing bowl. Squeeze out liquid. Peel and grate onion into potatoes. Add eggs, flour, and salt and stir to make a smooth batter that will drop heavily from the spoon. Heap the shortening in a heavy frying pan using enough to cover the pancakes amply. Drop the batter from a spoon into the hot shortening, making pancakes 3 inches in diameter. Fry over moderate heat until brown on the underside, turn to brown. Lift out and drain off excess fat on paper towel. Pancakes fried in deep fat should be puffed and crisp. Serves 4 to 6.

Variation 1: Use same mixture in greased shallow baking pan (8″ × 12″ cookie pan), bake 45 minutes at 350° or until nicely browned. Cut into squares and serve hot.

Variation 2: Substitute fine matzo meal for flour and fry as in basic recipe.

Variation 3: Turn either basic recipe or Variation 2 into well-greased small muffin pan and bake 45 minutes at 350°.

Indian Potato Pancakes

1 cup mashed potatoes, unsalted	3 tablespoons rice flour
1 teaspoon salt	1 teaspoon ghee
½ teaspoon turmeric	peanut oil or ghee for
½ teaspoon cayenne	frying

Peel, dice, and boil the potatoes. Mash them. Place the mashed potatoes, salt, turmeric, cayenne, rice flour, and teaspoon ghee in a bowl. Mix together very thoroughly until you have a firm dough. It may be necessary to add a dash or two more of flour. The dough will be too tender to roll, but it must hold together.

In a deep fryer, heat the peanut oil (or ghee).

While the fat is heating, pinch off bits of the dough and roll them into balls in the palms of your hands, then pat them gently into flat cakes about 2 or 2½ inches across. When the fat is hot enough to brown a bread cube in 2 minutes, slip in the pancakes one at a time, and fry gently for 2 or 3 minutes, turning once when brown. They will be a rich gold when done, and slightly crusty, and may or may not puff up a bit. Remove from the fat with a slotted spoon, drain on absorbent paper, and serve while still warm. Serves 4.

Paprika Potatoes

2 pounds potatoes	2 tablespoons flour
paprika sauce	1 cup water, or more
2 tablespoons fat	1 cup sour cream
2 tablespoons onion, chopped	½ teaspoon salt
1 teaspoon paprika	1 tablespoon tomato purée

Boil and peel potatoes; dice, and mix gently with paprika sauce, prepared as follows:

Melt fat. Fry onion until yellow. Stir in paprika and flour, and continue frying slightly. Add water, sour cream, salt, and tomato purée. Bring to a boil. Serves 5.

Scalloped Potatoes

1 large onion, thinly
  sliced or diced
3 tablespoons melted
  shortening (butter,
  preferably)
5 pounds potatoes,
  pared and thinly
  sliced

1 pound American
  cheese (cheddar type)
½ teaspoon salt and
  ⅛ teaspoon white
  pepper
milk as required

Use a large casserole of earthenware or glass ovenware with a tight cover. Melt the shortening in the baking dish, scatter onion bits over the bottom then arrange alternate layers of sliced potato and sliced cheese dusted with salt and pepper combination. The casserole may be filled to the top and pressed down before adding enough milk to come ¾ of the way up the side. Arrange strips of cheese in a sunburst over the top and bake, covered, 45 minutes at 375°. Uncover and bake 15 minutes longer or till nicely browned on top. When reheating cover the dish till hot then remove cover 5 minutes before serving. Serves 8 to 10.

Potato Soufflé

3 pounds potatoes
3 tablespoons butter
1 cup warm milk
4 eggs, separated

1 cup grated
  kefalotiri cheese
salt and pepper to taste

Boil the potatoes in their skins until tender. While they are still hot, remove skins, and purée potatoes by passing through a sieve or food mill. Melt the butter in a pot. Add the puréed potatoes and mix well. Add the milk and continue to stir. Beat the egg yolks until thick and add to the potatoes. Remove from the heat immediately. Add the cheese. Beat the whites until stiff. Cool the potatoes slightly, then fold the whites into them. Pour into a buttered mold and bake immediately in a preheated 350° oven for 20 to 25 minutes. Serves 6 to 8.

Note: This can be made in individual ramekins.

Small Potatoes in Dill Sauce   BULGARIA

1½ pounds young potatoes
  salt to taste
4 to 5 tablespoons fat
2 tablespoons flour
½ cup finely chopped dill

1 egg
¼ cup sour milk or yogurt
1 tablespoon vinegar or lemon
  juice

Clean and peel potatoes and boil until soft in lightly salted water. Pour off water and reserve it. Heat fat; add flour and brown.

Potato and Tomato Casserole   GERMANY

2 pounds potatoes, cooked
1 pound tomatoes, sliced
3 tablespoons cheese, grated
  salt and pepper

marjoram
1 onion, sliced and slightly fried
  butter, to dot

Peel and slice potatoes. In a buttered baking dish, arrange alternating layers of potatoes, tomatoes, and grated cheese. Sprinkle with salt, pepper, and marjoram. Top with cheese and fried onion rings, dot with butter. Bake in moderate (350°) oven for 30 minutes. Serves 4.

Potato Puffs   POLAND

10 baby Idaho potatoes,
  cooked in jackets
1 heaping tablespoon butter
2 tablespoons sour cream
3 eggs, separated

2 to 3 tablespoons sugar (to taste)
  dash of salt
  deep fat for frying
  sugar and sour cream
  for garnish

Allow potatoes to cool. Then peel and mash. Add butter, sour cream, egg yolks, and seasoning. Mix thoroughly; then fold in stiffly-beaten egg whites. Spoon into hot fat. Puffs will rise. They are done when nicely brown on all sides. Drain on paper towel. Serve with sugar and sour cream. Serves 6 to 7.

Potato-Cheese Puffs

1½ cups mashed potatoes
   (hot or cold)
3 tablespoons hot milk
½ cup grated cheese
   (or dry pot cheese)
2 eggs, separated
1 teaspoon salt

¼ teaspoon paprika
1 tablespoon finely chopped
   green pepper (or parsley)
1 small grated onion (or
   1 tablespoon juice)
2 tablespoons melted butter

Beat mashed potatoes with milk. Add egg yolks to cheese and beat till fluffy. Combine other ingredients. Fold in stiffly beaten egg whites and melted butter. Drop in small mounds on a well-greased cookie sheet and bake 20 minutes at 350° or till nicely browned. Excellent with a vegetable dinner. Serves 6.

Potato Soufflé with Cheese

2 pounds potatoes
6 tablespoons butter
2 tablespoons bread crumbs
½ pound sheep's cheese

¼ pound smoked bacon
dill
salt and pepper to taste

Boil potatoes in skins in salted water. Peel and slice. Brush flameproof dish with some of the butter; sprinkle with a few of the bread crumbs. Stir sheep's cheese with remaining butter in a small pan over low heat until foamy. Dice bacon, fry until brown and crisp, and mix with melted fat, remaining bread crumbs, chopped dill, salt, pepper, and potato slices. Place in prepared dish and cook over moderate heat for 15 to 20 minutes. Turn out of dish like a cake and cut. Serve hot. Serves 4 to 6.

Sour Potatoes

2½ pounds potatoes,
   peeled and sliced
   salted water to cover
½ teaspoon caraway
   seeds
¼ cup flour
¼ cup shortening

1 cup sour cream
1 tablespoon vinegar
½ teaspoon sugar
1 tablespoon chopped
   dill or chives
1 or 2 egg yolks

Boil potatoes in salted water with caraway seeds. Drain, and reserve liquid. Brown flour in shortening, stirring constantly, and stir in 1 to 1½ cups of potato water. Simmer for 10 to 15 minutes. Add the remaining ingredients and potatoes. Serves 6.

Potatoes Smothered in Sour Cream

2 pounds potatoes,
  peeled and sliced
2 medium onions,
  chopped
1 tablespoon butter

½ cup sour cream
1 heaping tablespoon
  chopped dill
salt and pepper to taste

Parboil potatoes in salted water 5 minutes. Drain. Brown onions lightly in butter and add to potatoes, with sour cream, dill, and seasoning. Cover tightly and simmer until done, about 30 minutes. Serves 6.

Note: These potatoes are also excellent if done with mushrooms. Slice 10 to 12 medium mushrooms and cook with 1 minced onion in butter until onion is lightly brown and mushrooms transparent. Add to potatoes, and proceed as directed above, using only 1 onion instead of 2. Omit the dill.

Stuffed Potatoes

4 large potatoes
  scant cup cottage
  or cream cheese,
  mixed with 2
  tablespoons grated
  cheese

2 eggs
2 tablespoons butter
¼ cup sour cream
  salt, pepper to taste

Cook unpeeled potatoes in boiling salted water for about 10 to 20 minutes, until parboiled, then peel. Carefully scrape out center, taking care that potatoes remain whole. Place in hollow a filling made of cottage cheese mixed with grated cheese and the eggs.

Melt butter in an ovenproof dish; place stuffed potatoes in it; season; pour in sour cream and bake in 350° oven for about 20 minutes. If desired, add sour cream after, instead of before, baking. In that case place flakes of butter on stuffed potatoes before baking. Serves 4.

Note: Use scraped-out potato for another dish.

Potato Straws INDIA

2 *large potatoes*   ½ *teaspoon salt*
 peanut oil   ¼ *teaspoon cayenne*

Peel, wash, and shred the potatoes through the coarse part of a grater. Drain off excess water. It is even better to squeeze them gently in the hands. Potatoes hold an amazing amount of water. Fry them quickly in deep hot peanut oil for 3 to 5 minutes when they should be golden brown. Remove with a slotted spoon, and drain on absorbent paper. Shake with salt and cayenne, and serve while hot if possible. They are good cold, properly drained. This makes 2 cups. Serves 4.

Potato Surprise ITALY

4 *medium potatoes*   ⅛ *teaspoon nutmeg*
¼ *cup butter*   1 *egg*
2 *tablespoons flour*   1 *egg yolk*
2 *cups milk*   1 *cup Swiss type cheese,*
½ *teaspoon salt*   *diced very fine*
¼ *teaspoon white pepper*   2 *tablespoons melted butter*

Parboil potatoes 10 minutes, drain, peel and cut into halves. Scoop out the potato halves and reserve pulp. Melt butter in frying pan, blend in flour, cook 2 minutes and add milk. Mix well, add salt, pepper, and nutmeg and cook 5 minutes. Remove from fire and let cool.

When cool, add whole egg and egg yolk and diced cheese and mix very well. Fill the potato half shells with this mixture and cover with potato pulp which was scooped out and reserved. Place stuffed potatoes in greased baking dish, sprinkle with melted butter and bake in moderate oven (375°) 25 minutes. Serve immediately. Serves 4.

Swedish Potatoes

6 to 7 potatoes
1 chopped onion
2 tablespoonfuls butter or margarine
  about ¾ pint thin cream or milk (1 ¾ cups)

salt
white pepper
chopped parsley

Peel and rinse the potatoes and dice uniformly. Brown the potatoes and onion slowly in the fat. Season. Add the liquid gradually and simmer until the potatoes are tender, about 15 to 20 minutes. Taste and add chopped parsley. Serves 4.

Swiss Potatoes

3 pounds potatoes,
  cooked
¾ pound Emmentaler
  cheese, sliced

2 cups sour cream
¼ cup butter

Peel and slice potatoes. Place one layer in buttered ovenproof dish. Add layer of small cheese slices. Alternate layers. Top with potatoes. Pour sour cream over. Dot with butter. Bake in 350° oven 30 to 40 minutes. Use as a side dish for salads. Serves 6 to 7.

Baked Sweet Potatoes
(Yellow or Red)

Select well-rounded sweet potatoes, allowing 1 per serving. Wash thoroughly and dry. Bake at 375° till tender enough to pierce with a toothpick. With the point of a paring knife slit each potato lengthwise then across. Press the pulp till it shows between the cuts. Insert ¼ teaspoon of butter or other shortening. Slip under the broiler flame to brown.

Sweet Potatoes, Baked Over

6 sweet potatoes, cooked
  salt and pepper
6 tablespoons brown sugar

3 tablespoons butter
3 tablespoons bread crumbs

Slice cooked sweet potatoes ½ inch thick. Place in layers in a buttered baking dish, sprinkling each layer with salt, pepper, brown sugar, and butter. Cover the top layer with buttered bread crumbs and bake in hot (450°) oven until well browned, about 20 minutes. Serves 6.

Candied Sweet Potatoes

3 pounds sweet potatoes
1 cup orange juice
1 teaspoon salt
  dash of ginger or
  cinnamon

1 cup brown sugar
½ cup margarine

Boil the sweet potatoes in their jackets. Skin and slice thickly and arrange the slices attractively in a greased baking dish. Pour the orange juice over. Sprinkle with the salt, ginger, and sugar and dot with margarine. Bake in a 375° oven until the sweet potatoes are candied (about 45 minutes). Serves 8 to 10.

Sweet Potato and Apple Casserole

Arrange alternate layers of parboiled and sliced sweet potatoes and ¼-inch slices of cored tart apples in a well-greased casserole. Pour in maple or corn syrup diluted with hot water to come half way up the side of casserole. Top with a layer of crumbs or cornflakes. Dot with butter or other fat and bake 40 minutes at 350° or till nicely browned.

Sweet Potatoes with Chestnuts   JEWISH

2 pounds sweet potatoes,
  pared
1 pound chestnuts
½ cup brown sugar

¼ cup water
½ cup bread crumbs
2 tablespoons butter or
  substitute

Slice sweet potatoes in 1-inch thick rounds. Boil 5 minutes in enough water to cover, adding ¼ teaspoon salt and covering the pot while boiling. Remove the shells from chestnuts and parboil at least 10 minutes. Drain and remove brown skins. Drain water from sweet potatoes, saving ¼ cup to mix with brown sugar and shortening. Arrange layers of sweet potato rounds and chestnuts in a baking dish or casserole, add the sugar mixture, top with crumbs and bake 30 to 40 minutes at 350° till brown. Serves 6.

Yam is the name for the Southern sweet potato which is less dry and much sweeter than the lighter colored ones. Both varieties can be used in these recipes.

Sweet Potatoes, Southern Style   GERMANY

6 medium sweet potatoes
2 tablespoons butter
½ cup sweet cream

salt
¼ cup sherry

Bake whole sweet potatoes in oven until done, 30 to 40 minutes. Cut lengthwise and scoop out insides. Mash this and mix with butter, cream, salt, and sherry. Stuff back in shells and bake for 5 minutes in hot (450°) oven. Serves 6.

Sweet Potato Pudding   ISRAEL

1 pound cooked sweet
  potatoes
1 pound firm apples,
  pared and cored
1 pound parboiled winter
  squash (or pumpkin)

salt to taste
4 tablespoons fat
½ cup honey or
  orange marmalade
½ cup water
½ cup white wine

Slice the potatoes, apples, and squash thickly and place in alternate layers in a casserole. Mix the remaining ingredients and pour over. Cover and bake in a 350° oven until the apples are done and the sweet potatoes glazed (about 30 minutes). Serves 4 to 6.

Yam Puffs

4 medium-sized cooked yams   Dash of pepper
1 egg, well beaten   Dry bread crumbs
½ teaspoon salt

Peel the potatoes and put through a ricer or mash. Combine ingredients. Cool the mixture. Drop by teaspoonfuls into bread crumbs. Toss with a fork until completely covered. Then drop into deep hot fat. Fry until browned.

Baked Pumpkin

Select medium-sized pumpkin. Cut into 2-inch wedges, melon fashion. Remove seeds and stringy part. Sprinkle each piece with a little brown sugar, add a dash of nutmeg. Bake 45 minutes at 350°. Bake the seeds, too. Just sprinkle a little salt on them and bake till nicely browned. The Balkan peoples eat baked pumpkin seeds much like roasted chestnuts.

Mashed Pumpkin

Pare and cube pumpkin. Boil in salted water to cover till tender. Mash and season to taste with salt, nutmeg and butter.
Variation: Place mashed and seasoned pumpkin in a shallow baking dish and brown under broiler flame before serving. Or, dot with butter and bake in the oven till lightly browned on top.

Pumpkin, Hunter Style

½ cup olive oil   ½ teaspoon salt
2 cloves garlic   ½ teaspoon pepper
1 pound pumpkin, sliced thin   1 teaspoon rosemary
    and cut into squares

Place olive oil in pan with garlic. Brown garlic and remove. Add pumpkin, salt, pepper, and rosemary and cook gently 20 minutes, stirring frequently. Serves 4.

Pumpkin Pudding

1 medium can cooked pumpkin	1½ tablespoons flour
1 tablespoon butter	1 cup milk
1 teaspoon salt	3 egg yolks
½ teaspoon pepper	1 tablespoon grated
¼ cup butter	Parmesan cheese

Place pumpkin and butter in saucepan and cook gently until pumpkin is dry. Cool and add salt and pepper. Melt ¼ cup butter, blend in flour, cook 1 minute, add milk, stirring thoroughly, and cook until thick. Add sauce to pumpkin and mix well. Add egg yolks, one at a time, mixing well after each addition. Add cheese. Place mixture in greased mold. Place mold over pan of boiling water and cook 45 minutes or until pudding is firm. Turn over onto serving dish. Serves 4 or 5.

Smothered Pumpkin

2 pounds pumpkin	1 tablespoon chopped herbs—
1 tablespoon butter	fresh dill, parsley, chives,
½ teaspoon sugar	tarragon
salt and pepper	1 teaspoon flour

Dice the parboiled pumpkin and simmer with butter and other ingredients, tightly covered, until tender. Use no water. Serves 6.

Variation: Prepare as above, but simmer in 2 cups of milk blended with 1 tablespoon flour, omitting herbs. When done, blend in 2 egg yolks, taking care not to let eggs curdle.

Sour Pumpkin

2 pounds pumpkin	1 cup dill pickle liquid
manié made with 1 table-	1 cup sour cream
spoon butter, 1 tablespoon	1 tablespoon chopped fresh dill
flour	and parsley

Dice parboiled pumpkin, drain, and simmer in a sauce made with the butter *manié*, pickle liquid, sour cream, herbs, and seasoning. Cook until tender, about 30 minutes. Serves 6.

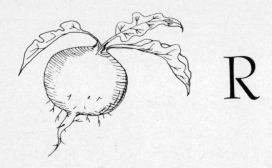

R

Radishes in Pepper Sauce

large radishes
2 tablespoons butter
2 tablespoons flour
1 cup cream

¼ teaspoon pepper
2 teaspoons sugar
½ teaspoon salt
chopped parsley

Choose radishes that are too large to serve as a relish. Clean them well and place in a saucepan in enough water to cover, adding about ½ to 1 teaspoon salt to the water, and cook until tender. Drain (but reserve the liquid), and chop them, then put aside. You should have 2 cups. In another pan, melt the butter, and to it add the flour, mixing until smooth. Slowly add the hot liquid from the radishes, stirring constantly to keep the mixture smooth, then blend in the cream. Add the radishes, pepper, sugar, and ½ teaspoon salt. Just before serving, heat almost to boiling and garnish with the parsley. Serves 4.

Stewed Radishes

4 to 5 bunches radishes
1 quart salted water

1 bunch parsley
2 tablespoons butter

Slice radishes very thin, and boil in salted water for 10 minutes. Drain. Chop parsley and fry in heated butter with radishes. Serve hot. Serves 4 to 6.

Rutabaga Casserole FINLAND

2 medium rutabagas,
  peeled and diced
  (about 6 cups)
¼ cup fine dry
  bread crumbs

¼ cup cream
½ teaspoon nutmeg
1 teaspoon salt
2 eggs, beaten
3 tablespoons butter

Cook the rutabagas until soft (about 20 minutes) in salted water to cover. Drain and mash. Soak the bread crumbs in the cream and stir in the nutmeg, salt, and beaten eggs. Combine with the mashed rutabagas. Turn into a buttered 2½-quart casserole, dot the top with butter, and bake in a moderate oven (350°) for 1 hour or until lightly browned on top. Serves 6 to 8.

Browned Rutabaga Cubes FINLAND

¼ cup butter
4 cups raw rutabaga
1 teaspoon salt

2 tablespoons dark
  brown sugar

Melt the butter in a frying pan. Add the rutabaga cubes and cover. Cook over low heat, stirring frequently until all sides are browned. Add salt and sugar, stirring well so they are evenly distributed. Continue to cook over low heat (covered) until the rutabaga is fork-tender (about 20 minutes). Serve hot. Makes 4 to 6 servings.

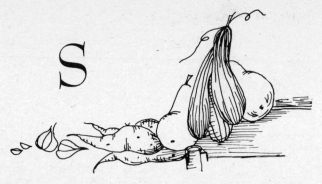

Boiled Salsify

> 8 ounces salsify for each portion water
>   plain flour
> 2 teaspoonfuls salt to each quart (5 cups) of water

Brush and peel or scrape the salsify. Put them immediately into water containing flour (2 ounces [½ cup] flour to 1 quart [5 cups] of water). Rinse the salsify and put into boiling salted water. Boil until tender, about 15 to 20 minutes for early salsify, 40 to 60 minutes for old salsify.

Drain the salsify.

Serve them with (creamed) butter or Hollandaise sauce or on a vegetable platter.

Fried Salsify or Oyster Plant

After having thoroughly drained it, cut it into three and one-half lengths, and put these on a dish.

Season with salt and pepper; add lemon juice, a few drops of oil, some chopped parsley, and leave to *marinate* for from 25 to 30 minutes, taking care to toss the salsify from time to time. This done, drain the lengths of salsify, dip them in some thin batter; plunge them in very hot fat, and drain them when the batter is quite dry. Serve them on a napkin with fried parsley

Note: It is not absolutely necessary to *marinate* salsify; the question is one of taste.

Sauté of Salsify or Oyster Plant   FRANCE

Cut it into 2-inch lengths; dry them very well, and toss these in butter in an omelet pan, until they are of a nice golden brown. Season, and serve in a *timbale* with fried parsley.

Sauerkraut   RUMANIA

2 pounds sauerkraut
7 tablespoons fat
salt to taste

Place sauerkraut in hot fat in a pan as wide as possible, turn with 2 forks while frying for 10 minutes (or until it becomes transparent). Heap up loosely in a dish, season with salt, and serve. Serves 6 to 8.

Hot Sweet Sauerkraut   ISRAEL

1 1-pound, 13-ounce can   1 onion, chopped
  sauerkraut   4 tablespoons brown sugar
6 tomatoes, cut up   raisins, if desired
2 cups tomato soup

Put all the ingredients into a heavy pot on very low heat. Simmer for about 6 hours, or overnight. Serve hot. Serves 6 to 8.

Note: This dish is good, but not as remarkable, if cooked for only an hour.

Sauerkraut   ISRAEL

1 large head of cabbage   2 tablespoons coarse salt
  (about 5 pounds)   water as needed
1 teaspoon caraway seed (optional)

Cut the cabbage fine. Pack into jars, with a sprinkling of salt and caraway seed between each layer. Pack the cabbage down as tightly as possible. Add water to overflowing. Close the jar with a glass top and screw cap on loosely. Add water each day if needed to keep jar full. The kraut will be ready in about a week's time if kept at room temperature.

Plain Sauerkraut A U S T R I A

2 pounds sauerkraut
½ cup water, or more
½ cup fat

1 tablespoon onion, chopped
1 teaspoon salt

Cook sauerkraut in water until soft. Melt fat. Brown onion slightly. Combine with sauerkraut and salt. Use as a side dish for potato dumplings or purée of peas. Serves 4 to 6.

Note: If sauerkraut is too sour, wash in cold water before using.

Sauerkraut with Rice B U L G A R I A

1 pound sauerkraut
⅓ cup oil or fat plus 2
  tablespoons fat for dish
  sauerkraut juice, to taste
  (optional)
¼ cup rice
¾ cup boiling salted water

3 tablespoons grated cheese
  (Kaskaval or sirene, latter
  crumbled)
1 tablespoon chopped parsley
  pepper to taste
¾ cup milk
3 eggs

Fry sauerkraut in oil or fat for about 10 minutes. If desired, pour in a little sauerkraut juice so that it is spicier. Meanwhile boil rice in salted water for 20 minutes. Drain. Sprinkle with cheese and chopped parsley; add pepper.

In a well-greased dish place half of sauerkraut, then rice, then remaining sauerkraut. Beat milk and eggs and pour over sauerkraut. Place in 350° oven and bake for about 30 minutes. Serves 5 to 6.

Sauerkraut, Viennese Style A U S T R I A

2 pounds sauerkraut
2 tablespoons fat
3 tablespoons flour
½ teaspoon onion, chopped

1 large potato, grated
  water as needed
¼ teaspoon salt

Cover sauerkraut with cold water. Cook 1 hour, or until soft. Melt fat; add flour and onion, and brown. Combine with sauerkraut stock, potato, and sauerkraut. Bring to a boil; add water and salt. Cook gently 5 minutes (¼ teaspoon caraway seeds may be added). Serves 5.

Note: Sauerkraut is even better reheated the next day.

Sauerkraut with Wine   AUSTRIA

⅓ cup onion, chopped   *¼ teaspoon salt (or more)*
½ cup butter or fat   *dash pepper*
2 pounds sauerkraut   *¼ cup sugar*
1¼ cups white wine

Fry onion in butter. Add sauerkraut, wine, salt, pepper, and sugar. Simmer 1 hour. Serves 6.

Glazed Shallots   POLAND

1 pound shallots (or very   *bouillon to cover (about 1*
small white onions)   *cup)*
2 tablespoons butter   *salt and pepper to taste*
2 level tablespoons sugar

Blanch onions, and when cool enough to handle, peel and brown lightly in butter. In a shallow casserole melt the sugar and allow to brown. Add onions, bouillon, salt, and pepper, and more sugar if necessary—for a sweet-salty taste. Simmer, tightly covered, until onions are tender, 25 to 30 minutes. There should be almost no liquid left. If too much liquid remains, remove cover and allow to simmer, open, until sauce has been reduced to consistency of honey. Serves 4.

Sorrel   FRANCE

Having shredded the sorrel and washed it in several waters, set it to cook gently in a little water. This done, thoroughly drain it on a sieve and mix it with a pale *roux*, consisting of 2 ounces of butter and 1 ounce of flour. Add 1¼ pints of consommé, salt, and a pinch of sugar to it, and *braise* it in the oven for 2 hours.

Then rub it through a fine sieve; thicken it with the yolks of 6 eggs or 3 whole eggs beaten to a stiff froth and strained. Heat, and finish with ⅙ pint of cream and 5 ounces of butter.

Sorrel

Prepare like Spinach with Sweet Cream.* Instead of sweet cream use 1 cup sour cream and a dash of sugar. When done, beat in 2 or 3 egg yolks and let stand for a minute or two, covered, after removing from fire. Garnish with slices of hard-cooked egg if desired.*See page 195.

Spinach AUSTRIA

3 pounds spinach	½ teaspoon parsley, chopped
½ cup salted water	½ teaspoon onion, chopped
White Sauce	4 tablespoons flour
3 tablespoons butter	spinach stock (or milk) as needed

Clean and wash spinach. Cook in water 10 to 15 minutes. Strain and save stock; rinse with cold water. Mash through strainer or chop. Prepare white sauce. Add spinach and cook 2 to 3 minutes. Use as a side dish for potatoes, croutons, dumplings, eggs any style. Serves 6.

Note: A little garlic juice or pepper may be added to white sauce.

Spinach FRANCE

Spinach should only be prepared at the last moment, if possible.

After having parboiled it in plenty of boiling salted water, cool it, press out all the water, and, according to circumstances, either chop it up or rub it through a sieve.

If it has to be served with the leaves left whole, merely drain it through a sieve, without either pressing or cooling it.

Baked Spinach and White Sauce JEWISH

4 tablespoons flour	3 eggs
4 tablespoons butter	3 cups chopped raw spinach
1½ cups milk	Salt and pepper to taste
¼ cup light cream	

Make a white sauce of flour, melted butter, milk, and cream. Beat eggs lightly and stir into sauce. Add spinach and seasoning. Turn into a buttered mold. Set mold in a pan of hot water and bake 45 minutes to 1 hour at 375°. Unmold and serve hot. Serves 3 to 4.

Spinach Au Gratin   G R E E C E

3 pounds spinach
7 tablespoons butter
¼ to ½ pound kefalotiri cheese,
  grated
  toasted bread crumbs
3 eggs either hard-cooked or
  raw (optional)

Béchamel Sauce
1 can evaporated milk
1 can water
¼ cup butter
½ cup flour
1 egg, beaten
  salt and pepper to taste

Clean and wash the spinach; cut each leaf into 3 or 4 pieces, and drop into rapidly boiling water. Let the spinach boil for 3 or 4 minutes, then strain it; press out all excess fluid and return it to the pot. Melt 5 tablespoons of the butter, pour it over the spinach.

To prepare the sauce, pour the evaporated milk and water (measured in the milk can) into a pot; scald and keep hot. Melt the ¼ cup butter in another pot. Blend in the flour. Add the hot milk, stirring constantly until the mixture is smooth and thick. Season with the salt and pepper. Cool slightly, then sitr in the beaten egg, blending it in well.

Spread a thin layer of the béchamel in a buttered pan; sprinkle with a little cheese. Spread in the spinach; sprinkle with more cheese. Spread the rest of the béchamel over all; sprinkle with the remaining cheese and then with the bread crumbs. Melt the remaining 2 tablespoons butter and drizzle over the casserole. Bake in a preheated 400° oven for about 20 minutes.

Note: You may add the hard-cooked eggs to this, if you like. Slice them and place them on the spinach before adding the final layer of sauce. Or beat the uncooked eggs and mix them with the spinach before you layer that into the casserole.

Boiled Spinach

> 6 to 8 ounces fresh spinach for each portion
>   or 3 to 4 ounces deep-frozen, whole spinach (½ cup)
>   water
> 2 teaspoonfuls salt to each quart (5 cups) of water
>   butter or margarine (optional)

Clean the fresh spinach and rinse it thoroughly.

Put it into boiling salted water and cook until tender, about 5 minutes. Drain the spinach.

Pour the liquid away. The spinach may be fried in butter. Taste for seasoning.

Thaw deep-frozen spinach and reheat it directly in the butter over gentle heat.

Spinachburgers

½ pound spinach
3 eggs
2 tablespoons flour

8 to 10 slices of dry white
  bread
fat for frying

Clean and wash spinach leaves and chop fine. Beat eggs with flour and mix in chopped spinach. Dip each slice of bread into this mixture and fry immediately in very hot fat until golden. Place slices on a dish around boiled carrots or lightly cooked whole, small tomatoes. Serves 4 to 6.

Spinach Cheese Dish

2 pounds spinach
1 teaspoon salt
6 tablespoons cooking oil
6 eggs, lightly beaten

½ pound salt goat cheese,
  finely grated
½ teaspoon black pepper

Chop the spinach and mix with the salt. Allow to drip for 5 minutes. Pour on the oil and spread on a shallow baking pan. Add the eggs and the pepper to the finely grated cheese. Make six hollows in the spinach and put the cheese mixture in each. Bake in a 400° oven for 30 minutes. Serves 6.

Creamed Spinach   SCANDINAVIA

> 1 ½ *pounds fresh spinach*
>   *or 1 large packet deep-frozen spinach (9 ounces)*
>   *water*
> 2 *teaspoonfuls salt to each quart (5 cups) of water*
> *Sauce*
> 1 ½ *tablespoonfuls butter or margarine*
> 2 *tablespoonfuls plain flour*
>   *about ½ pint milk (about 1 ¼ cups)*
>   *salt*
>   *white pepper*
>   *grated nutmeg (optional)*

Clean and rinse the fresh spinach. Put it into boiling salted water and cook it until tender, about 5 minutes. Drain the spinach and pour the liquid away. Leave the spinach whole or chop the cooked leaves.

Fry the fat and flour. Add the liquid and cook the sauce for 3 to 5 minutes. Add the cooked spinach and reheat it. Deep-frozen spinach is thawed in the sauce and reheated. Taste for seasoning. Serves 4.

Spinach with Sweet Cream   POLAND

3 pounds spinach, cleaned and
  parboiled in salted water for
  5 minutes

White Sauce
1 *tablespoon butter*
1 *tablespoon flour*
½ *cup sweet cream (milk if*
  preferred)
  salt and pepper to taste
  dash of sugar

Drain parboiled spinach and rise under cold water to restore color. Chop fine and press through a sieve. Melt butter, blend in flour, add cream, and stir until smooth. Season, add spinach, and simmer tightly covered for 15 to 20 minutes. Serves 6.

Note: Serve garnished with slices of hard-cooked egg if desired.

Spinach Croquettes

2 rolls or 2 slices bread
1 tablespoon butter
2 cups chopped cooked spinach
2 cups bread crumbs
2 eggs, lightly beaten

1 tablespoon creamed or
  melted butter
salt and pepper to taste
bread crumbs for rolling
butter for frying

Cube the rolls or bread and make croutons by frying cubes in 1 tablespoon butter. Combine with the spinach, the bread crumbs, eggs, creamed butter, and seasoning. Shape into oval croquettes, roll in bread crumbs, and fry in butter to a golden brown. Serves 6.

Spinach Curry

½ pound fresh spinach
1 cup lightly salted water
3 tablespoons ghee
1 cup yogurt
3 cups water
2 tablespoons chick pea flour
1 teaspoon fenugreek seed (essential for the best)

½ teaspoon mustard seed
½ teaspoon turmeric
½ teaspoon cayenne
3 cloves
1 1-inch piece cinnamon stick
  (optional)
    tomatoes (optional)

Wash and chop the spinach coarsely. Boil the salted water, and add the chopped spinach.

Cook briskly for 5 or even 10 minutes, until the spinach is quite limp. Set aside, but do not drain; let sit in its water, and forget it. Mix the yogurt, water, and chick pea flour. Heat the ghee. Add the spices to it.

Stir until all sputters satisfactorily, then add the yogurt liquids. Stir until boiling. Lower the heat, and add spinach, water, and all.

Simmer for 20 minutes. Use bits of tomato. Great for color accent. And taste. Serves 4.

Spinach Dumplings

1 pound spinach
¾ cup flour
¼ cup butter
½ to 1 cup hot milk
5 rolls (or corresponding
  amount of white bread)
2 tablespoons chopped parsley

salt and pepper to taste
1 quart meat or vegetable
  bouillon
grated cheese or bread
  crumbs browned in ¼ cup
  butter

Chop spinach very fine. Brown flour in half the butter. Pour milk over rolls or bread; squeeze out and fry in remaining butter with parsley. Season. Mix all these prepared ingredients together. Shape into dumplings with a spoon and place in boiling bouillon. Slowly simmer until they rise to surface and then for 5 minutes longer. Sprinkle with grated cheese or bread crumbs Serves 4 to 6.

Florentine Eggs   AUSTRIA

2 pounds spinach	½ teaspoon salt
½ cup butter	1 teaspoon lemon juice
salt	dash cayenne pepper
10 eggs, poached	1 teaspoon grated Parmesan
Béchamel Sauce	cheese
2 tablespoons butter	1 tablespoon butter, melted
3 tablespoons flour	1 tablespoon grated cheese
1½ cups milk	1 teaspoon bread crumbs
1 teaspoon Worcestershire	
sauce	

Wash spinach; cook in hot butter with salt 10 minutes, shaking pan frequently. Grease ovenproof dish; sprinkle with bread crumbs. Place spinach in dish. Top with eggs. Prepare béchamel sauce. Pour over eggs. Pour melted butter over. Sprinkle with cheese and bread crumbs. Bake in 400° oven 5 minutes to give it yellow crust. Serves 7.

Spinach with Garlic   POLAND

Prepare and chop spinach. Instead of white sauce, simmer in a brown sauce made as follows:

1 tablespoon butter	1 clove garlic, mashed
1 tablespoon flour	salt and pepper to taste
½ cup strong bouillon	

Brown the butter. Mix in the flour smoothly. Add bouillon and stir over low heat until thickened. Then add garlic and seasoning. Combine chopped spinach with the brown sauce and simmer, tightly covered, for 15 to 20 minutes. Serves 6.

Pancake Roll with Spinach   SCANDINAVIA

2 to 3 eggs
½ pint water (1¼ cups)
6 ounces plain flour (1½ cups)
1 teaspoonful baking powder
1 teaspoonful salt
½ pint milk (1¼ cups)

Filling
1 large (9 ounce) packet deep-frozen spinach
3 tablespoonfuls butter or margarine
salt
white pepper

Beat the eggs. Add the water, flour, baking powder and salt. Whisk to a smooth batter. Add the milk.

Pour the batter into a greased 8-by 12-inch baking tin. Bake in the oven (480°) until the batter is set and browned, about 20 minutes.

Fry the thawed, drained spinach in the fat. Season with salt and pepper. Spread the spinach over the cooked batter pudding and roll it up like a Swiss roll. Serves 4.

Spinach Pancakes   CZECHOSLOVAKIA

1 pound spinach, cleaned
¼ cup butter
2 eggs, separated

salt to taste
⅓ cup flour

Steam spinach 3 to 5 minutes. Drain and chop very fine. Cream butter with egg yolks, add salt, spinach, and flour. Mix well. Fold in stiffly beaten egg whites. Bake on a greased griddle. Make pancakes small (about 3 inches in diameter). Serves 4 to 6.

Spinach Parmesan   ITALY

1 pound spinach, washed
  and chopped, or 1 package
  frozen chopped spinach
2 tablespoons butter
¼ teaspoon salt

⅛ teaspoon nutmeg
2 eggs, lightly beaten
3 tablespoons grated
  Parmesan cheese

Cook spinach in 1 cup water 5 minutes, drain, and chop fine. Place in saucepan with butter, salt, and nutmeg and cook 4 minutes, stirring well. Shut off flame and keep pan on hot stove plate. Add eggs, mix well, add Parmesan cheese and continue stirring 2 or 3 minutes. Serve immediately. Serves 4.

Spinach and Potatoes Au Gratin BULGARIA

1 pound spinach leaves	1½ pounds potatoes
½ cup grated white cheese	6 to 7 tablespoons oil
(kefalotyrie)	1 cup yogurt or milk
1 tablespoon fat	3 eggs

Cook spinach leaves in very little salted water until they wilt, then chop fine. Mix crumbled cheese and fat with spinach. Cook unpeeled potatoes separately in boiling salted water for 20 to 40 minutes, depending on size. Peel and slice very thin. In an ovenproof dish place 1 tablespoon oil, then half of potato slices, then spinach and cheese mixture, then remaining potatoes. Mix remaining oil with yogurt and eggs and pour over potatoes. Bake in 350° oven for about 20 minutes until a brownish crust forms. Serves 4 to 6.

Spinach Pudding CZECHOSLOVAKIA

2 pounds spinach,	salt to taste
cleaned	dash of mace
4 eggs, separated	¼ cup butter
2 rolls	2 tablespoons bread crumbs
1⅓ cups milk	

Soak rolls in milk. Steam spinach for 3 to 5 minutes. Drain and grind. Beat egg yolk until creamy, add rolls, salt, mace, and spinach. Fold in stiffly beaten egg whites. Grease a covered pudding form well, sprinkle with bread crumbs. Pour in mixture, cover, and cook in a pan of boiling water for about 45 minutes. Serve with melted butter and fried bread crumbs. Serves 4 to 6.

Spinach Puffs

½ pound fresh spinach
½ cup chick pea flour
½ cup whole wheat flour
1 teaspoon salt

½ teaspoon turmeric
½ teaspoon cayenne
1 teaspoon ground coriander
2 tablespoons peanut oil

Wash the spinach carefully, removing the stems and yellow leaves. Chop very fine, but do not grind (for this makes water). Set aside.

Mix together the chick pea flour, whole wheat flour, salt, turmeric, cayenne, and coriander in a saucepan. Add the spinach and peanut oil.

Mix well. Then start adding water, in very small amounts, a few drops at a time, until the mixture holds together but is not sticky. Form into 2-inch balls, rolling between the palms of the hands. For ease in shaping, it is best to film the hands with a little ghee. Deep fry these, a few at a time, in hot peanut oil.

Spinach and Rice

½ cup olive oil
1 cup chopped onions
2 pounds spinach
1 cup rice

1 cup diced tomatoes
1 clove garlic, chopped
    salt and pepper
2 cups hot water

Put the oil and onions in a pan, cover, and let stew for about ten minutes. Wash and cut up the spinach, and put over the onions. Cover with the rice. Put the tomatoes and garlic over the rice, add the salt and pepper, and pour in the water. Cover and simmer about an hour. Serves 6.

Spinach and Ricotta Balls

1 pound spinach, washed
    and chopped
¾ pound ricotta
½ teaspoon salt
2 tablespoons grated
    Parmesan cheese

2 egg yolks
2 tablespoons flour
2 quarts simmering water
¼ cup melted butter
2 tablespoons grated
    Parmesan cheese

Cook spinach in 1 cup water 5 minutes. Squeeze spinach dry and mix with ricotta, salt, cheese, and egg yolks. When well mixed, shape as very small eggs, dust with flour and drop into simmering water, a few at a time. The little balls will come to the surface of the water. Counting from the time that they rise to the surface, simmer 4 minutes and remove from water. Repeat until all the little balls are cooked. Sprinkle with melted butter and Parmesan and serve immediately. Serves 4.

Spinach Ring (with Cream)   JEWISH

2 eggs
1 tablespoon cornstarch
1 tablespoon brown sugar
  salt and pepper to taste

1 cup whipped cream
3 cups finely chopped spinach
1 tablespoon butter

Beat eggs lightly. Combine with sugar and cornstarch. Fold into cream and add seasoning. Stir in spinach. Pour in buttered ring mold. Set ring in a pan of hot water and bake at 375° for 40 minutes or until set. Unmold just before serving. Serves 6.

Spinach Roulade   AUSTRIA

4 egg yolks
4 tablespoons sour cream
4 tablespoons spinach, cooked
  and puréed
1 tablespoon cheese, grated
½ teaspoon salt

4 egg whites, stiffly beaten
Filling
4 eggs, scrambled
  salt to taste

Mix yolks, sour cream, spinach, cheese, and salt. Fold in egg whites. Butter a baking sheet. Spread mixture on top. Bake in 350° oven 8 minutes. Loosen with thin knife. Spread scrambled eggs on top; salt. Roll and cut into slices 2 inches thick on a warm platter before serving. Serves 5.

Spinach Omelet

4 eggs, separated
2 teaspoons hot water
½ pound fresh spinach,
   cleaned and chopped

salt to taste
2 teaspoons cold water
¼ cup butter

Beat egg yolks with salt and hot water. Add spinach. Add cold water to egg whites, beat until stiff; fold into yolk-spinach mixture. Grease 2 frying pans well with butter, and pour half the batter into each. Bake in a preheated 350° oven for about 30 minutes, or until eggs are set. Serves 2.

Omelets with Spinach

The Omelet
2 eggs
½ cup milk
½ cup flour
   salt to taste

The Purée
1½ cups puréed spinach
1 tablespoon butter
2 tablespoons cheese
2 to 3 tablespoons sour cream

Cook 3 thick pancakes out of omelet mixture. Purée spinach. Place 1 pancake in a buttered dish, then ½ of spinach purée, then the second omelet, remaining spinach purée, finishing with third omelet. Grate cheese over top layer, pour sour cream over and brown in 350° oven for 20 minutes. Serve warm. Serves 4 to 6.

Spinach Mashed Potatoes

6 medium potatoes, peeled
1 teaspoon salt
1 10-ounce package frozen
   chopped spinach

½ to 1 cup hot milk
butter

Cook the potatoes until tender with the salt in just enough water to cover. Drain and mash them. Meanwhile put the spinach into another saucepan, pour the milk over it, and cook over low heat until it is done. Add the spinach-milk mixture to the mashed potatoes and whip until fluffy. Serve immediately. Serves about 6.

Spinach Soufflé

1 cup raw spinach, chopped
   salt and pepper
5 tablespoons butter
7 tablespoons flour

1 cup milk, scalded
7 eggs, separated
4 to 5 scallions, white
   parts only, chopped

Clean and wash the spinach. Select only the tender leaves and chop these to measure 1 cup. Season lightly with salt and pepper, and place in a strainer. Let drain for 1 hour. In a small pot, melt the butter. Add the flour, stirring constantly to a smooth paste. Add the hot milk and stir to make a thick sauce. Add a little salt and pepper. Remove from heat. Add the spinach and the scallions to the sauce. Beat the egg yolks until very thick. Beat the whites until stiff. Fold the yolks into the sauce, then fold in the whites. Pour into a buttered mold. Bake immediately in a preheated 350° oven for about 30 minutes. Serve immediately. Serves 6 to 8.

Sweet-Sour Spinach

1 pound spinach
1 large onion
2 tablespoons shortening
2 tablespoons flour
½ cup cider vinegar

2 tablespoons brown sugar
1 teaspoon salt
1 cup drained canned
   tomatoes

Wash and drain spinach. Shred or chop leaves and stems. Brown diced onion in shortening. Stir in flour and blend till light brown. Add vinegar in which sugar has been dissolved. Add salt. Stir till smooth. Add tomatoes and chopped spinach and cook 3 minutes. Serves 4.

Acorn Squash

JEWISH

Cut halves through stem end. Remove seeds. Add 1 teaspoon butter, dust with salt and paprika, and bake 40 to 60 minutes at 375° or till tender.

Variation 1: Boil halves in salted water to cover till tender. Drain and brush the inside with melted butter or other shortening. Bake 10 minutes to brown. Or slip under the broiler.

Variation 2: Fill baked or boiled halves with cooked diced beets, creamed white onions, boiled rice, or creamed spinach with grated cheese topping.

Calabash and Dumplings

ISRAEL

2 pounds calabash (or any
   winter squash)
4 tablespoons brown sugar
½ teaspoon salt
¼ teaspoon cinnamon or
   nutmeg
5 tablespoons margarine

water
Dumplings
¾ cup flour
2 tablespoons semolina
   pinch of salt
½ cup water or milk

Cut the calabash into 1-inch cubes, sprinkle with sugar and seasoning, dot with margarine, and half cover with water. Cook until the vegetable is soft (about 1½ hours). Mix all the dumpling ingredients and drop by the teaspoonful into boiling water. Cook for 5 minutes. Serve with the calabash. Serves about 6.

Squash

4 pounds squash
  dash salt
3 tablespoons butter or fat
5 tablespoons flour
1 teaspoon parsley, chopped
1 teaspoon dill, chopped

1 teaspoon onion, chopped
  dash paprika
½ cup water
  vinegar to taste
½ cup sour cream

Halve and peel squash. Cut in thin strips like noodles. Salt; let stand 45 minutes. Melt butter or fat; blend in flour, parsley, dill, onion, and paprika; add water. Cook gently until thick. Add squash and vinegar. Simmer 15 to 20 minutes; add sour cream. Serves 6.

Squash Alias Asparagus

12 small summer squash
2 tablespoons margarine

2 packages powdered asparagus soup
2 cups milk

Peel the squash and cut into asparagus-sized strips. Put into individual casseroles. Dab with a bit of margarine. Boil the dried asparagus soup and milk (or used canned asparagus soup, diluted to sauce consistency). Pour over squash and bake in a 350° oven 30 minutes. The dish tastes like asparagus. Serves 6.

Bottle Squash

6 bottle squash (small),
  or other winter squash
  dash of cinnamon
  honey to taste

salt to taste
dash of ginger
water

Cut the squashes into cubes and sprinkle with all the seasonings and honey. Add a very little water and cook until the vegetable is soft and the liquid absorbed (about ½ hour). Serves 4 to 6.

Squash Au Gratin

3 pounds small squash
  (zucchini)
1 cup vegetable or olive oil
  flour
1 recipe Thick Béchamel Sauce

1½ cups grated kefalotiri
  cheese
toasted bread crumbs
3 tablespoons butter, melted
salt and pepper to taste

Select tender squash. Scrape the skin, wash. Cut into small slices. Season with salt and pepper. Heat the oil in a frying pan. Dip the squash into the flour, shaking off the excess, and fry until rosy. Prepare the béchamel.

Butter a medium-sized pan. Spread in it a thin layer of béchamel, sprinkle with cheese. Cover with a layer of squash. Continue to spread these layers alternately, ending with a thick layer of béchamel. Sprinkle with the cheese and then the bread crumbs. Drizzle the melted butter over the top, and bake in a preheated 325° oven for 20 to 30 minutes.

Squash Croquettes or Patties

2 pounds small squash
1 tablespoon butter
3 tablespoons chopped onion
1 cup grated kefalotiri or
  Parmesan cheese
1 cup toasted bread crumbs

1 tablespoon chopped parsley
2 eggs
salt and pepper to taste
flour
oil for frying

Clean and wash the squash. Boil in lightly salted water until soft; drain well. Mash and set aside. Melt the butter in a pan, and sauté the onions until limp and golden but not browned. Add the onions, cheese, bread crumbs, parsley, eggs, and salt and pepper to the squash, and mix well. If the mixture is too soft, add more bread crumbs. Let it stand for 10 minutes, then shape into croquettes or patties. Roll in flour, fry until golden.

Squash with Eggs

1 onion, diced
2 tablespoons shortening
   (butter, oil or vegetable)
   pinch of salt
2 cups diced squash, cooked
4 tablespoons cold water,
   approximately

4 to 6 eggs, separated
⅛ teaspoon salt
   minced or sprigs of parsley
   or dill

Cook onion in hot melted shortening in a frying pan. When light brown add salt and stir. Turn off heat and skim out fried onion. Cook diced squash in cold water in a well-covered pot 10 minutes or till tender. Drain off liquid. Add cooked squash to frying pan and beat eggs separately, adding salt to egg whites while beating stiff but not dry. Combine beaten yolks and egg whites and pour over squash. Cook over low to moderate heat 3 to 5 minutes or till eggs are set and the top frothy. With a spatula turn up half the omelet over other half and serve with fried onions, parsley, or dill. Serve immediately. Serves 4.

Fried Italian Yellow Squash

4 very thin slices squash,
   cut into 4-inch pieces
½ cup flour

½ teaspoon salt
1 egg, lightly beaten
1 cup olive oil

Roll squash in flour, dip into salted egg, and fry in hot oil until light brown in color on both sides. Serves 4.

Squash Lathera

3 pounds zucchini squash
1¼ cups oil
2 medium onions, chopped
1½ pounds ripe tomatoes,
   peeled and strained, or
   1 tablespoon tomato paste
   diluted with 1 cup water

2 to 3 cloves garlic, chopped
2 tablespoons chopped parsley
   salt and pepper to taste
   water as needed

Clean and wash the squash, cut each into 4 or 5 round slices. Heat the oil in a pot and sauté the onions until lightly browned. Add the tomatoes (or diluted tomato paste) and the garlic; bring to a boil. Add the squash, parsley, salt, pepper, and ½ cup water. Cover the pot. Simmer until all the liquid has been absorbed and only the oil remains as a sauce (about 45 minutes). Serves 6.

Note: You may fry the squash first, if you wish. In that case, use half of the oil for the onions and the other half for the squash, and cook the sauce for 15 to 20 minutes before adding the fried squash and the parsley. Do not add more water. Cook for about 20 minutes more, or until the liquid is absorbed and only the oil remains.

Squash Medyas (Slit and Stuffed)

12 small summer squash
   (vegetable marrow or
   zucchini type)
 2 tablespoons grated yellow
   cheese (optional)

2 cups cottage cheese
4 eggs
   salt and pepper
   butter (optional)
½ cup sour cream

Cook the unpeeled tender squash in as little water as possible, and drain them while still firm. Slit lengthwise ("medyas" means "cut in two") and remove the seed section, leaving a scooped-out boat shape for filling. Mix the cheeses and eggs with salt and pepper and fill the cavities. Put the scooped-out seed sections in a well-buttered casserole and place the medyas on top. Dab each medyas with a little butter if you wish. Bake in a hot oven until the filling has set. Top with sour cream and bake 5 minutes more. Delicious hot or cold. Serves 12.

Sautéed Squash

1 pound squash (small
  green variety)
⅛ teaspoon salt
3 tablespoons fine cracker
  crumbs or matzo meal

3 tablespoons hot melted
  shortening
3 tablespoons sugar
  pinch of cinnamon

Cut into ¼-inch thick rounds (unpared squash) or lengthwise into ¼-inch thick slices. Sprinkle with salt very lightly and roll each piece in crumbs or matzo meal. Sauté in hot melted shortening on both sides of slices till tender and lightly browned. Sprinkle with sugar and cinnamon as cooked slices are removed from pan to baking dish. Return to hot frying pan and cover till serving time or heat in moderate oven 5 to 10 minutes. This dish is frequently served cold. Serves 4.

Squash Soufflé

1½ pounds squash
½ cup butter
½ cup milk, scalded
½ cup toasted bread crumbs
1 teaspoon baking powder

4 eggs, separated
¼ to ½ pound grated Par-
  mesan
salt and pepper to taste

Wash and peel the squash. Bring to a boil in a pot of water; cook about 10 minutes or until tender. Chop finely or mash. Brown the butter in a pot. Add the squash and mix well; mix in the hot milk. Mix together the bread crumbs and baking powder; add to the squash. Beat the egg yolks and add them with the cheese to the squash. Season with salt and pepper. Beat the whites until stiff, and fold gently into the mixture. Pour immediately into a buttered mold. Bake in a preheated 350° oven for 30 minutes. Serve immediately. Serves 6 to 8.

Squash with Tomato   JEWISH

3 cups diced squash
¼ teaspoon salt
4 tablespoons cold water
1 cup diced fresh tomato or
   ½ cup stewed

1 teaspoon sugar
1 tablespoon butter
1 tablespoon flour

Cook in a covered pot squash, salt, water, and tomato 10 minutes. Add sugar. Brown flour in hot melted butter and stir in. Cook 3 minutes longer, uncovered, stirring to prevent sticking. Serves 4.

Variation: Serve with boiled potatoes, whole or finely diced.

Squash in Tomato Sauce   ISRAEL

2 tablespoons chopped onion
3 tablespoons margarine
2 tablespoons flour
2 cups tomato juice
2 teaspoons bouillon cube, crushed

1 teaspoon salt
   dash of paprika
1 teaspoon sugar
10 small squash
1 teaspoon chopped parsley

Fry the onion in the margarine. Add the flour, and when the mixture bubbles, add the tomato juice and stir until thickened. Add the bouillon cube, and the seasonings. Slice the squash (do not peel) and put into a casserole. Sprinkle with the parsley and cover with the sauce. Bake in a 375° oven 30 minutes, or until the squash are tender. Serves 6.

Baked Summer Squash   JEWISH

Cut the tops off white summer squash, allowing 1 small squash per serving, or use the larger variety and serve filling only. Scoop out centers, leaving half-inch-thick shells. The seeds of young squash are very tender and need not be discarded. Cook the scooped out portions in a little salted water, in a tightly covered pot, till soft. Mash thoroughly and combine with ½ the quantity bread crumbs. Add 1 egg, per cupful, 1 tablespoon grated cheese, minced parsley, and a dash of cayenne. If additional liquid is necessary, add cream or evaporated milk. Fill the cavities of squashes, adjust the tops and bake 30 to 40 minutes at 350°. Remove the "lids" and slip under broiler flame to brown lightly. Serve with "lids" on to retain the heat.

Baked Winter Squash   JEWISH

Select a medium-sized squash, wash and cut into 2-inch cubes. Remove seeds and pare. Arrange in a buttered baking dish, sprinkle with salt, pepper, and cracker crumbs. Dot with butter and bake 45 minutes to 1 hour at 350° F. Oil or vegetable shortening may be substituted for butter.

Two pounds squash serves 6.

Variation: Cut squash into wedges from stem to blossom end. Remove seeds and stringy part. Dust cut side with salt and pepper and arrange on a baking sheet. Bake 1 hour at 350° or till tender. Add melted shortening just before serving. These baked slices are very attractive. Allow a 2-inch wedge per serving.

Yellow or Crookneck Squash   JEWISH

Select young squash for best flavor. Do not pare. Wash and slice into ¼-inch rounds. Boil in as little water as possible, keeping the pot covered for 5 minutes. Remove cover, salt to taste, and add butter. If not tender enough, cook a few minutes longer over low heat. Do not cook too long. Serve hot.

Succotash   JEWISH

1 cup cooked fresh corn, cut from cob	2 tablespoons butter
1 cup cooked fresh lima beans	½ teaspoon salt
	minced parsley

Combine corn and beans and cook 3 minutes with the other ingredients. Serves 4.

Variation 1: Add ½ cup stewed tomatoes and ½ teaspoon brown sugar.

Variation 2: Substitute cooked green beans for limas, cutting them into ½-inch lengths or smaller.

Variation 3: Use same proportions of canned corn kernels and baby limas, well drained.

Baked Tomatoes

12 small, even-sized tomatoes
 6 lumps butter
  salt and pepper to taste

1 tablespoon chopped dill
or chives

Cut tops off tomatoes and scoop out seeds. Fill with butter and herbs, season, and cover again with the tops. Bake in shallow dish, uncovered, in medium-hot oven for about 30 minutes. Serves 6.

Devil's Tomatoes

3 tomatoes
 salt and pepper
½ tablespoon flour
 butter for frying
5 tablespoons butter
1 cooked egg yolk

1 whole egg
2 teaspoons powdered sugar
¼ teaspoon salt
1 teaspoon mustard
2 tablespoons vinegar

Scald, peel, and slice tomatoes. Season well. Sprinkle with flour and fry in butter. Keep hot while making sauce, as follows:
Cream butter, mash yolk, beat and add whole egg. Mix in other ingredients. Cook in double boiler, stirring continuously until sauce thickens. Pour over tomatoes and serve. Serves 2.

Tomatoes Filled with Eggs and Cheese
CZECHOSLOVAKIA

8 tomatoes
  salt to taste
  pepper to taste
1 cup grated Swiss or
  American cheese

¼ cup butter
8 eggs
1 tablespoon minced parsley

Cut out a circle at the stem end in tomatoes. Scoop out insides carefully, sprinkle with salt, pepper, and half of the cheese. Put in a bit of butter, and drop an egg into each tomato. Sprinkle with more salt, the remaining cheese, and parsley. Bake in a preheated 350° oven for 30 minutes or until eggs are set. Excellent as a meatless dish with potato or legumes purée. Serves 4 to 8.

Tomato Omelet
GREECE

1½ pounds ripe tomatoes
  salt and pepper to taste

4 tablespoons butter
6 eggs

Wash and peel the tomatoes, scoop out the seeds and discard. Cut into small pieces. Place in a frying pan with a little salt and pepper and cook until reduced to a pulp. Add the butter, and while this is browning, beat the eggs with salt and pepper. Add to the pan. Lower the heat and stir gently. Allow to cook until set to your taste. Remove from the heat. Gather the tomatoes from the edges of the pan, spread on the top of the omelet; fold in half. Serve immediately with fried potatoes. Serves 3.

Fried Tomatoes
CZECHOSLOVAKIA

½ cup white wine or water
2 eggs, separated
⅔ cup flour

salt to taste
5 firm tomatoes, sliced
shortening for frying

Mix wine, egg yolks, flour, and salt. Fold in stiffly beaten egg whites. Dip tomatoes in mixture; fry to a golden brown. Serve with mashed potatoes. Serves 2 to 4.

Tomatoes Au Gratin SCANDINAVIA

> 8 to 12 tomatoes
> salt
> white pepper
> 2 tablespoonfuls chopped parsley, dill, or chives
> 1 to 2 tablespoonfuls butter or margarine

Wash and dry the tomatoes. Cut a cross in each tomato or divide it into two halves. Sprinkle herbs inside the tomatoes and dot each one with a pat of fat.

Place the tomatoes on a buttered, fireproof dish. Bake until tender, about 10 minutes.

Serve at once as a separate course with mushroom sauce. Serves 4.

Grilled Tomatoes JEWISH

Cut large firm tomatoes in halves crosswise. Dust with salt and cracker crumbs. Add a dot or two of butter and broil 3 to 5 minutes under broiler flame to melt butter and brown crumbs. Allow 1 tomato for two servings.

Tomatoes with Mushroom Stuffing POLAND

For 6 large or 12 smaller tomatoes, use:

> 12 medium mushrooms,
>   chopped
> ½ medium onion, chopped
> 1 heaping tablespoon butter
>
> 2 tablespoons bread crumbs
> 2 to 3 tablespoons sour cream
>   salt and pepper to taste

Prepare tomatoes. Blanch, cut off tops, and scoop out seeds. Season with salt and pepper. Simmer chopped mushrooms and onion in butter until transparent and limp—about 5 minutes. Combine with bread crumbs and sour cream, season to taste, and fill the tomatoes. Cover with tomato tops and arrange in shallow buttered baking dish. Bake in 375° oven 20 to 25 minutes. Serves 6.

Tomato-Cheese Pie

Pastry
½ cup margarine
2 cups sifted flour
½ cup grated yellow cheese
1 egg yolk
2 tablespoons ice water
  pinch of salt
  dash of cayenne

Filling
4 large tomatoes, thinly sliced
2 large onions, thinly sliced
5 tablespoons margarine
2 eggs
1½ cups milk
¾ cup grated yellow cheese
  salt, cayenne, and
  pepper to taste

For the pastry, cut the margarine into the flour. Add the cheese and rub gently until crumbly. Mix the egg yolk with the ice water, salt, and cayenne, then add gradually to the first mixture. Roll out the dough. Line a spring pan with this pastry and press the edges down with a fork.

Cover the dough with tomato slices. Fry two-thirds of the onion in the margarine. Mix with the raw onion and sprinkle on the tomatoes. Mix the eggs, milk, ½ cup of the cheese, and the seasonings. Pour over the onions. Bake in a 375° oven 35 minutes. Sprinkle on the remaining cheese and bake for 5 minutes more. Serve warm, preferably.

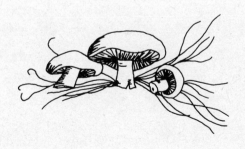

Mixed Vegetables

Vegetables Au Gratin SCANDINAVIA

With Sauce
1 to 1½ pounds cooked vegetables, whole or in pieces, e.g., cauliflower,
broccoli, fennel, Jerusalem artichokes, leeks, asparagus or salsify.
Sauce
2 tablespoonfuls butter or margarine
3 tablespoonfuls plain flour
 about ½ pint vegetable water (about 1¼ cups)
 about 5 tablespoonfuls cream
 salt
 white pepper
1 to 2 egg yolks
Gratin Top
1 to 2 tablespoonfuls butter or margarine
1 to 2 tablespoonfuls grated cheese

Fry the fat and flour for the sauce. Add the liquid and cook
the sauce for 3 to 5 minutes. Season to taste. Let the sauce
cool a little and stir in the egg yolks.

Put the well-drained vegetables into a greased, fireproof dish
and pour the sauce over them. Dot with fat and sprinkle grated
cheese on top. Brown in the oven (or under radiant grill or
broiler) for about 10 minutes.

Served as a separate dish. Serves 4.

Vegetables in Aspic

> 1½ pounds cooked mixed vegetables, such as cauliflower, French
>   beans, peas, carrots and asparagus
> Aspic
> 2 egg whites
> 1½ pints vegetable stock (3¾ cups)
> 10 leaves gelatin, soaked
>   or 2 tablespoonfuls powdered gelatin
> 2½ to 5 tablespoonfuls white wine
>   (2½ tablespoons = 7½ teaspoons) (optional)

Strain and clear the vegetable stock. If wine is to be used, add it to the stock and taste for seasoning.

Pour a thin layer of aspic into a large mold or into several small molds and allow it to set for 2 to 3 hours.

Arrange the vegetables on top and pour on sufficient cool aspic to cover them. Stand in a cold place until set.

Turn out the aspic. Garnish. Serve as a separate course with a sauce such as sour cream flavored with mustard and horse-radish, mayonnaise, horse-radish cream or sharp sauce.

Aspic may be garnished with parsley, cucumber, and hard-boiled eggs or radishes, tomatoes, and hard-boiled eggs.

Vegetables Au Naturel

1 head cauliflower	1 pound whole green beans
1 pound young carrots	½ cup butter
1 pound fresh peas	¼ cup finely chopped parsley

Cook the whole head of cauliflower in salted water to cover until tender-crisp. Meanwhile, cook the carrots, peas, and green beans in separate saucepans. Place the cauliflower in the center of a large serving platter, arrange the carrots on either side of it, then mound the green beans and peas around it. Pour the butter over all and sprinkle with the parsley. Serve at once. Serves 10 to 12.

Creamed Vegetables

> *1 to 1½ pounds cooked vegetables in pieces, e.g., cauliflower,*
> *Jerusalem artichokes, carrots, savoy cabbage, white cabbage,*
> *runner beans or peas*
> *chopped herbs*
> *Sauce*
> *1½ tablespoonfuls butter or margarine (4½ teaspoons)*
> *3 tablespoonfuls plain flour*
> *about ¾ pint vegetable water and milk (1¾ cups)*
> *salt*
> *white pepper*

Fry the fat and flour. Add the liquid and cook the sauce for 3 to 5 minutes. Season with salt and white pepper.

Add the vegetables and reheat them in the sauce or pour the sauce over the hot vegetables. Sprinkle herbs on top.

Serves 4.

Mixed Vegetable Curry

> *1 cup fresh green peas*
> *1 cup carrots, scraped and diced*
> *1 cup potatoes, peeled and diced*
> *2 cups string beans, snapped into 1-inch pieces*
> *4 tablespoons peanut oil or ghee*
> *2 teaspoons cumin seed*
> *1 teaspoon salt*
> *2 teaspoons mustard seed*
> *2 teaspoons turmeric*
> *1 teaspoon coriander seed*
> *1 teaspoon cayenne*
> *½ cup yogurt*

Boil the peas, carrots, potatoes, and string beans together in enough lightly salted water to cover. Set aside. Do not drain.

In a separate pot, heat the peanut oil or ghee. Add the spices to it. Blend well, then add the mixed vegetables in their juices. Bring to a boil and add the yogurt.

Stir well and simmer for 20 minutes. Too thick? Add water to thin as desired. Serves 4.

Cutlets for Vegetarians   AUSTRIA

4 *white rolls*	1 *egg*
1 *cup milk*	⅓ *cup bread crumbs*
6 *tablespoons butter*	4 *tablespoons spinach, chopped*
¼ *teaspoon onions, chopped*	⅓ *cup flour*
1 *teaspoon parsley, chopped*	2 *eggs*
¾ *pound mushrooms, diced*	1 *tablespoon milk*
1 *tablespoon fat*	¾ *cup bread crumbs*
salt, pepper	½ *pound fat*

Remove crusts of rolls; soak in milk. Squeeze dry and fry in butter. Fry onions and parsley. Sauté mushrooms in fat. Mix fried parsley, onions, and rolls with salt, pepper, egg, bread crumbs, and spinach. Shape patties; dip in flour and eggs mixed with milk, and then in bread crumbs. Fry in hot fat.

Serves 4 to 5.

Note: The same recipe may be used with any single vegetable. In that case, use larger amounts, such as 3 pounds of mushrooms, 2 pounds of spinach, 2 pounds of cabbage, etc.

Eggs with Vegetables   BULGARIA●YUGOSLAVIA

1 *large onion*	½ *pound tomatoes*
2 *tablespoons butter*	8 *eggs*
2 *green peppers, fried,*	*salt*
skinned, and chopped	¾ *cup cottage cheese*
1 *to 2 small peperonis, finely*	1 *to 2 tablespoons chopped*
chopped and seeded	*parsley*

Chop onion fine and fry in butter. Add chopped peppers and raw, chopped peperonis. Simmer 10 minutes. Peel tomatoes and cut into eighths. Add and simmer 5 minutes. Break eggs into mixture, add salt, crumbled cheese, and parsley, and scramble. Serve with white bread. Serves 4 to 6.

Vegetable Fritters SCANDINAVIA

1 to 1½ pounds cooked vegetables in pieces, e.g., cauliflower,
* Jerusalem artichokes, salsify or leeks*
Fritter Batter
4 ounces flour (1 cup)
½ teaspoonful salt
1 gill ale or water (½ cup + 2 tablespoons)
1 egg
* oil or coconut butter to fry*

Mix the ingredients for the batter.

Drain the vegetables thoroughly and dip them into the batter. Put them into the hot fat, not too many at a time. Fry them until they are golden brown, about 5 minutes. Lift them out using a fritter spoon and drain them on absorbent paper.

Arrange the fritters on a hot serving dish and garnish with tomato and parsley.

Serve immediately with mayonnaise, sharp sauce, tomato sauce or mushroom sauce. Serves 4.

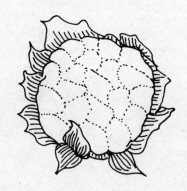

Vegetable Loaf   JEWISH

2 tablespoons melted shortening
1 cup diced or chopped onion
1 cup minced celery
1 cup grated raw carrots
1 cup finely ground English
  walnuts (or mixed nuts)
1 cup dry whole wheat or rye
  bread crumbs

1 teaspoon each salt and
  poultry seasoning
2 eggs
1 cup evaporated milk or
  cream
1½ cups tomato or mushroom
  sauce

Cook onions in hot melted shortening till light brown and add vegetables, nuts, crumbs, and seasonings. Sauté. Beat eggs and stir in cream. Combine both mixtures and turn into a well-greased loaf pan or shape into balls or patties for individual portions. Bake at 350° for 40 to 45 minutes or till nicely browned. Turn out loaf and serve with tomato sauce or fresh mushroom sauce. Or, use a can of cream of mushroom soup, heated just before serving. Garnish with sliced hard-cooked eggs or cooked green peas around the loaf. Serves 4 to 6.

Vegetable Macédoine   POLAND

½ cup each diced carrots,
  kohlrabi, celery root,
  parsnip, and parsley root
  salt and sugar to taste
2 tablespoons butter
1 scant cup bouillon

½ cup green peas, cooked
  separately
½ cup snap beans or asparagus
  tips, cooked separately
1½ teaspoons flour

Combine carrots, kohlrabi, celery root, parsnip, and parsley root with 1 tablespoon butter, sugar, seasoning, and bouillon. Simmer, tightly covered, until tender. Combine with peas, snap beans, and/or asparagus tips. Dust in the flour and simmer a few minutes longer or until sauce thickens. Remove from heat. Add remaining butter and allow to melt. Serve garnished with croutons as a side dish. Serves 6.

Vegetable Meal-In-One JEWISH

1 cup diced green beans
1 cup diced carrots
1 cup diced eggplant
1 cup stewed or 1½ cups
  sliced fresh tomatoes
1 teaspoon salt

4 tablespoons butter or other
  shortening
4 eggs, well beaten
2 cups cooked rice, drained,
  tightly packed

Wash and drain diced vegetables. Combine and add tomatoes, sprinkle with salt and stir once or twice. Butter baking dish or casserole and turn in vegetable mixture. Melt remaining shortening in a saucepan and drizzle over top of vegetables. Pour beaten eggs over top and bake 25 to 30 minutes at 350° or till eggs are set. Serve with mounds of cooked rice around or underneath. Serves 5 or 6.

Variation: Substitute cooked fine noodles or macaroni for rice.

Mixed Vegetables AUSTRIA

2 pounds assorted vegetables
  (kohlrabi, carrots, string
  beans, wax beans, green
  peas, cauliflower, asparagus
  celery, Brussels sprouts, etc.)

6 tablespoons butter
1 tablespoon parsley, chopped
3 tablespoons Parmesan
  cheese, grated

Clean, dice, and boil vegetables separately in salted water until soft. Drain. Melt butter. Add parsley, vegetables, some cheese. Mix gently. Sprinkle with remaining cheese. Serves 6.

Note: Vegetables used are optional and may be mixed according to season and taste.

Vegetable Pancakes ISRAEL

⅔ cup chopped, cooked leeks
⅔ cup chopped, cooked
  spinach
⅔ cup chopped, cooked pumpkin

½ cup flour
2 eggs
2 teaspoons sugar
  salt to taste
  cooking oil

The vegetables should be cooked separately, then chopped. Mix the flour, eggs, sugar, and salt and divide among the vegetables. Form into small patties and fry in deep hot oil. Serves 4 to 6.

Cheese and Vegetable Ring   JEWISH

2 tablespoons butter or
   vegetable shortening
2 cups fine noodles, cooked
1 cup grated American cheese
   (cheddar type)
2 cups each cooked green beans,
   peas, carrots (canned may be used)
½ cup chopped spinach or
   other greens

½ cup dry skim milk or
   2 cups milk
2 cups water (if using dry
   skim milk)
2 tablespoons flour
½ teaspoon salt
   dash of white pepper (optional)
3 eggs, well beaten
   minced parsley for garnish

Use a 9-inch ring mold (or a casserole dish). Grease the inside
and bottom well and cover with half the cooked noodles. Sprinkle
half the amount of grated cheese evenly, add half the amount
of mixed vegetables then repeat, reserving some of the grated
cheese to sprinkle over the top. Combine milk, flour and seasonings in a saucepan.

Cook over low heat till sauce begins to thicken. Stir in the
well-beaten eggs till smooth and pour into the ring mold slowly,
turning so that the sauce is absorbed evenly by the layers of
noodles and vegetables. Bake 30 minutes at 350° or till lightly
browned on top. Turn off oven heat. After 5 minutes remove
from oven and turn out on serving plate. Fill center with cooked
diced carrots, peas or both and garnish with minced parsley.
If a casserole is used surround with mounds of alternating carrots
and peas. Serves 5 or 6.

Vegetable Soufflé   AUSTRIA

½ cup green peas
1 cup Brussels sprouts
½ medium-sized cauliflower head
4 to 5 carrots, cut into strips
2 to 3 medium-sized
   mushrooms, sliced
2 tablespoons butter

Béchamel Sauce
3 tablespoons butter
3 tablespoons flour
1¼ cups milk
5 egg yolks
5 egg whites, stiffly beaten
salt

Boil green peas, Brussels sprouts, cauliflower flowerets, and
carrots in salted water. Drain; set aside to cool. Sauté mushrooms
in butter. Prepare béchamel sauce. Fold in vegetables and
mushrooms. Place mixture in buttered ovenproof glass dish and
bake in 300° oven 45 minutes. Serves 5.

MIXED VEGETABLES

Vegetarian Hash SWEDEN

2 to 3 carrots

4 to 5 potatoes

1 pickled beetroot

1 to 3 onions

1 small can mushrooms, 4½ oz., chopped (optional)

2 to 3 tablespoonfuls butter, margarine or oil

salt

white pepper

chopped parsley

Peel and wash the carrots and potatoes. Cut them and the beetroot into small dice. Peel and chop the onions.

Brown the onions (and mushrooms) in some of the fat. Lift them out. Then brown the carrots and potatoes in the remaining fat. Return the onions (and mushrooms) to the pan and let them all fry together gently until they are tender, about 20 minutes. Add the diced beetroot. Season to taste.

Arrange on a vegetable platter and sprinkle with chopped parsley. Serve with fried eggs, pickled beetroots or a salad. Serves 4.

Indian Chop Suey INDIA

6 cups raw vegetables in the following combination:

snow peas

Chinese cabbage

Chinese beans

eggplant

5 tablespoons peanut oil

2 teaspoons salt

sweet red pepper

sweet green pepper

zucchini (or any Chinese squash)

2 teaspoons cumin seed

1 teaspoon cayenne

Remove the strings from the snow peas as you would for string beans, and use the snow peas whole. Cut the Chinese beans into 2- to 3-inch pieces; cut the eggplant, peppers, and zucchini into strips the same length. Do not be confined by these suggestions. Also happy in the pot are cauliflower, separated into flowerets; regular string beans, slivered Indian style; a potato or two; and whole okra pods, stemmed.

Heat the peanut oil, and add the spices to it. (omit turmeric.) When the spices are warmed, add the prepared vegetables and stir until all are well coated with oil. Cover, and cook for 10 minutes. Test with a sharp knife for tenderness; do not over-cook. Depending upon the thickness of the vegetables, they should be ready in about 10 to 15 minutes.

Zucchini

Zucchini

JEWISH

1 pound zucchini
½ teaspoon salt
1 tablespoon butter

This small green squash is exceptionally good when young and tender. Do not pare. Remove stem end and blossom point. Cut into ¼-inch slices and cook 5 minutes in very little water in a covered saucepan. Season with salt and butter while hot.

Zucchini

INDIA

2 pounds young zucchini
3 tablespoons ghee or peanut
   oil
1 teaspoon salt

1 teaspoon turmeric
1 to 2 scallions, including the
   tender green tops, finely
   chopped

Wash and cut the zucchini into ½-inch slices. Set aside. Then, in a saucepan, heat the ghee or peanut oil, and add the salt, turmeric, and scallions to it. Stir well for 1 minute, then add the zucchini.

Stir for another minute, cover, and let simmer slowly, without adding water. The zucchini will be tender and ready to serve in 10 to 15 minutes. It may be reheated over and over again with no harm.

Note: What is also nice is to add 1 green pepper, chopped in chunks about half the size of the zucchini circles. Sweet red peppers will give you a happy color combination as well. For a more substantial dish, add 2 small potatoes, peeled and chopped. And a few bits of tomato are always welcome, also. However, tomatoes should not be added until about 5 minutes before the dish is done. Serves 4.

Baked Zucchinis

1 ½ pounds zucchinis
½ pint boiling water
1 tablespoon vinegar
2 egg yolks

5 tablespoons butter, melted
½ cup sour cream (or yogurt)
½ cup grated Parmesan (or
    similar fat, firm cheese)

Wash zucchinis, cut off both ends, grate coarsely, and cook until soft in boiling water with vinegar. Drain well and place in greased ovenproof dish. Boil yolks, butter, sour cream or yogurt and grated Parmesan cheese in a small pan, stirring constantly. Pour over zucchinis. Cook in 425° oven until brown (about 10 minutes). Serve immediately. Serves 4 to 6.

Zucchini in Casserole

4 medium zucchini
1 tablespoon butter
1 ½ cups cold cream sauce
2 eggs, lightly beaten

2 tablespoons grated Parmesan cheese
¼ teaspoon salt
¼ teaspoon pepper

Slice zucchini and fry in butter until light brown, taking care not to overcook. Mix together cream sauce, eggs, Parmesan, salt, and pepper and fold in fried zucchini.

Butter and flour a casserole, pour into it the zucchini mixture and place casserole in pan of water in moderate oven (375°) 40 minutes. Let stand 5 minutes after removing from oven before turning out on serving dish. Serves 4.

Dalmatian Zucchini

2 pounds zucchinis
½ pound tomatoes, peeled
    and sliced thin
2 tablespoons parsley,
    chopped fine

1 clove garlic, chopped fine
    salt and pepper to taste
¼ cup olive oil

Wash and dice the zucchinis, without peeling or scraping. Place in a casserole or ovenproof dish. Cover with tomato slices. Sprinkle with parsley and garlic. Dust with salt and pepper. Pour oil and very little water over the dish. Cover and cook over low heat. Do not stir, but shake the casserole occasionally. Serve either hot or cold. Serves 4.

Marinated Zucchini

4 *large zucchini*	1 *tablespoon chopped parsley*
1 *cup olive oil*	½ *teaspoon salt*
1 *clove garlic, chopped*	½ *teaspoon pepper*
1 *tablespoon chopped basil leaves*	1 *cup wine vinegar*

Cut zucchini into 1-inch slices, fry in hot oil until light brown and drain on paper. In a casserole place 1 layer fried zucchini, dot with chopped garlic, basil, and parsley, sprinkle with salt and pepper and repeat procedure until all zucchini are used. Boil vinegar 5 minutes and pour over zucchini. Let marinate at least 12 hours, drain and serve. (The zucchini will keep fresh in this marinade 15 days at least.) Serves 8.

Mashed Zucchini with Yeast, Fried

1½ *pounds zucchinis*	½ *bunch parsley*
salt to taste	½ *bunch dill*
½ *to* ¾ *ounces crumbled yeast*	*flour*
(or 1 to 1½ packages dry	¼ *cup grated kaskaval or*
yeast)	*kefalotyrie*
2 *eggs*	*fat for frying*

Grate zucchinis, sprinkle with salt, and let stand for 10 to 15 minutes. Squeeze out liquid. Add yeast, eggs, chopped herbs, and sufficient flour for a soft dough. Add cheese. Allow dough to rise until double in bulk and with a spoon cut out patties and fry in hot fat. Serves 4 to 6.

Zucchini, Mashed and Fried

2 *pounds zucchinis*	½ *bunch parsley, minced*
2 *eggs*	½ *bunch dill, minced*
3 *tablespoons flour*	*fat for frying*
⅓ *cup crumbled white cheese*	*salt to taste*
(kefalotyrie)	

Grate zucchinis on a coarse grater; sprinkle with salt and let stand for 5 to 10 minutes. Squeeze out as much liquid as possible. Mix with eggs, flour, cheese, and herbs. Place spoonfuls of mixture in hot fat and fry until golden brown on both sides. Serve with 1 cup yogurt, mixed with 2 or 3 grated garlic cloves, chopped parsley, and salt. Serves 6.

ZUCCHINI

Zucchini with Mint ITALY

4 medium zucchini
2 tablespoons olive oil
½ teaspoon salt

½ teaspoon pepper
1 teaspoon chopped mint
leaves

Parboil zucchini 10 minutes and cut into strips. Place in skillet with oil, salt, pepper, and mint and cook 5 minutes, stirring frequently. Serves 4.

Zucchini Parmesan ITALY

3 large zucchini
1 tablespoon butter
½ teaspoon salt

3 tablespoons grated Parmesan cheese

Parboil zucchini 10 minutes. Slice and place in buttered baking dish. Sprinkle with butter, salt, and Parmesan and bake in moderate oven (375°) 5 minutes, or until cheese has melted. Serve immediately. Serves 4.

Zucchini Pie ITALY

4 large zucchini
2 tablespoons flour
1 cup olive oil
3 tablespoons grated Parmesan cheese

1 cup tomato sauce
½ pound mozzarella, sliced thin

Cut zucchini into 1-inch slices, sprinkle with flour and fry in olive oil until light brown. In greased casserole place 1 layer of fried zucchini, sprinkle with Parmesan cheese, add a little of the sauce, cover with thin layers of mozzarella and repeat procedure until zucchini and other ingredients are all used, ending with mozzarella. Bake in moderate oven (375°) 30 minutes. Serves 4.

Grains and Lentils

Pearl Barley with Dried Mushrooms   POLAND

2 ounces dried mushrooms   1 heaping tablespoon butter
1 egg   salt and pepper to taste
2 cups barley

Soak mushrooms and cook in 4 cups salted water until tender. Beat egg lightly and mix with barley. Allow to dry. Add butter to the water in which mushrooms cooked. Let it melt, and then pour the boiling liquid over the barley. Simmer very slowly for 10 minutes. Cut mushrooms into thin strips, add to the pot, and mix lightly. Cover and bake in 350° oven for 1 hour. Serves 6 to 7.

Barley and Mushroom Pie   POLAND

Prepare, but do not bake. Make dough as follows:

2 cups flour   2 tablespoons sour cream
2 tablespoons butter   salt

Mix thoroughly until dough is workable. Line a buttered dish as if for pie. Fill with the barley and mushroom mixture, cover with thin layer of dough, perforate with fork, and bake in medium-hot oven for 1 hour. Serves 6 to 8.

Note: Pearl barley is also excellent cooked according to the basic directions given at beginning of this section, the kernels first coated with slightly beaten egg and allowed to dry out. Add a tablespoon of butter and a tablespoon of chopped fresh dill before putting into oven.

Whole Barley Pudding   FINLAND

This is the traditional dessert or supper main dish in the province of Satakunta in western Finland, but you may prefer to serve it as a breakfast dish or in place of a starch dish in any menu. Serve with butter.

½ cup whole pearl barley   *2 tablespoons butter*
1½ cups water   *½ teaspoon salt*
2⅔ cups milk

Cook the barley and water slowly for 30 minutes or until the barley begins to expand. Stir in the milk, bring to a boil, and pour into a casserole. Dot with the butter, add the salt, and bake in a slow oven (250°) for 4 hours or until all the liquid is absorbed. Stir occasionally as the casserole bakes. Makes about 6 servings.

Cornmeal Mush   RUMANIA

6 cups cornmeal (as coarse   *3 quarts water*
  as possible)   *dash salt*

Roast cornmeal dry in pan until it turns a darker color. Pour very slowly into boiling salted water, stirring with a whisk. It should take about 20 minutes to add the last of the cornmeal. Cook about 20 minutes longer on top of a double boiler until the mush no longer looks wet.

Rinse a dish with water, pour in corn mush, form dumplings with a spoon which has been dipped in water or milk, and place on serving dish. Serve with cold milk. (When served with cold milk, this is the breakfast of the Rumanian peasants.) Serves 8.

Note: People who don't expect to eat again until late in the day often stow away 3 cups apiece of this mush. You may reduce the amount to suit your family's appetites.

Corn Pone with Cheese　　　　　　　　RUMANIA

1 cup cornmeal
1 cup cheese
2 tablespoons butter

Boil a soft corn mush. Coat an ovenproof dish with butter. Place in it a layer of mush, then cheese (grated or in pieces, according to type). Place a layer of mush on top, then flakes of butter, and bake in 350° oven until top turns brown (about 45 minutes). Serve hot in baking dish. Serves 4 to 6.

Buckwheat Groats　　　　　　　　　　POLAND

1 cup whole groats
1 egg (optional)

1 tablespoon butter
2 cups boiling salted water

Use the whole-kernel groats rather than the so-called "refined" grinds, which cook up to a mush or gruel. Heat dry in a heavy skillet, stirring constantly to avoid scorching. Coat with the butter. Pour boiling water over groats, stir once, cover, and cook in 350° oven for 1 hour. For cooking on top of range, turn heat down as low as possible or cook over asbestos. Serves 3 to 4.

Note: Another way to cook groats is to coat kernels with beaten egg instead of butter, let them dry out, and then proceed as above, adding butter to the water.

Buckwheat Groats with Cheese　　　　POLAND

1 cup whole-kernel groats,
　blanched
2 cups sour cream
1 tablespoon melted butter

salt and pepper to taste
½ pound farmer or pot cheese
2 egg yolks

Combine blanched groats with sour cream and butter. Season, and put half into the bottom of well-buttered baking dish. Cream farmer cheese with egg yolks, spread over groats in the casserole, and then cover with remainder of the groats. Bake covered in (350°) oven for 50 minutes to 1 hour. Serve with sour cream. Serves 4.

231

Kasha-Varnitchkes

1 cup coarse buckwheat groats
2 egg yolks
4 cups boiling water
1 teaspoon salt

4 tablespoons butter
1 cup cooked noodle squares
  or bow-knots

Brown the groats in a heated heavy skillet or frying pan, stirring constantly to prevent burning. Stir in the egg yolks till grains are coated. Add the hot water slowly, stirring constantly. Add salt. Cook till tender over moderate heat. Add shortening and cooked noodle squares. Turn into a casserole and brown under broiler flame till nicely and evenly browned. Serves 3 or 4.

Boiled Lentils

¾ pint lentils (1 pound) (2¼
  cups)
2½ pints water (6¼ cups)
1 to 1½ teaspoonfuls salt
1 small onion, sliced
1 small carrot, sliced

2 cloves
1 bay leaf
  white pepper
  parsley
1 saltspoonful thyme (¼ teaspoon) (optional)

Clean and wash the lentils. Soak them in the salted water for about 12 hours.

Cook them until tender, about 1 to 1½ hours, in the same water containing onion, carrot, and spices. Season to taste.

Sprinkle chopped parsley on top. Serves 4.

Purée of Lentils

1 pound lentils
3 tablespoons butter
½ teaspoon salt

¼ teaspoon pepper
1 to 2 egg yolks (optional)
1 cup light cream

Wash lentils; cook in unsalted water until soft. Rub through strainer. Add butter, salt, and pepper. Blend in egg yolks mixed with cream. Keep in hot-water bath until served. Serves 5 to 6.

Purées can be made with white sauce, too.

To avoid skin forming on surface, dot purées with lumps of butter.

Sweet-Sour Lentils   J E W I S H

1½ cups lentils
1 quart cold water (¾ cup if
  using pressure cooker)
2 tablespoons butter or
  vegetable shortening

2 tablespoons flour
¼ teaspoon salt
  juice of 1 lemon (a bit of
  grated rind)
2 tablespoons sugar

Cook lentils in cold water 45 minutes to 1 hour or till tender. Drain, reserving liquid. (Cooks in 10 minutes in pressure cooker.) Heat shortening in saucepan and add flour, stirring till deep brown. Add some of the liquid strained from cooked lentils, stirring smooth. Add salt, sugar, and lemon juice and rind. Cook 1 minute before adding to lentils. Turn into a casserole and bake 15 minutes at 350°, or till the liquid has been absorbed. Garnish with minced parsley or sprinkle with paprika and serve hot. Serves 4.

Plain Boiled Rice   INDIA

1 cup long-grain raw white
  rice (washed in cold—not
  hot—water)

5 cups water
1 teaspoon salt
1 tablespoon butter or ghee

Use a pot deep enough to allow for a nice, rolling boil. It is important that each grain have enough room to move freely.

Put the rice, cold water, and salt all together into the pot, and, when the water boils briskly, add the butter or ghee. Stir once at this point; no more. Constant stirring gums up the works.

Now look at the clock. In exactly 15 minutes, lift out a few grains and roll them in your fingers. If the grains yield to the touch, then the rice is ready. If they resist and do not bend to the fingers, and if the core of the grain feels gritty, boil a few minutes longer, then test again. It is unlikely that the rice will be overdone in 15 minutes, but if you allow it to boil for 20 minutes or more, you could be in trouble. Unless, of course, you like glue.

Cheese-Rice Casserole

1 cup rice
2 quarts boiling water
1½ teaspoons salt
1 tablespoon butter

1¼ cups grated American
  cheese
2 eggs, beaten slightly
1 cup milk

Drop the rice in the boiling salted water and cook till tender, from 20 to 25 minutes. Drain well. Arrange in buttered casserole in alternate layers with the grated cheese. Combine the eggs and milk and pour over the rice mixture. Set the dish in a pan of hot water and bake for 30 minutes at 350°. It is done when a knife inserted in the center comes out clean. Serves 6 to 8.

Curried Rice

6 ounces rice (⅞ cup)
2 tablespoonfuls chopped onion
1 teaspoonful curry powder
2 tablespoonfuls butter or margarine

1 large apple, diced
2 peeled tomatoes, in sections
1 teaspoonful salt
¾ pint boiling water (1¾ cups)

Fry the rice, onion, and curry in the fat. Add the apple, tomatoes, and salt. Stir and pour the boiling water on to the mixture. Cover with a tightly fitting lid and cook the rice gently until tender, about 18 to 20 minutes.

Fried Rice

6 tablespoons peanut oil
1½ teaspoons salt
2 eggs, well beaten
2 cups bean sprouts (optional)
1 cup onions, chopped fine
2 teaspoons seasoning powder

4 teaspoons light soy sauce
10 cups cold cooked rice
½ cup fresh scallions, chopped fine
2 teaspoons heavy soy sauce
½ teaspoon pepper

Put peanut oil in hot skillet or cast-iron Dutch oven; add salt and eggs, and stir-fry 1 minute or until firm.

Add bean sprouts, onions, seasoning powder, and light soy sauce, and fry for 2 minutes.

Add cooked rice and scallions, mix well, and keep stirring for 4 minutes.

Add heavy soy sauce and pepper. Mix well. Serves 6.

Lemon Rice   INDIA

¼-*pound stick of butter or*
   4 tablespoons ghee
1 teaspoon salt
1 teaspoon black mustard seed
   (but yellow will do)

2 teaspoons turmeric
3 cups cooked rice
   juice of 1 lemon, strained

Melt the butter or ghee. Add the seasonings to it, and stir well until the seasonings blend and the mustard seeds dance. Then add the rice. Stir well until all heats through, then add the lemon juice. Serves 4.

Rice Patties   POLAND

2 cups rice, cooked in milk
2 tablespoons dried mush-
   rooms
1 tablespoon butter
2 whole eggs, lightly beaten

salt and pepper to taste
1 tablespoon chopped fresh dill
   (or dill and parsley)
— *bread crumbs*
butter for frying

Cook rice. Soak and cook mushrooms. Drain, reserving liquid, and chop. While rice is cooling, cream butter and eggs. Combine with mushrooms. Season, add dill, and mix with rice. Shape into patties, roll in bread crumbs, and fry in butter to a golden brown. Serve with a mushroom sauce made with the mushroom liquid, 2 teaspoons butter browned with 1 tablespoon flour, and 2 to 3 tablespoons sour cream. Blend these well, let bubble up once, and pour over the rice patties. Serves 6.

Pulao   INDIA

2 to 3 tablespoons ghee
1 cup raw rice

2 cups water
1 teaspoon salt

Heat the ghee in a pot, and add the rice to it. Stir constantly until the rice is pale gold, taking care not to scorch. Then add the water and salt.

Bring to a boil, stir once, lower the heat, and simmer, covered, for about 15 minutes. The water will be absorbed and the rice will be flaky and tender. Serves 4.

Baked Rice Pudding   FINLAND

1 cup uncooked rice
3 cups milk
¼ cup melted butter
½ cup sugar
3 eggs, beaten
½ teaspoon salt

½ cup sliced unblanched
  almonds
1 teaspoon cinnamon
1 whole blanched almond
  light cream

Cook the rice according to the directions on the package. Drain and rinse with cold water.

Combine the milk, melted butter, sugar, eggs, and salt. Stir in the rice and pour into a well-buttered 2-quart casserole. Combine the sliced almonds and cinnamon and sprinkle over the pudding. Bake in a moderate oven (350°) for about 1 hour or until the pudding has thickened sufficiently. Press the whole almond into the pudding and cover the mark left. Serve either hot or chilled with the light cream to pour over it. Serves 6 to 8.

Spanish Rice   JEWISH

1½ cups cooked rice
1 onion, diced
3 tablespoons shortening
1 cup finely cut green pepper

½ cup finely cut celery
½ cup tomato sauce or 1 cup
  canned or fresh tomato

Fry or sauté onion in shortening, stirring several times till light brown. Add other ingredients. Add to cooked rice with tomato sauce, canned or fresh tomato. Cook over low heat 5 minutes. Serves 4 or 5.

Steamed Rice   AUSTRIA

1 cup rice
2 tablespoons butter or oil
½ teaspoon salt

2 cups water
¼ onion

Wipe rice. (Do not wash.) Fry in fat until glazed. Add salt, water, and onion. Simmer, covered, 30 minutes. Remove onion before serving. Serves 4.

Semolina Porridge   S C A N D I N A V I A

1¾ pints milk (4½ cups)
3½ ounces semolina (½ cup + 2 teaspoons)
  salt
  sugar
2 to 3 bitter almonds, grated (optional)

Bring the milk to a boil and whisk in the semolina. Cook the semolina gently for 4 to 8 minutes according to the type of grain. Stir from time to time. Flavor with salt and sugar and bitter almonds, if desired.

Serve with milk, sugar, and cinnamon. The porridge may also be accompanied by jam or fruit purée. Serves 4.

Boiled Soybeans   J E W I S H

½ cup soybeans per serving   *cold water to cover*
⅛ teaspoon salt   *onion (optional)*

Cook till tender and serve whole, with or without liquid, with butter or grated cheese added while hot.

Variation 1: Mash or put through potato ricer and add butter or other shortening.

Variation 2: Drain cooked soybeans and add ¼ cup tomato sauce, Creole sauce, fried onion rings. Slip under broiler flame to brown lightly.

Soybean Loaf   J E W I S H

2 cups cooked, mashed   *½ cup evaporated milk*
  soybeans combined with   *or cream*
  liquid   *1 onion, diced and fried*
1 cup fine crumbs   *minced parsley*
1 egg   *salt and white pepper to taste*

Combine. Turn into greased loaf pan and bake at 350° till nicely browned. Serves 4 or 5.

Relishes and Pickles

Pickled Beets

JEWISH

3 pounds beets
1 pint vinegar
½ cup sugar

1 tablespoon stick cinnamon
1 teaspoon whole allspice
6 whole cloves

Cook beets in water until tender. Slip off skins. Dice or slice. Bring to boil the vinegar, sugar, spice mixture in a bag. Add beets. Boil 5 minutes. Remove spice bag. Fill jars. Seal, store. Yields 2 pints.

Horseradish Relish

ISRAEL

½ cup grated fresh
   horseradish
½ cup citrus vinegar
1 teaspoon salt

2 cups grated boiled beets
2 tablespoons sugar
   pinch of pepper

Grate the horseradish root out-of-doors or it will draw more tears than a bushel of onions. Mix all the ingredients together.

Pickled Onions

JEWISH

4 quarts small white onions
3 pints boiling water
1 cup salt
3 tablespoons whole all-
   spice
3 tablespoons whole white
   mustard seed

¼ cup grated horseradish
1 quart white vinegar
3 tablespoons peppercorns
¼ cup sugar

Peel onions. Pour boiling water and salt over onions and let stand 24 hours. Drain, cover again with boiling water for 5 to 10 minutes. Drain and pack jars. Boil vinegar, water, sugar, and spices for 3 minutes. Remove allspice and peppercorns. Add a bit of red pepper to each jar. Fill jar with liquid. Seal, store.

Peppers in Vinegar   RUMANIA

50 round red peppers
2 cups oil
¾ cup sugar
3 quarts wine vinegar

another ½ cup oil per jar
vinegar solution to pour over:
1 part vinegar to 3 parts
water

Wash peppers; dry and prick several times with a needle. Fry in oil for 3 minutes, turning frequently. Drain. Cook in mixture of sugar and 2 quarts vinegar for about 10 minutes. Drain peppers and place in wide jars pressing them together. Dilute remaining vinegar with an equal amount of water and pour over peppers to cover them. Pour ½ cup of oil into each jar. Seal jars well. Store in a cool place.

If you do not wish peppers to be so strong, you can cut them in 3 or 4 pieces and remove seeds before frying. Then proceed as above.

Vegetable Purée with
Whole Small Peppers   BULGARIA

20 pounds tomatoes
1 pound small hot peppers
1 cup oil
⅓ cup sugar

salt to taste
dry dill to taste
oil to pour over

Cut tomatoes into small pieces or chop. Put through a strainer and cook to reduce juice a little. Remove stalks from whole peppers and prick several times with a needle. Add to tomatoes. Add oil, sugar, salt, and dill and cook until tomato juice is thick and peppers are very soft. Fill into small, dry glasses and pour oil onto each about 1 inch above contents.

Dill Pickles

50 medium cucumbers
(approximately 3 ½ inches
long)
3 quarts pickling solution
For each jar:
2 or 3 bay leaves
¼ teaspoon celery or mustard
seeds

½ teaspoon whole mixed spice
1 tablespoon vinegar
2 cloves garlic
bunch of dry dill
2 grape leaves

Wash and drain cucumbers and pack into quart jars. To each jar add bay leaves, mustard seeds, mixed whole spice, vinegar, and garlic in the quantities listed. Bring pickling solution to a boil and fill packed jars. Top each jar with small bunch of dried dill and grape leaves. Adjust covers and seal at once. Can be used after 8 or 10 days.

Yields approximately 6 to 7 quarts.

Easy Method Pickles

For each jar:
cucumbers (3 to 3 ½ inches
in size)
1 tablespoon coarse salt
1 teaspoon brown sugar

1 tablespoon vinegar
3 cloves garlic
3 bay leaves
dry dill

Pack cucumbers into quart jars. Add spices to each jar in the amounts listed. Pour into each jar as much boiled water, slightly cooled, as is required to fill to the top. Adjust rubber rings and covers but do not seal. Keep jars at room temperature until fermentation stops and the liquid in jars becomes cloudy. Tighten covers and store in a cool place. Fermentation period is hastened if jars are placed in the sun. Pickles are ready to eat within 10 days.

Variation: For a spicy pickle, add 1 small red hot pepper to each jar and ¼ teaspoon whole mixed spice at top before adding water.

Cucumber Raita   I N D I A

1 pint yogurt
1 cucumber
1 teaspoon salt

1 teaspoon cumin seed (or
   1 teaspoon powdered cumin)

Place the yogurt in a mixing bowl, and whip lightly. Peel
and chop the cucumber, very, very fine. Add to the yogurt
along with the salt and cumin seed. The cumin seed should
not be added right from the spice bottle, or it will taste like
bits of straw. To release the taste, put in a very small, ungreased
pan and roast gently, tossing and turning until the cumin
browns. Then crush slightly, and add to the recipe. Or substitute
1 teaspoon of powdered cumin. It will make for a slight difference
in flavor—nothing serious. The roasted cumin is superior.

Tomato Relish   J E W I S H

12 firm green tomatoes
 4 sweet red peppers
 2 green peppers
 2 cups cider vinegar

1½ cups brown sugar
1 tablespoon salt
½ cup prepared mustard

Dice tomatoes. Remove seeds and stems from peppers, cut
or chop. Bring vinegar and sugar to a boil, add salt and mustard,
and pour over the vegetable mixture. Bring to a quick boil, turn
down heat and simmer 20 to 30 minutes. Stir occasionally. Turn
into hot sterilized jars and seal. Yields 4 pints.

Carrot and Green Pepper Relish   J E W I S H

½ cup vinegar
2 tablespoons brown sugar
1 tablespoon onion juice
   dash of salt

1 cup shredded raw carrot
½ cup chopped green pepper
3 tablespoons salad oil

Bring vinegar and sugar to a quick boil. Add onion juice and
salt. Add to chopped pepper and carrot. Mix well and stir in
salad oil as soon as cold. Chill before serving.

Celery Relish

4 sweet red peppers
4 sweet green peppers
2 quarts chopped celery
2 cups chopped white
   onions
2 cups shredded cabbage

1 tablespoon salt
3 cups vinegar
2 cups sugar
1 tablespoon mustard seed
3 cloves garlic

Remove seeds and stems from peppers. Chop or cut fine. Bring all the vegetables to a boil in enough water to cover. Add all seasonings, vinegar, and sugar. Cook slowly 20 minutes or until celery is tender. Remove garlic and turn into hot sterilized jars. Seal while hot.

Yields approximately 3 pints.

Note: If a toothpick is used to spear garlic cloves, it will be easy to identify and remove.

Cucumber Relish

12 large cucumbers
 6 green peppers
 3 large onions
½ cup salt
1 cup horseradish

1 cup sugar
1 tablespoon mustard seed
1 teaspoon celery seed
   vinegar

Peel and remove the seeds from the cucumbers. Put the cucumbers, green peppers, and sliced onions through coarse food chopper or chop in a large wooden bowl. Add the salt, mix well, and let stand overnight. In the morning, drain, add the horseradish, sugar, mustard, and celery seeds and enough vinegar to cover. Mix thoroughly and pack in sterilized pint jars. Seal at once. Makes a mild relish.

Yields 4 to 5 pints.

Coconut Chutney INDIA

1 cup fresh coconut,
   chopped in chunks
2 green chili peppers, chopped
2 tablespoons fresh ginger
   root, chopped

1 teaspoon salt
1 teaspoon sugar
   juice of 1 lemon

Blend together the coconut, chili peppers, ginger root, and just enough water to blend the coconut. Add the salt, sugar, and lemon juice.

This one is a creamy white. It may seem thin. Pour into a jar; within a matter of 15 minutes or so, the coconut milk settles at the bottom. If you prefer the thinner texture, just shake it up before serving. If you like it thick, spoon the coconut chutney from the top and throw away the water.

Ginger Chutney INDIA

This makes a very small amount—about ½ cup. You will find many special uses for this exotic chutney, just as for the famous English hot mustard.

1 cup green ginger root,
   chopped
2 green chili peppers,
   chopped

1 teaspoon salt
3 teaspoons sugar
   juice of 1 lemon

Blend until smooth the ginger root, chili peppers, salt, sugar, and lemon juice. This one is blended all in one swoop.

Sesame Seed Chutney INDIA

1 cup sesame seed
¼ cup water
2 chili peppers, chopped
2 tablespoons fresh ginger
   root, chopped

1 teaspoon salt
   juice of 1 lemon
1 tablespoon sugar

Blend the sesame seed, water, chili peppers, and ginger root together. When blended, add the salt, lemon juice, and sugar.

Salads

Autumn Salad

FINLAND

½ head fresh cauliflower,
  chopped
¼ pound fresh mushrooms,
  chopped
2 medium carrots, peeled and
  shredded

1 small onion, minced
½ teaspoon salt
½ teaspoon sugar
  French dressing

In a bowl, toss together the raw cauliflower, mushrooms, carrots, onion, salt, and sugar until mixed. Chill. Serve on lettuce, adding French dressing to taste. Serves 4 to 6.

Beet Salad

YUGOSLAVIA

2 pounds young beets
2 tablespoons vinegar
2 tablespoons water
  salt to taste

1 teaspoon caraway seeds
2 teaspoons grated horse-
  radish

Boil beets until tender (30 to 60 minutes, depending on size). Peel and slice fine. Dilute vinegar with water and pour over still-warm beets. Season with salt and caraway seeds and stir in grated horseradish. Let stand for 3 to 4 hours. If you prefer a milder flavor, add a little sugar and grate an apple with the horseradish. Serves 4 to 6.

Molded Beet Salad

2 cups beet juice
2 packages lemon gelatin
1½ cups water
1 cup shredded or grated
  cooked beets

½ pound cream cheese
1 cup whipping cream or
  evaporated milk (chilled)

Heat beet juice. Dissolve gelatin in boiling water and add beet juice and grated beets. Whip chilled evaporated milk with a rotary beater. Add cheese and beat a few minutes together. Combine. Chill in cup molds. When set, unmold on lettuce or other salad greens. Serves 6 to 8.

Green-Bean Salad

3 pounds (approximately)
  green beans
½ cup parsley

1 tablespoon chopped garlic
1 cup oil
½ cup vinegar

Clean the green beans and wash them well. Drop into rapidly boiling water. Cover and cook over a high heat for about 20 to 30 minutes (or until tender). Remove from the heat; drain. Place in a bowl with the remaining ingredients; mix together and serve. Serves 6 to 10.

Greek Haricot Beans

1 cup dried beans
½ cup olive oil
  salt and pepper
1 cup bean liquid
2 tablespoons tomato purée

1 bay leaf
1 clove garlic
1 lemon
1 onion, finely chopped

Soak the beans overnight. Cover with fresh water and cook until almost tender (1 to 2 hours), then drain, reserving the liquid. Heat the oil and add the beans, pepper, and salt. Brown well. Add about 1 cup of the liquid from the original cooking, the tomato purée, bay leaf, and garlic and simmer until the beans are soft and the sauce thick. Add the lemon juice and finely chopped onion. Cool and serve as a salad course. It is also good hot. Serves 3 to 4.

Haricot Beans and Lentil Salads FRANCE

Thoroughly drain the vegetable, whatever its kind; season with oil and vinegar, and add some chopped parsley. Serve separately some thinly sliced, washed, and pressed onion.

Bean Salad ISRAEL

2 pounds cowpea beans
  salted water to cover
4 cloves garlic, crushed
1 red chili pepper, finely
  chopped

6 tablespoons olive oil
  juice of 1 or 2 lemons
  chopped parsley

Soak the beans overnight. Drain, cover with salted water, and cook until the skins burst and swim to the top (2 to 3 hours). Remove the skins and drain. Cool. Add the crushed garlic and finely chopped chili pepper and dress with olive oil, lemon juice, and chopped parsley. Serve cold. Serves 4 to 6.

Cabbage and Apple Salad SCANDINAVIA

8 ounces white, savoy or celery cabbage, shredded (⅔ cup)
2 apples, sliced
  juice of 1 orange (and ½ lemon)
1 gill thick cream, whipped (½ cup plus 2 tablespoons)

Mix the cabbage, apple and fruit juice. Fold in the cream carefully. Serves 4.

Cabbage-Carrot-Tomato Salad   GREECE

½ to 1 cabbage
3 to 6 tomatoes
3 to 5 large, tender carrots,
  shredded
⅓ to ½ cup oil

¼ cup (or less) vinegar or
  lemon juice
salt to taste
Calamata or black olives
parsley

Shred the cabbage. Place in a strainer and wash under running water for several minutes; drain well. Wash the tomatoes and cut into wedges. Wash and scrape the carrots. Place the carrots in the center of a platter; surround them with a ring of cabbage and then with a ring of tomatoes, or put the tomatoes in the center and lay the carrots around them. Sprinkle with salt. Before serving, add a dressing of oil and vinegar or oil and lemon. Garnish with Calamata olives and parsley. Serves 6.

Cold Cabbage Salad   AUSTRIA

1 head cabbage (2 pounds)
½ teaspoon salt
½ teaspoon caraway seeds

1½ tablespoons oil
3 tablespoons vinegar

Wash and shred cabbage. Pour boiling water over; drain. Mix salt, caraway seeds, oil, and vinegar, and pour over cabbage. Let stand 1 to 2 hours before serving. Serves 5.

Red Cabbage Salad   POLAND

1 medium head red cabbage,
  shredded
salted, boiling water
juice of 1 lemon

salt and pepper to taste
sugar to taste
olive oil

Throw shredded cabbage into boiling water. As soon as the water boils again, drain and allow cabbage to dry off. Sprinkle with lemon juice to restore bright red color. Chill. An hour before serving, season with salt and pepper. Add sugar to taste and several tablespoons of olive oil, depending on one's preference. Serves 6.

Red Cabbage and Pineapple Salad JEWISH

1 small head red cabbage
1 tablespoon lemon juice
¼ teaspoon salt
8 slices canned pineapple

2 tablespoons chopped nuts
½ cup sour cream
    lettuce or salad greens

Shred cabbage, add lemon juice and salt and let stand about ½ hour before serving. Place a generous spoonful of cabbage on top of each slice of drained pineapple. Top with sour cream mixed with pineapple syrup. Garnish with salad greens and chopped nuts. Serves 8.

Carrot and Cabbage Slaw JEWISH

1 large carrot
1 pound cabbage
¼ teaspoon salt
2 tablespoons lemon juice or
    vinegar

4 tablespoons evaporated milk
    or cream

Shred carrot and cabbage into a large bowl. Add salt, lemon juice, or vinegar and evaporated milk or light cream. Stir lightly with 2 forks and serve. Serves 4.

Cole Slaw and Carrot Salad JEWISH

2 cups finely shredded cabbage
1 large carrot, scraped and
    shredded
1 small green pepper, diced or
    chopped

¼ teaspoon salt
½ cup salad dressing

Combine. Serve on escarole. Serves 4 to 6.

Carrot Salad with Apples CZECHOSLOVAKIA

2 cups shredded carrots
2 cups shredded apples
¼ cup sugar

juice and peel (grated)
of 2 lemons
salt to taste

Toss all ingredients together and serve immediately. Oranges may be substituted for lemons. Serves about 4.

Cauliflower Salad ISRAEL

1 medium head cauliflower
3 cups water
2 teaspoons salt
Dressing:
2 tablespoons olive oil

1 cup wine vinegar
salt and white pepper
1 teaspoon mustard
dash of sugar

Separate the flowerets of the cauliflower and cook rapidly in salted water about 8 minutes. Drain well.

Make the dressing by shaking together all the ingredients. Pour this over the cauliflower and chill thoroughly. Serves 4 to 5.

Celery Root Salad JEWISH

Select firm celery roots. Scrub clean and pare. Cut into strips or dice. Add mayonnaise or French dressing. Serve on lettuce and garnish with parsley.

Variation 1: Add sour cream to salad dressing.

Variation 2: Add shredded blanched almonds or pecans for added calories.

Variation 3: Boil celery root first. Dice or cut fine and add mayonnaise.

Raw Celery Root Salad CZECHOSLOVAKIA

1 large (1 pound) celery
  root
½ small onion, chopped

¼ cup mayonnaise
1 tablespoon lemon juice

Clean, peel, and grate celery root. Add onion, and toss with mayonnaise and lemon juice. This may also be used as a sandwich spread. Serves 2.

Chick Peas and Fava Bean Salad   ISRAEL

1 cup chick peas   1 teaspoon salt
1 cup broad (fava) beans   pepper to taste
  water, as needed   French dressing

Soak the chick peas and beans separately, overnight. Cook each separately in water to cover 2 to 3 hours. When the peas and beans are tender, drain. Mix them together and add salt and pepper. Pour the dressing over while the legumes are still hot. Cool. Serves 6 to 8.

Chicory Salad   AUSTRIA

3 heads chicory   ¼ cup vinegar
¼ cup oil   ¼ teaspoon salt, or to taste

Clean and wash chicory; slice or cut into pieces. Mix oil, vinegar, and salt; pour over salad and toss well. Serves 6.

Chicory [Belgian endive]
with Gorgonzola Cream   SCANDINAVIA

1 head of chicory, washed and trimmed
2 hard-boiled egg yolks, cold
1¾ ounce gorgonzola, sieved or grated (10½ teaspoons)
1¾ ounce butter or margarine (10½ teaspoons)

Sieve the egg yolks. Add the cheese and fat. Beat the mixture until creamy. Separate the chicory. Fill the leaves with the cream, just before serving. Garnish with grapes and rings of sweet red or green pepper. Serves 4.

Cucumber Salad   AUSTRIA

5 cucumbers   ½ cup vinegar
  dash salt   dash pepper, paprika
½ cup oil

Plain: Peel cucumbers; slice very thin; salt. Cover; let stand 30 minutes. Drain. Mix oil with vinegar; sprinkle with pepper and paprika. Pour over cucumbers. Serves 5 to 6.

Note: For extra flavor, sprinkle with chopped chives or grated garlic.

With Potatoes: Prepare salad as above. Mix with 1½ pounds potatoes, cooked and sliced thin.

With Sour Cream: Prepare salad as above, eliminating oil and vinegar dressing. Mix with 1 cup sour cream. Add 1 to 2 tablespoons vinegar, if desired.

Cucumber in Lime Gelatin   JEWISH

1 package lime gelatin
1 cup boiling water
1 large cucumber
1 cup grated raw carrot
1 cup finely chopped cabbage
1 cup chopped apple

¼ cup chopped nuts or
  peanuts
½ cup canned shredded pineapple
salt to taste
shredded salad greens

Dissolve gelatin in boiling water. Grate unpared cucumber, combine with carrot, cabbage, apple, nuts, drained pineapple, and salt to taste. Combine with gelatin. Turn into a ring mold rinsed in cold water. Chill till firm. Unmold and serve on shredded salad greens marinated with dressing. This salad may be turned into individual molds. Serves 8.

Carlton Salad   SCANDINAVIA

1 apple, diced
1 orange or ½ grapefruit, diced
4 ounces white cabbage, shredded (⅓ cup)
4 ounces green grapes, cut in two and the seeds removed (⅔ cup)
  lettuce
  orange sections
7 tablespoonfuls mayonnaise (scant ½ cup)
7 tablespoonfuls thick cream, whipped (scant ½ cup)

Mix the ingredients and stir carefully into the mayonnaise blended with cream.

Garnish with lettuce and orange. Serves 4.

Congress Salad

2½ tablespoons mustard
⅓ cup oil
1 teaspoon sugar
⅓ cup vinegar
1 pound potatoes, cooked,
  peeled, and diced

1 pound carrots, cooked,
  peeled, and diced
¾ pound pickles, peeled and
  diced

Blend mustard, oil, sugar, and vinegar together. Beat with fork. Add cooled potatoes, carrots, and pickles. Let stand ½ hour before serving. Serves 5.

Note: Same ingredients, chopped, may be used as filling for green peppers, tomatoes, and cucumbers.

Country Salad

10 to 12 small plum tomatoes
2 to 3 cucumbers
2 small onions
1 green pepper

½ pound feta cheese
  (more or less to taste)
salt and pepper to taste
olives

Clean and cut the tomatoes into bite-sized pieces. Cut the cucumbers. Mince the onions and peppers. Cut up the feta cheese. Place all these in a bowl, add olives. Season. Toss well. Serve with oil-and-vinegar dressing. Serves 6 to 8.

Danish Salad

½ pound green peas
¼ pound macaroni

1 cup mayonnaise
1 tablespoon parsley, chopped

Cook peas and macaroni separately in boiling water until tender. Drain and cool. Cut macaroni in inch-long pieces and add peas. Mix well with mayonnaise. Sprinkle with chopped parsley. Serves 4.

Diplomat Salad

2 to 3 tomatoes, peeled and
    diced
2 to 3 slices fresh or canned
    pineapple, cut in pieces
1 large or 2 small bananas,
    sliced
2 truffles, cut in thin strips
1 cup mayonnaise (preferably
    homemade)

¼ cup Rhine wine
1 large or 2 small apples,
    cored, pared, and diced
3 medium potatoes, cooked
    in jackets, peeled, and
    sliced thin
Worcestershire sauce to taste
    (1 teaspoon or less)
    dash of cayenne pepper

Combine fruits, potatoes, and truffles. Dilute mayonnaise with wine (add according to taste), season with Worcestershire sauce and cayenne pepper, and add to mixture. Toss lightly and refrigerate for 3 to 4 hours. Serves 6.

Eggplant Salad

2 to 3 large eggplants
1 onion, finely grated
    salt and pepper to taste

lemon juice or vinegar to taste
1 (or more) cups olive oil, as needed

Wash the eggplants and put into a pan (or wrap in aluminum foil) and bake until soft. Put the onions into cold water to soak and remove some of the strength. Remove the skins from the cooked eggplant and mash the pulp thoroughly. Drain the onion well and add to the eggplant. Add salt and pepper, and beat. Add lemon or vinegar alternately with the oil, and beating all the while, until you have a thick mixture. Serve in a bowl or as a side dish.

Charred Eggplant Salad

*1 large eggplant
  (about 1 pound)
1 clove garlic, crushed, or
  1 green onion, chopped
1 tablespoon lemon juice
4 tablespoons olive oil*

*salt and pepper to taste
red pimiento, chopped
  (optional)
mayonnaise or tahina
  (optional)*

Put the unpeeled eggplant on the open flame and turn it when the skin begins to char. When all the skin has been blackened and the eggplant is soft, put it on a board, make an incision, and let the excess juice drain off. Wash the eggplant under the tap to remove the charred skin. If you are a great gourmet you will now open the eggplant and remove the seed sections also. Add garlic (if you do not intend to use onion) and lemon juice during the chopping, until the mixture is pure white. Some people add the olive oil during the chopping, but the ceremony calls for adding it at the table, along with chopped onions and salt and pepper to taste. Non-Romanian Israelis serve this course in green pepper boats, garnished with red chopped pimiento, on a lettuce leaf and with or without mayonnaise or tahina stirred in. Serves 4 to 6.

Farmers' Chop Suey

*1 cucumber
2 tomatoes
1 green pepper
4 stalks celery and leaves*

*2 spring onions
sprig of parsley
2 cups shredded lettuce
sour cream*

Score unpared cucumber and slice very thin. Dice tomatoes. Cut pepper, celery, and onions fine. Add parsley and shredded lettuce. Combine all in a salad bowl, add a dash of salt and pepper. Serve with plenty of sour cream. Serves 4.

Variation: Add diced boiled potatoes.

Finocchio Salad Rings   I S R A E L

1 large finocchio (fennel)
  dash of celery salt
½ pound Bel Paese cheese
1 medium tomato, diced

4 black olives, sliced
lettuce
olive oil

Separate the thickened stalks at the base of the finocchio. Sprinkle with celery salt. Put slices of the soft Bel Paese cheese on each stem, and press in pieces of tomato and black olive. Fit 3 stalks together to make a roll. Chill and then cut into ½-inch rings. Serve on lettuce with a little olive oil. Serves 8.

Cooked-Greens Salad   G R E E C E

2 bunches dandelion greens
  or chicory or endive
  or escarole

oil
lemon
coarse salt

Bring to a boil ample water with some coarse salt in a large pot. Wash the greens and pick them over; toss into the rapidly boiling water and boil in a covered pot over a very high heat (this retains the green color) until tender. Do not overcook. Boil for 20 to 30 minutes. Drain, and serve hot in individual vegetable dishes. Add oil and lemon to taste.

Mixed Green Salad   S C A N D I N A V I A

½ to 1 head of lettuce, whole leaves or shredded
1 piece fresh cucumber, sliced
2 tomatoes, quartered
  or 1 bunch radishes, whole or sliced
  or ½ to 1 sweet pepper, in strips
  full quantity vinaigrette, lemon dressing or another dressing

Arrange all the ingredients in a large bowl or distribute between four individual bowls. Toss the salad in the dressing immediately before serving or serve the dressing separately. Serves 4.

255

Tossed Green Salad

1 clove garlic
1 teaspoon prepared mustard
½ teaspoon salt
  dash of pepper
  dash of paprika
⅓ cup olive oil
  juice of 1 lemon
2 hard-cooked eggs,
  chopped

1 large head lettuce
1 bunch parsley, chopped
1 bunch chives, chopped
1 red pimiento, chopped
  or sliced
1 green pepper, chopped
2 red radishes, sliced
1 small carrot, finely sliced

Rub a wooden bowl with the garlic. Add the mustard, salt, pepper, paprika, olive oil, lemon juice, and eggs and mix well. Put plastic or wooden servers in the bowl to keep the dressing from touching the salad. On top of the servers, arrange whole or torn leaves in the shape of a lettuce head. Garnish each layer of lettuce with the parsley, chives, pimiento, green pepper, radishes, and carrot. Mix the salad at the table to ensure its crispness. Serves 6 to 8.

Cottage Cheese in Green Peppers

Cut nicely shaped green peppers lengthwise through the center. Do not remove stem, but do remove seeds and fibers. Fill pepper halves with cottage cheese seasoned with salt, pepper, minced parsley or chives and as much sour cream or beaten egg white as needed to make a fluffy mixture. Allow ½ cup cheese for two pepper halves of medium size. Sprinkle with chopped nuts or decorate with mint leaves or parsley.

Gypsy Salad

¼ cup olive oil
1 tablespoon wine vinegar
½ teaspoon prepared mustard
2 anchovy filets, chopped
½ heart escarole, shredded fine

½ heart endive, shredded fine
1 heart fennel, cut into small
  pieces
2 radishes, sliced

Mix well oil, vinegar, mustard, and chopped anchovies. Pour over mixed greens in salad bowl. Mix well. Serves 2.

Kohlrabi Salad   CZECHOSLOVAKIA

8 small young kohlrabi,
  peeled and grated
Dressing
½ cup water
2 tablespoons vinegar

1 tablespoon oil
  salt to taste
½ teaspoon sugar
  OR
⅔ cup mayonnaise

Toss together all ingredients. Serves 4.

Lemon-Leaf-Lettuce Salad   FINLAND

1 quart salad greens
2 tablespoons lemon juice
1½ teaspoons sugar
¼ to ½ teaspoon salt

dash freshly ground pepper
2 tablespoons heavy cream
  (optional)

Wash, dry, and crisp the greens. Tear into bite-sized pieces
and put in a salad bowl. Sprinkle with the lemon juice and
toss well, then sprinkle with the sugar, salt, and pepper, and
toss again until well mixed. Add the cream if you wish, and
toss until evenly blended. Serves 3 to 4.

Lettuce with Sour Cream   CZECHOSLOVAKIA

2 to 3 heads Boston
  lettuce
1 cup sour cream

¼ teaspoon salt
½ teaspoon sugar
2 tablespoons vinegar

Wash lettuce and break up into a bowl. Mix the remaining
ingredients and pour over lettuce. Toss. Serves 4 to 6.

Lakme Salad   FRANCE

Take equal quantities of red peppers and tomato sauce; plain-
boiled rice, kept very white, and with each grain distinct; and
chopped, washed, and pressed onion.

Season with oil and vinegar, and flavor with curry powder.

Mimosa Salad

2 apples, diced
1 slice pineapple, in pieces
4 ounces celeriac, coarsely grated (8 fluid ounces) (1 cup)
2 hard-boiled egg yolks
   green salad
7 tablespoonfuls mayonnaise (scant ½ cup)
7 tablespoonfuls thick cream, whipped

Mix the ingredients and stir carefully into the mayonnaise blended with cream. Sieve the egg yolks over the salad and garnish with green salad. Serves 4.

Fresh Mushroom Salad

1 pound small mushrooms,
   well shaped
2 quarts salad greens
   (approximately)
2 tablespoons grated fresh
   onion

1 teaspoon sugar
2 tablespoons cream
   dash white pepper
   salt

Parboil the mushrooms for 2 minutes in enough salted water to cover. Drain and dry thoroughly. Slice very thin and arrange in a salad bowl over the washed and crisped greens. Combine the onion, sugar, cream, and white pepper, and sprinkle over the salad. Toss. Add salt to taste, if needed, toss again, and serve at once. Serves 4 to 6.

Niçoise Salad

Take equal quantities of string beans, potato dice, and quartered tomatoes. Decorate with capers, small, pitted olives. Season with oil and vinegar.

Orange-Carrot Salad I S R A E L

1 pound firm, fresh carrots
  juice of 3 oranges
  juice of ½ lemon

dash of ginger (optional)
salt and sugar to taste

Peel the carrots and grate coarsely. Cover with the orange and lemon juice, adding sugar and salt to taste. Add a dash of ginger if desired. Refrigerate for several hours (this salad improves with keeping up to three days) so that the carrots absorb the juices. Serve on crisp lettuce leaves or in lemon baskets garnished with a sprig of mint. Serves 4 to 6.

Orange-Onion-Olive Salad I S R A E L

4 oranges, skinned and
  thinly sliced
4 sweet onions, thinly sliced

black olives
olive oil
lemon juice

On top of each orange slice, put a slice of sweet onion. Garnish with black olives and drizzle with olive oil and lemon juice. Serves 4 to 6.

Onion Salad

1 cup water
½ cup vinegar
1 pound onions, sliced
Dressing
2 tablespoons oil

1 to 2 tablespoons vinegar
  salt to taste
¼ teaspoon sugar

Bring water and vinegar to a boil. Add onions, bring again to full boil. Drain. Mix dressing, pour over onions. Chill. Serves 3 to 4.

Parsnip Salad

1⅓ cups water
⅔ cup vinegar
2 peppercorns
2 allspice
2 cloves
1 bay leaf

salt to taste
1 pound parsnips, pared
  and sliced
  boiling water to cover
1 to 2 tablespoons oil
1 large onion, chopped

Bring water with vinegar, spice, and salt to a boil. In another pot, pour fresh boiling water over parsnips; simmer for 2 minutes. Drain parsnips, place in boiling vinegar water, cover, and simmer for about 30 minutes. Remove spice, add oil. Chill. Before serving, sprinkle onion over top. Serves 4 to 6.

Baked Pepper Salad

1 pound long green or red
  peppers
3 tablespoons oil
3 tablespoons vinegar

1 onion, chopped
2 cloves garlic, chopped
1 tablespoon chopped parsley
  salt to taste

Wash peppers and dry. Roast on electric plate or in pan without fat, until outer skin becomes blackish. Place peppers whole or in pieces in a marinade of oil, vinegar, onion, garlic, parsley, and salt. Let stand for 1 hour. Serves 4 to 6.

Peppers Stuffed with Eggplant Salad

1 pound long green peppers
2 eggplants
3 to 4 cloves garlic, mashed
1 tablespoon vinegar

3 tablespoons oil
salt to taste
3 to 4 tomatoes, quartered
chopped parsley

Cook peppers in 375° oven about 10 minutes. Pour cold water over; remove seeds and skin. Chill.

Cook eggplant in 375° oven ¾ hour or until soft when pierced with a fork. Scrape out insides and chop. Mix with garlic, vinegar, oil, and salt. Fill peppers with the mixture. When completely cold, place on a plate with tomato quarters between. Sprinkle each row with chopped parsley. Serves 4 to 6.

Potato, Apple, and Caper Salad

6 medium potatoes, cooked
   in salted water in jackets
2 medium apples
1 heaping tablespoon capers

¼ cup olive oil
¼ cup dry white wine
   lemon juice to taste
   salt and pepper

Peel potatoes and allow to cool. Core and peel apples. Slice potatoes and apples very thin, mix with capers, olive oil, wine, and lemon juice to taste. Season with salt and pepper. Refrigerate 1 hour. Serves 6 to 7.

Potato Salad

3 pounds potatoes
¾ cup oil
  salt and pepper to taste
⅓ cup vinegar or lemon juice
1 teaspoon grated onion

2 to 3 tablespoons chopped
  parsley
2 to 3 hard-cooked eggs, sliced
olives
parsley sprigs

Wash and scrub the potatoes, then boil until tender; cool, and slip off the skins. Slice or cut into pieces; place in a salad bowl. Beat together the oil, vinegar (or lemon juice), salt, pepper, and onion until well blended; mix in the parsley. Pour the dressing over the potatoes and toss lightly. Garnish with egg slices placed alternately on the salad with olives and parsley sprigs. Serves 6 to 8.

Potato Salad

6 to 8 boiled potatoes, diced
2 hard-boiled eggs, sliced
1 yellow onion, chopped
  or 1 leek, sliced
1 to 2 sticks celery, sliced
  (optional)

7 fluid ounces mayonnaise (⅞ cup)
or
3½ fluid ounces mayonnaise
  (scant ½ cup)
3½ fluid ounces sour cream
  (scant ½ cup)

Toss the ingredients in the dressing.
Chill before serving.
The salad may be garnished with green salad and chopped parsley. Serves 4.

Potato Salad

2 pounds potatoes boiled in
  their skins and peeled
1 large dill pickle
2 tablespoons chopped onion
1 large sour apple

3 tablespoons vinegar
½ cup mayonnaise (more
  if desired)
salt and pepper

Dice all the ingredients, dilute the mayonnaise with the vinegar, stir into the salad, add salt and pepper. Serves 4 to 6.

Potato Salad   POLAND

6 medium potatoes   ¼ cup olive oil
  salt and pepper to taste   3 tablespoons vinegar
½ medium onion, minced, or
  equivalent amount chopped
  chives

Potatoes for salad should be cooked in their jackets, peeled, and allowed to cool. Avoid Idahos and other mealy potatoes—new potatoes are excellent. Slice thin, season, add minced onion or chives and olive oil and vinegar. Mix and refrigerate for 1 hour. Serves 6.

Radish Salad   CZECHOSLOVAKIA

1 pound radishes   ½ teaspoon sugar
  juice of 1 lemon   salt to taste
1 tablespoon water   1 tablespoon oil

Grate radishes coarsely. Mix all other ingredients, and pour over radishes. Toss well. Chill before serving. Serves 6 to 8.

Radish Salad   GERMANY

2 bunches red radishes   1 teaspoon chives, chopped
1 tablespoon olive oil   salt and pepper
2 tablespoons vinegar   ½ cup sour cream, optional

Wash radishes and slice or grate them. Sprinkle with salt and let stand for 5 minutes. Mix oil, vinegar, chives, and seasoning to form a marinade, pour over radishes and let stand. If desired, add sour cream immediately before serving. Serves 4.

Russian Salad

1 cup diced cooked potatoes	3 hard-cooked eggs, diced
2 dill pickles, diced	mayonnaise mixed with
1 cup cooked peas	sour cream, to taste
½ cup diced cooked beans	salt and freshly ground
1 cup diced cooked carrots	pepper

Toss the vegetables together with the mayonnaise and sour cream. Add salt and plenty of pepper. Serve instead of potato salad. Serves 6.

Salad

greens of every variety (Bibb lettuce, iceberg lettuce, escarole, endive, chicory, watercress, baby-spinach leaves)	carrots, diced fine
	celery, chopped
	tomatoes, chopped (or small whole cherry tomatoes)
cucumber, chopped	fresh green peas—a generous handful (please do not skimp)
radishes, sliced	
green pepper, diced	
sweet red pepper, diced	scallions (if you like raw onions)
chopped cabbage (preferably a combination of green, red, and Chinese cabbage)	

Put the greens into an enormous bowl. Pick and choose from among these, but do use as many as possible. These should constitute about half of your total mixture. Wash carefully and pull into bite-sized pieces. Add the remaining ingredients to the greens.

Toss all together very well and set aside until serving time. This will keep easily for a day or so if stored in a large plastic bag in the refrigerator.

Serve with:

Indian Dressing	4 tablespoons honey
juice of 4 lemons, strained	2 tablespoons sugar
4 teaspoons salt	1 teaspoon cayenne

Place all the ingredients in a jar. Shake all together well. The lemon juice will dissolve the honey, and the dressing will not be sweet, despite the way it sounds. Nor should this amount of cayenne be too much for any but the most tender taste—it is needed to awaken the raw vegetables. Set aside until the salad is ready to serve.

When you are ready to serve the salad, pour the dressing over all and toss and toss and toss until all the vegetables are coated.

This is enough dressing for the 20 cups of vegetables. For small, individual servings of salad, use only a spoon or two. The trick here is not to drown the salad but only to coat it properly and gently.

Serbian Salad   YUGOSLAVIA

1 pound tomatoes	3 tablespoons oil
4 green peppers	2 tablespoons vinegar
2 cucumbers	chopped parsley, salt,
1 large onion	pepper to taste

Cut tomatoes into round slices. Remove seeds from peppers; then cut into rings or strips. Cut cucumbers (peeled or unpeeled) into fine slices and onion into fine rings. Mix everything and dress with oil and vinegar. Sprinkle with parsley, salt, and pepper. Serves 4.

Spinach Salad   BULGARIA

1 cup young spinach leaves	2 to 3 tablespoons oil
3 to 4 shoots young onions,	2 hard-cooked eggs, chopped
chopped fine (or 1 cup	salt and pepper to taste
finely chopped chives)	olives to garnish (optional)
¼ cup yogurt	

Wash spinach thoroughly. Cut into fine strips. Mix with onion shoots (or chives). Mix yogurt and oil; add hard-cooked eggs; season and pour over spinach leaves. Garnish with olives, if desired. Serves 3 to 4.

Sauerkraut Salad GERMANY

½ pound prepared sauerkraut
3 tablespoons olive oil
2 apples, grated

1 onion, chopped
1 teaspoon sugar
salt and pepper

Drain sauerkraut. Make marinade of other ingredients and add. Let stand 15 minutes before serving. This salad goes particularly well with fish. Serves 4.

Sauerkraut GERMANY

2 pounds cabbage
3 tablespoons butter
1 onion, chopped
apple, sliced

salt and pepper
1 potato, raw
½ cup white wine

Pluck apart cabbage and wash well. Shred. Melt butter in a fairly large pot and turn cabbage in it thoroughly. Add onion, apple, and seasoning to taste. Fill pot with water. Cook until tender, about 10 minutes. Grate into this raw potato, to give a nice texture. Add wine before serving.

Variation: Instead of wine, paprika, sugar, and cream may be used to season. Or champagne may be substituted for white wine. Serves 4.

Sicilian Salad ITALY

4 hard ripe tomatoes
½ clove garlic, chopped
¼ cup olive oil
½ teaspoon salt

½ teaspoon pepper
½ teaspoon wine vinegar
1 tablespoon basil leaves

Wash tomatoes and cut into large pieces. Sprinkle with garlic, oil, salt, pepper, and vinegar and add basil leaves. Chill 5 minutes and serve. Serves 4.

Squash-Yogurt Salad ISRAEL

10 small summer squash
   water to cover
 1 tablespoon chopped fresh
   mint leaves

1 tablespoon chopped fresh
   dill
   salt and pepper
 2 cups leben (yogurt)

Cut the squash very thin. Just cover with water, bring to a boil, and remove from heat (squash should only be parboiled).

Drain. Chill thoroughly, sprinkle with herbs and seasoning, pour the yogurt over, and serve very cold. Serves 6 to 8.

Tomato Salad   BULGARIA

2 pounds tomatoes
2 to 3 small onions, chopped
3 tablespoons chopped parsley

2 tablespoons oil
salt and coarsely ground
  pepper to taste

Peel tomatoes and, without crushing, cut into slices with a very sharp knife. Place these slices in straight rows on a flat plate. Mix onions with parsley and sprinkle onto tomatoes. Mix oil with salt and pepper and pour over tomato slices.

This dish looks especially attractive because of its arrangement and fresh colors. Serves 4 to 6.

Tomato Salad   FRANCE

Select some medium-sized and rather firm tomatoes, and scald them. Then skin them; cut them in two crosswise; press them to clear them of juice and seeds; cut them into thin strips; season them with oil and vinegar, and add some chopped tarragon.

Tomato Salad   AUSTRIA

3 pounds tomatoes
½ teaspoon salt
  dash cayenne pepper
¼ cup oil
½ cup vinegar

¼ teaspoon French mustard
¼ teaspoon sugar
  several drops Worcestershire
  sauce (optional)
¼ teaspoon parsley, chopped

Wash tomatoes. Cut horizontally into thin slices. Mix salt, cayenne, oil, vinegar, mustard, sugar, and Worcestershire sauce. Pour over tomatoes. Sprinkle with parsley. Chill in refrigerator 30 minutes before serving. Serves 6.

Cottage Cheese Filled Tomato   JEWISH

Slice off stem ends of tomatoes, remove pulp and fill with seasoned cottage cheese. Top with sour cream and minced parsley and serve on a bed of lettuce, green pepper rings, other greens.

Baked Custard over Tomatoes FINLAND

3 medium tomatoes,
   sliced
   salt

3 tablespoons melted butter
4 eggs
2 cups milk

Arrange the tomatoes in a buttered casserole. Sprinkle with salt and brush with the butter. With a fork, beat together the eggs, milk, and ½ teaspoon salt. Pour this mixture over the tomatoes and bake in a moderate oven (350°) for 15 minutes or until the eggs have set. Serve immediately. Serves 3 to 4.

Tomatoes Stuffed with Egg RUMANIA

8 tomatoes
5 eggs
1 teaspoon mustard
2 gherkins, chopped
   lemon juice to taste

salt and pepper to taste
3 tablespoons oil
3 olives
   mayonnaise or chopped
   olives for garnish (optional)

Choose fleshy tomatoes all about the same size. Cut off tops and carefully hollow out tomatoes (use tomato pulp for another dish). Hard-cook 4 eggs; chop them very fine or put through mincer. Mix with mustard, chopped gherkins, lemon juice, salt, and pepper. Make a mayonnaise out of remaining egg and oil; stir into mixture and fill tomatoes with it. Put tops on tomatoes and garnish with mayonnaise or chopped olives, if desired. Serves 4 to 6.

Stuffed Tomatoes with Mayonnaise AUSTRIA

5 tomatoes
2 apples, peeled and diced

3 stalks celery, diced
2 to 3 tablespoons mayonnaise

Place tomatoes in boiling water a few seconds. Peel; cut out stems. Scoop. Mix apples, celery, and mayonnaise. Stuff into tomatoes. Serve on green lettuce leaves. Serves 5.

Fine Mixed Vegetable Salad HUNGARY

1 pound potatoes, boiled,
  peeled
¼ pound pickled cucumbers
2 hard-cooked eggs
2 green peppers

½ pound tomatoes, peeled
2 heads lettuce
5 to 6 tablespoons mayonnaise
  salt and pepper to taste
1 cup chopped parsley

Slice potatoes, cucumbers, and eggs thin.

Remove white membrane and seeds from peppers and cut into thin strips. Cube tomatoes. Cut one head of lettuce into strips. Mix mayonnaise with salt, pepper, and parsley. Add to prepared ingredients and mix well. Garnish with leaves from remaining lettuce. Serves 4.

Parisian Vegetable Salad AUSTRIA

1 cup green peas, cooked
1 cup green beans, cut up small and cooked
1 cup carrots, diced and cooked
1 cup green peppers, diced raw
½ cup celery, diced and cooked
  (or diced raw celery stalks)
  hard-boiled eggs, quartered
  lettuce leaves (green)

French dressing
1 teaspoon mustard
¼ teaspoon paprika
¼ teaspoon pepper
½ teaspoon onion, chopped
2 tablespoons oil
2 tablespoons vinegar
¼ teaspoon salt
½ teaspoon sugar
2 tablespoons water

Mix vegetables. Place in center of salad bowl. Decorate with circle of quartered eggs and lettuce leaves. Prepare French dressing by blending all ingredients thoroughly. Serve separately from salad. Serves 5 to 6.

Note: Any vegetable in season may be used.

Waldorf Salad SCANDINAVIA

2 apples, diced
4 ounces celeriac, coarsely grated (8 fluid ounces) (1 cup)
  or 2 sticks celery, sliced
4 ounces chopped walnuts or hazelnuts (1 cup)
  green salad
7 tablespoonfuls mayonnaise (scant ½ cup)
7 tablespoonfuls thick cream, whipped

Mix the ingredients and fold carefully into the mayonnaise blended with cream.

Garnish with green salad. Serves 4.

SALADS

Watercress Salad

1 bunch watercress
  salt to taste
¼ cup oil

¼ cup vinegar (or lemon
  juice)

Clean and wash watercress; cut stems; drain thoroughly. Salt watercress. Mix oil and vinegar; pour over and toss well. Serves 6.

Zevulun Lettuce Salad

1 ½ heads of lettuce
3 bananas
⅓ cup sour cream
2 tablespoons freshly
  grated horseradish

½ cup mayonnaise
4 tablespoons water
  juice of 1 ½ lemons
2 tablespoons sugar
½ cup salted roast peanuts

Cut the lettuce heads into quarters and put into a salad bowl, round side up. Cut the bananas in half lengthwise and put between the lettuce, after dipping the fruit in lemon juice. Mix the sour cream with the horseradish, mayonnaise, water, lemon juice, and sugar. Pour this over the lettuce, top with a sprinkling of peanuts, and serve. Serves 6.

Zucchini Salad

½ pound very young zucchinis
1 to 2 young carrots
  dill to taste, chopped fine
  parsley to taste, chopped

2 to 3 tablespoons oil
1 to 2 tablespoons vinegar
  salt to taste
  radishes for garnish (optional)

Grate young zucchinis and carrots. Add dill and parsley. Mix oil, vinegar, and salt. Pour over vegetables. Garnish with slices of radish. Serves 3 to 4.

Sauces and Dressings

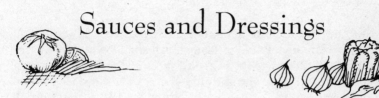

Sauce Antalouse

1½ pounds fresh tomatoes
  water
1 tablespoon diced fresh green
  pepper

1 tablespoon diced fresh red
  pepper
2 cups mayonnaise
  salt and pepper to taste

Cut the tomatoes into 2 to 3 pieces. Place in a pot with very little water, and salt. Cook until soft, then strain. Put the pulp and juice back into the pot. Cook down until you have about ½ cup paste. Cool. Add with all the other ingredients to the mayonnaise and mix well. Serve cold.

Sauce Béarnaise

GERMANY

4 tablespoons white wine
3 tablespoons wine vinegar
1 clove
3 shallots
1 small stem tarragon

½ bay leaf
  salt
  peppercorns
2 egg yolks
10 tablespoons butter

Bring wine, vinegar and spices to a boil. Strain. When cool, stir in egg yolks and half the butter. Place in double boiler, over hot, *not boiling*, water and gradually add remaining butter, beating constantly until thick.

271

Béchamel Sauce

6 tablespoons butter
7 to 8 tablespoons flour
4 cups milk, scalded

1 to 2 egg yolks
salt and pepper to taste

Melt the butter, but do not brown. Add the flour slowly, mixing constantly. Remove from the heat. Slowly mix in the scalded milk. Return to the heat and stir until the sauce thickens. Beat the egg yolks well, and add them with salt and pepper to the mixture, stirring constantly until blended. If you do not serve the sauce immediately, stir it occasionally to prevent a crust from forming.

Butter Sauce

Mix 2 ounces of sifted flour with 2 ounces of melted butter. Dilute with 1 quart of boiling water, salted to the extent of ¼ ounce per quart. Stir briskly to ensure a perfect blending, and do not allow to boil. Add immediately the yolks of 6 eggs mixed with ¼ pint of cream and the juice of half a lemon. Rub through a fine sieve, and finish the sauce with 5 ounces of best fresh butter.

Be careful that the sauce does not boil after it has been thickened.

Lemon-Butter Sauce

3 tablespoons butter, melted
3 tablespoons lemon juice
½ teaspoon grated lemon rind

1 tablespoon brown sugar
dash of salt and pepper
1 tablespoon minced parsley

Combine by stirring well in a saucepan after butter has melted. Serve with vegetables.

Sour Cream Dressing

    7 tablespoonfuls sour cream or soured cream
      salt
      white pepper
    1 tablespoonful clipped chives or chopped onion
    1 teaspoonful lemon juice

Mix the ingredients. Taste for seasoning.
Use with vegetables and salads.

Sour Cream and
Mayonnaise Dressing

    3 tablespoonfuls mayonnaise
    3 tablespoonfuls sour cream or soured cream
    1 tablespoonful clipped chives
    ½ saltspoonful allspice (good pinch)

Mix the ingredients. Taste for seasoning.
Use with vegetables and salads.

Sour Cream Salad Dressing

2 teaspoons sugar   3 tablespoons lemon juice
½ teaspoon salt   ⅛ teaspoon paprika
½ teaspoon dry mustard   1 cup heavy sour cream

Combine ingredients in the order listed, stirring till smooth.
Cover and store in refrigerator to use on frozen cream cheese
salads. Can be used with fresh or canned fruit salads, vegetable
salads, fish salads. Will keep for a week or two in a covered
container in refrigerator. Yields 1¼ cups.

Creole Sauce

2 medium onions,
  sliced or diced
2 medium green peppers,
  diced fine
2 tablespoons shortening
2 tablespoons flour
½ cup thinly sliced fresh
  mushrooms

2 large tomatoes, skinned
  or ½ cup purée
¼ teaspoon salt
  dash of pepper
1 teaspoon prepared mustard
  or horseradish

Brown onions and peppers in hot melted shortening. Stir in flour. Add remaining ingredients except mustard. Cook over moderate heat 5 minutes and add 1 cup hot water and mustard. Stir 1 minute and remove from heat. Yields 2 to 2½ cups.

Cumberland Sauce

1¼ cups currant jelly
  (or cranberry jelly)
¼ cup red wine
4 tablespoons orange juice

⅓ teaspoon dry mustard
2 tablespoons orange rind,
  cut into fine strips
¼ teaspoon salt (optional)

Mix currant jelly with red wine, orange juice, and mustard. Add orange rind and salt; set in refrigerator.

Curry Dressing

1 tablespoon vinegar
3 tablespoons oil
  salt
  white pepper or paprika

½ teaspoonful grated onion
1 saltspoonful curry (¼ teaspoon)
  cayenne pepper

Mix the ingredients. Taste for seasoning.

Danish Salad Dressing   SCANDINAVIA

> 2 tablespoonfuls butter or margarine
> 2 tablespoonfuls plain flour
> ½ pint cream and water (1¼ cups)
> 1 egg yolk
> 1 tablespoonful vinegar or beetroot juice
> 1 teaspoonful prepared mustard
> ½ teaspoonful salt
>   sugar (optional)

Fry the fat and the flour. Add the liquid, bring to the boil and cook for 3 to 5 minutes. Cool slightly and stir in the egg yolk.

Season to taste.

Dill Sauce   POLAND

1 tablespoon butter
1½ teaspoons flour
¼ cup broth
1 cup sour cream

salt to taste
2 tablespoons chopped fresh
dill
2 egg yolks (optional)

Melt butter, stir in flour, blend thoroughly, and dilute with broth. Combine with sour cream, stirring constantly until smooth. Add dill, season to taste, and let bubble up once. For a more delicate taste add the beaten egg yolks, taking care not to let sauce curdle. Makes 1¼ to 1½ cups.

French Dressing   GERMANY

½ teaspoon salt
¼ teaspoon pepper
2 tablespoons lemon juice

4 tablespoons olive oil
3 tablespoons sweet cream

Combine all ingredients, in order given, and mix well. Serve with green or vegetable salad.

Sauce Hollandaise

¼ cup vinegar	4 egg yolks
¼ cup water	1 cup butter
1 teaspoon shallots, chopped	salt to taste
5 peppercorns	1 tablespoon lemon juice

Cook vinegar and water with shallots and peppercorns until reduced to half. Strain; cool. Add egg yolks and beat in top of double boiler until thick. Remove from flame. Add melted butter drop by drop and season with salt and lemon juice.

Variation: Cook liquid as above. Add yolks and butter cut into pieces. Beat in double boiler until thick. Add lemon juice, salt, ¼ teaspoon cayenne pepper, and ½ tablespoon Worcestershire sauce.

Note: For variety, add mustard, anchovies, chives, horseradish, or tomato purée.

If the sauce curdles, add 1 tablespoon cold water and stir until smooth again.

Lemon Dressing

1 tablespoonful lemon juice
3 tablespoonfuls oil or water or half quantity of each
   sugar (optional)

Mix the ingredients by shaking or whisking them together. Taste for seasoning.

The dressing may be flavored with chopped herbs, ground ginger, or finely crushed cumin.

Lemon dressing is used with raw vegetable salads.

Basic Mayonnaise Recipe

6 egg yolks	salt and white pepper to taste
12 tablespoons olive oil	dash of sugar (optional)
lemon juice to taste	

Beat 1 egg yolk and 2 tablespoons olive oil with rotary beater or in electric blender, pouring the olive oil in gradually. When thick, add a few drops of lemon juice and blend in thoroughly. Add second yolk and two more spoonfuls of oil, following the same procedure. Continue until all ingredients have been used. Season to taste and chill.

Mustard Dressing   SCANDINAVIA

1 tablespoon vinegar
3 tablespoons oil
  salt

white pepper or paprika
2 to 3 tablespoonfuls mustard

Mix the ingredients. Taste for seasoning.
Use with vegetable salads.

Mushroom Sauce   FINLAND

2 tablespoons butter
2 cups finely chopped
  mushrooms
1 small onion, finely chopped

2 tablespoons flour
2 cups cream or milk
  salt

Melt the butter in a pan and stir in the mushrooms. Cook over medium heat for 1 to 2 minutes; add the onion and cook until limp (about 2 minutes more). Stir in the flour, then the cream or milk. Add salt to taste. Simmer for 10 to 15 minutes or until smooth and thickened. Makes about 3 cups.

Remoulade Sauce   GERMANY

½ cup mayonnaise
1 teaspoon mustard
1 teaspoon salad herbs, chopped

1 teaspoon capers
1 small pickle, chopped
  cream

Blend the first five ingredients and then thin with cream to desired consistency.

Fruit Dressing   SCANDINAVIA

1 tablespoon vinegar
3 tablespoons oil
salt
white pepper or paprika
2 tablespoonfuls grapefruit or orange juice

Mix the ingredients. Taste for seasoning.
Use with raw vegetable salads.

Cold Garlic Sauce   GREECE

8 to 10 cloves garlic, peeled
salt to taste
⅔ cup blanched almonds

1 slice of white bread,
    crust removed, soaked in
    water
¼ cup oil
¼ cup vinegar

Grind garlic with a little salt in a mortar or other strong dish.
Add almonds and continue to grind until you have a smooth
mixture. Add squeezed-out bread, oil, and vinegar. Stir until
smooth and store in a cold place. Serve this sauce with cold
cooked beets or cold cooked meat. Makes 1 cup.

Herb Dressing   SCANDINAVIA

1 tablespoon vinegar
3 tablespoons oil
salt
white pepper or paprika
1 to 2 teaspoonfuls chopped herbs, e.g., dill, chives,
    mustard and cress or chervil

Mix the ingredients. Taste for seasoning.
Use with vegetable salads.

Russian Dressing   SCANDINAVIA

> 7 tablespoonfuls mayonnaise (3½ ounces)
>   (about ½ cup)
> 2 tablespoonfuls chili sauce
> 2 teaspoonfuls lemon juice
> 1 teaspoonful onion juice or grated onion

Mix the ingredients. Taste for seasoning.

Basic Salad Marinade   JEWISH

½ cup salad oil (corn,
  peanut, or soy bean)
¼ cup olive oil (optional)
½ cup lemon juice
  or wine vinegar

3 tablespoons brown sugar
  dash of salt and pepper
¼ teaspoon paprika
  clove of garlic (cut and
  left in marinade)

Combine all ingredients in a tightly covered bottle or jar and shake well. Beat when prepared in advance and chilled. Yields approximately 1½ cups. Store in refrigerator.

For *Vegetable or Egg Salads*, add onion juice or grated onion, minced parsley, chopped pickle relish, chopped stuffed olives.

For *Green Salads*, add grated Parmesan or Roquefort cheese.

Cream Sauce   FRANCE

Boil 1 pint of Béchamel Sauce, and add ¼ pint of cream to it. Reduce on an open fire until the sauce has become very thick; then strain through a fine sieve. Bring to its normal degree of consistency by gradually adding, away from the fire, ¼ pint of very fresh cream and a few drops of lemon juice.

Cheese Dressing SCANDINAVIA

> *full quantity vinaigrette*
> *2 to 3 tablespoonfuls mashed blue-veined cheese*

Mix the ingredients. Taste for seasoning.
Use with vegetable salads.

Tomato Sauce ITALY

3 tablespoons olive oil
½ stalk celery, finely chopped
1 small onion, chopped
1 teaspoon parsley, minced
1 clove garlic
1 large can Italian tomatoes

1 medium can tomato purée
½ teaspoon salt
½ teaspoon pepper
½ teaspoon basil leaf, minced
½ teaspoon oregano
1 bay leaf

Place oil, celery, onion, parsley, and garlic in saucepan and brown lightly. Add tomatoes and tomato purée, salt and pepper and simmer gently for about 45 minutes. Add the basil, oregano, and bay leaf. Cook for 10 minutes longer. Makes sufficient sauce for 1 pound of spaghetti or macaroni.

Variation: ⅛ pound butter may be substituted for the olive oil, if preferred.

Thousand Island Dressing SCANDINAVIA

> *7 tablespoonfuls mayonnaise (3 ½ ounces)*
>   *(about ½ cup)*
> *1 tablespoonful chili sauce*
> *1 teaspoonful clipped chives or chopped onion*
> *1 hard-boiled egg, chopped*
> *1 tablespoonful chopped, stuffed olives (optional)*
> *1 saltspoonful paprika (¼ teaspoon)*
> *salt*
> *white pepper*

Mix the ingredients. Taste for seasoning.
Use with green salads.

Sauce Vinaigrette   GERMANY

2 hard-cooked eggs, chopped
  a few cucumber pickles, chopped
1 tablespoon parsley, chopped
1 small onion, chopped

2 tablespoons vinegar
4 tablespoons olive oil
  mustard, sugar, salt,
  pepper, to taste

Mix all chopped ingredients thoroughly with vinegar, oil and seasonings. If sauce is too sharp, dilute with a few teaspoonfuls of water.

White Sauce for Vegetables   ITALY

½ cup butter
1 tablespoon flour
1 cup milk

½ cup vinegar
3 peppercorns
2 tablespoons heavy cream

Melt half the butter in small saucepan, blend in flour, add milk gradually and cook over low fire, stirring constantly until slightly thickened. Remove from fire and keep warm.

Place vinegar and peppercorns in another small pan and boil gently until reduced half in quantity. Strain vinegar and add to white sauce. Add remaining butter a little at a time, stirring constantly, then add cream. Mix well and serve. Makes 1½ cups.

Yogurt Dressing   SCANDINAVIA

7 tablespoonfuls yogurt
½ tablespoonful vinegar (1½ teaspoon)
1 tablespoonful chopped onion

1 saltspoonful salt
1 saltspoonful sugar

Mix the ingredients. Taste for seasoning.
Use with green salads.

❧ Specialties ❧

Ghee INDIA

1 pound of butter
  (this will make at least ½
  pound pure ghee)
1 1-quart heavy-bottom
  saucepan

1 cooking spoon, not slotted
1 clean glass container
1 spare container (to hold the
  residue)

Melt the butter in the pan directly over medium heat. It will not burn, but will begin to bubble and foam. By the time it reaches a slow, rolling boil, the milk solids will move to the top. Take the pan from the heat and carefully skim off the foam with the spoon, discarding it in the spare container. Repeat this process several times to remove as much of the foam as possible. Then return the pot to the heat and let it gently come to a boil again. More solids—scantier this time—will again rise to the top. Skim off again. By this time, you should have taken off all the residue. If not, try again. Then put the pot back on the stove and turn off the heat; let rest for a minute or two. A thin, skinlike film will form. Remove it gently with the spoon. Discard.

What remains in the pot is a clear, very warm liquid, the sweetly aromatic ghee, floating on the heavier solids, which sit in the bottom like lead. As soon as the ghee has cooled down—but before it gets completely cold—strain through a fine-meshed tea strainer into the glass container. Stop pouring when the heavier solids move to the strainer. Cool; cover. The straining should have caught what few solids remain between top and bottom.

Garam Masala INDIA

2 cardamom pods, seeded
1 teaspoon whole cloves
30 whole peppercorns

2 teaspoons whole cumin seed
1 2-inch piece cinnamon stick

Measure all the ingredients, discarding the pods of the cardamom. Grind as finely as possible in a mortar and pestle.

Index